RICHARD HOLMES

DR. JOHNSON & MR. SAVAGE

Richard Holmes is the author of *Shelley: The Pursuit* (1974), for which he won the Somerset Maugham Award; *Footsteps: Adventures of a Romantic Biographer* (1985), which Michael Holroyd described as "a modern master-piece"; and *Coleridge: Early Vision*, the highly acclaimed winner of the 1989 Whitbread Book of the Year Prize. One of the most widely praised books published in England last year, *Dr. Johnson & Mr. Savage* received the James Tait Black Award. Holmes is a Fellow of the Royal Society of Literature and was made an OBE in 1992. He lives in London and Norfolk, with the novelist Rose Tremain.

VINTAGE

INTERNATIONAL

RICHARD HOLMES

DR. JOHNSON
&
MR. SAVAGE

VINTAGE INTERNATIONAL

Vintage Books   A Division of Random House, Inc.   New York

To the Rose in the Grove

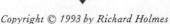

All chapter head illustrations are by William Hogarth from
Hogarth's Graphic Works, compiled by Ronald Paulson,
The Print Room, 1989.

The Library of Congress has cataloged the Pantheon edition
as follows:
Holmes, Richard, 1945–
Dr. Johnson and Mr. Savage / by Richard Holmes.
p. cm.
Includes bibliographical references and index.
ISBN 0-679-43585-9
1. Johnson, Samuel, 1709–1784—Friends and associates. 2. Savage,
Richard, d. 1743—Friends and associates. 3. Friendship—
England—History—18th century. 4. Authors, English—
18th century—Biography. 5. Influence (Literary, artistic, etc.)
6. Murderers—Great Britain—Biography. 7. Biography as a
literary form. I. Title. II. Title: Doctor Johnson and Mr. Savage.
III. Title: Johnson and Mr. Savage.
PR3533.H515 1994
828'.609—dc20
[B] 94-6219
CIP
Vintage ISBN: 0-679-75770-8

Random House Web address: http://www.randomhouse.com/

Printed in the United States of America
10 9 8 7 6 5 4 3 2 1

CONTENTS

. . . For as Johnson is reported to have once said, that 'he could write the Life of a Broomstick'.

—Boswell

PROLOGUE

When Samuel Johnson was compiling his great *Dictionary of the English Language*, which defines more than forty thousand words, he decided to illustrate his definitions with suitable literary quotations. 'I therefore extracted,' he explained in his Preface, 'from Philosophers principles of science, from Historians remarkable facts, from Chymists complete processes, from Divines striking exhortations, and from Poets beautiful descriptions.'

To do this, he read and annotated over two hundred thousand passages from innumerable English authors across four centuries. He marked up these passages, and handed them to his clerks in his attic at Gough Square to be entered into eighty large vellum notebooks.

He was working at great speed, and he chose his illustrations entirely at random. Most of them are from the great classics of English literature, such as Shakespeare, Milton, Dryden and Pope. But of the 116,000 quotations eventually included, he chose seven from the works of his strange friend Richard Savage. These quotations, and the seven words they illustrate, may have a curious significance. Since they were chosen rapidly and at random, from such a vast source, they could be thought to reveal unconscious links and symbolic meanings. If considered as a form of 'association-test', these seven words must instinctively have brought Richard Savage to Johnson's mind. Thus, to an analyst they might suggest something about the nature of that most puzzling relationship. Here are the seven words, and their illustrations, in alphabetical order.

1. 'Elevate'   to raise with great conceptions.
Savage: 'Now rising fortune *elevates* his mind,
He shines unclouded, and adorns mankind.'

2. 'Expanse'   a body widely extended without inequalities.
Savage: 'Bright as the Etherial, glows the green *expanse*.'

3. 'Fondly'   with great or extreme tenderness.
Savage: 'To be *fondly* or serenely kind.'

4. 'Lone'   solitary, unfrequented, having no company.
Savage: 'Here the *lone* hour a blank of life displays.'

5. 'Squander'   to scatter lavishly, to spend profusely, to throw away in idle prodigality.
Savage: 'They often *squandered*, but they never gave.'

6. 'Sterilise'   to make barren, to deprive of fecundity or the power of production.
Savage: 'Go! *sterilize* the fertile with thy rage.'

7. 'Suicide'   self-murder, the horrid crime of destroying one's self.
Savage: 'Child of despair, and *Suicide* my name.'

CHAPTER 1

DEATH

Everyone knows the great Dr Johnson, and the scholars seem to know him in minutest detail; almost no one knows anything definite now about the obscure, minor poet Richard Savage.[1] But Johnson and Savage were friends – intimate friends – in London for about two years in the 1730s. In those dark days in the city, dark for them both in many senses, the position was almost exactly reversed. Johnson was then unknown, and Savage was notorious. Thereby hangs a small, but haunting mystery of biography.

Sir John Hawkins, Johnson's earliest official biographer, thought the friendship was the single most inexplicable fact about Johnson's entire career. 'With one person, however, he commenced an intimacy, the motives to which, at first view, may probably seem harder to be accounted for, than any one particular in his life. This person was Mr Richard Savage . . .'[2]

James Boswell, in a moment of rare agreement with Hawkins, thought much the same: 'Richard Savage: a man, of whom it is difficult to speak impartially, without wondering that he was for some time the intimate companion of Johnson; for his character was marked by profligacy, insolence, and ingratitude . . .'[3]

One of the few facts that can be stated without contradiction about Richard Savage was that he died in 1743. So one might begin with his obituary.

Mr Richard Savage, Gent. Report has just reached us in the Bristol mails, of the Demise of Mr Richard Savage, son of the late Earl Rivers, in the debtor's Confinements of Bristol Newgate gaol. Mr Savage will be recalled as the unhappy Poet and author cf 'The Wanderer', convicted at the Old Bailey on a capital charge of Murder, and sometimes Volunteer Laureate to her Gracious Majesty Queen Caroline.

Much obscurity attends the Passage of his early life. We have it on his own Authority that he was born in the parish of St Andrew's, Holborn, in 1698, the bastard Son of the present Mrs Anne Brett, then Lady Macclesfield (though she never acknowledged his Claim), and the late 4th Earl Rivers of Rivers House, Great Queen Street, Holborn. These Circumstances are obliquely referred to in his memorable poem 'The Bastard' first given to the World shortly after his Trial in 1728.

Mr Savage first came to Notice with two Spanish dramas, and his Tragedy of 'Sir Thomas Overbury' produced at Drury Lane by Mr Cibber in 1723. He was befriended by the essayist Sir Richard Steele, and published a number of poetical Works in *The Plain Dealer* magazine of Mr Aaron Hill, who proclaimed his Merits and drew attention to his Plight. He became associated with Mr Alexander Pope of Twickenham, and is rumoured to have supplied many of the Scurrilities that furnished the latter's poetical Satire of 'The Dunciad'.

As a frequenter of the Coffeehouse, the Salon, and the Green Room, Mr Savage found his Name connected with many of the illustrious Ladies of the day, including the actress Mrs Anne Oldfield, the poetess Martha Sansom, and that assiduous writer of Scandalous romances, Mrs Eliza Haywood.

In November 1727, in consequence of an Affray at Robinson's Coffeehouse, Charing Cross, he was arrested on a capital charge of Wounding and Murder, found guilty by a Grand Jury Court at the Old Bailey under the direction of Judge Page, and condemned to suffer execution at Tyburn. His Case became celebrated among the *Literati* and Beau Monde of the capital, and in consequence of the Intercession of his kinsman Lord Tyrconnel and the renowned Patroness of poets my Lady Hertford, he received the Royal Pardon in February 1728.

In relating his Misfortunes, it is remarkable that Mr Savage always afterwards stated that his Mother Mrs Anne Brett, the former Lady Macclesfield, had unaccountably urged the Execution of his sentence against all representations of Mercy, and that it was only the gracious Intercession of her Majesty Queen Caroline which saved him from the Hangman's Noose. Mr Savage immediately thereafter tasted the delights of Celebrity, and applied precipitously for the position of Poet Laureate; which, failing to obtain, he appointed himself 'Volunteer Laureate' to the Queen thereby obtaining an Allowance of £50 per annum until her majesty's death in 1737. These Facts we have on the Authority of Mr Thomas Birch of the Royal Society.

Mr Savage now came under the Patronage of his generous kinsman Lord Tyrconnel, to whom his poem 'The Wanderer' is dedicated. But in consequence of some Misunderstanding, he shortly reverted to his previous condition of Poverty, and with the Cessation of the Queen's allowance, he was thrown once more upon his Wits and his Friends, in the Town. He once again began to publish a number of poetical Works, in the new *Gentleman's Magazine* of Mr Edward Cave at St John's Gate, Clerkenwell, among which was his poem 'Of Public Spirit' (1737); but was menaced with a charge of Obscene Libel for his poem 'The Progress of a Divine'.

The condition of his Poverty being unrelieved, he threw himself with increasing confidence on the Generosity of his many friends, among whom Mr Solomon Mendez of Hackney, and Mr James Thomson, the distinguished author of 'The Seasons', at Richmond; though it is to be feared that some Nights were passed in the Cellars and on the Bulks of Covent Garden, in the company of Beggars, Thieves, and other Denizens of Grub Street.

Mr Savage had for some time revolved a plan of Retirement to the country, where he hoped to re-write and refurbish his original Tragedy of 'Sir Thomas Overbury'. Accordingly through the Generosity of Mr Alexander Pope, a Subscription of £50 per annum was organized among his friends, and in the summer of 1739 Mr Savage departed for Wales. Here he settled at Swansea and its Environs, where he is supposed to have met his Friend the poet Mr John Dyer, and paid court to the celebrated Beauty of Llanelli, Mrs Bridget Jones. But his Funds once again running low, Mr Savage returned to Bristol to write his Tragedy and informed his Friends of his imminent Return to the Capital, at which much of his Subscription was unaccountably discontinued.

In January 1743 Mr Savage was precipitately arrested for Debt, and conveyed to the Newgate Prison in Bristol, where he received the personal Attentions of the Gaoler Mr Dagge, and died suddenly in his Room on 1st August 1743, being buried at Mr Dagge's expense in St Peter's Churchyard, six feet from the south Door of the church.

Mr Richard Savage never married, and had no known Offspring, though he is survived by his reputed mother Mrs Anne Brett, the former Lady Macclesfield, of Old Bond Street, London. His personal Papers have been obtained by his editor Mr Edward Cave, of the *Gentleman's Magazine*.

The facts, and even the rumours, given here accurately represent the public knowledge of Richard Savage's career at the time of his death, and are indeed historically correct as far as they go. But the obituary itself is a biographer's fiction. Nothing like it can be found in the memorial columns of the contemporary journals of 1743. I have simply invented it.

This imaginary obituary suggests some of the mysteries and questions that always surrounded Savage's life. But it is forced to omit the single most surprising fact, because at that time it had not become true. Among the 'Denizens of Grub Street' whom Savage encountered in the late 1730s was an unknown young literary novice called Samuel Johnson, who assured his own fame by writing Savage's biography a year later in 1744.

A life like Savage's is mysterious in itself, but also mysterious in the way it came to be told and reinterpreted, one version layered upon another, like a piece of complex geology. Its stratified truth was not ready to emerge immediately on his own death, or even in his own century. It depends on the series of its tellers or excavators, of whom our imaginary obituarist of 1743 is one; Samuel Johnson in 1744 is another; Johnson's own biographers, Sir John Hawkins (1787) and James Boswell (1791), are a third and fourth; and so on down a line of scholars, Victorian antiquarians and modern academics to our own time. Through these rich and varied workings of research and story-telling the buried figure of Savage slowly rises back to life again.

The subject of this book is one particular version, the 'original' version, Johnson's Savage. But it is also the question of *versions* itself. It is the biography of a biography. It concerns the kind of human truth, poised between fact and fiction, which a biographer can obtain as he tells the story of another's life, and thereby makes it both his own (like a friendship) and the public's (like a betrayal). It asks what we can know, and what we can believe, and finally what we can love.

If there was no official obituary of Savage in 1743, it is still possible to discover how his contemporaries felt about him very close to the time of his death, from public knowledge about his scandalous reputation and from popular hearsay. This must be the start, or first layer, of the investigation.

What emerges initially is a tale of controversy, sensationalism, disputed facts, and a good deal of eighteenth-century moralising about social justice and personal cruelty. Three documents vividly substantiate this: a poem, a letter, and an advertiser's announcement. Each of these is an early example of the memorial process at work, by which a private life begins to take its place in a nation's history.

Savage's life was seen from the start as containing the elements of a crime thriller, which would appeal to a popular as much as a literary readership. Savage, as his very name seemed to suggest, was a poet-killer with a peculiar violence in his relationships. His story begins in an aristocratic divorce court, emerges in the world of publicity and the new monthly magazines, continues in a murder trial, touches upon fashion, politics and royalty, and ends suddenly and disgracefully in a debtors' prison. More than any other English poet since Christopher Marlowe, Savage's reputation was notorious and his true identity problematic, though for very different reasons to Marlowe's. His 'case' was exemplary to his age, even if no one could quite agree what it exemplified, or who – ultimately – was to blame for its tragedy.

In the month of his death, the *Gentleman's Magazine*, which had to some degree sponsored the final stages of his career and had a literary investment in his story, published a verse 'Epitaph on the late R——d S——e Esq'. This emphasised the tragic aspects of the affair. It referred obliquely to his poetic powers, his wit, his illegitimacy, his trial, his laureateship, and his 'cruel' and vengeful mother.

The anonymous Epitaph writer begins by invoking Phoebus, the god of Poetry – which is like placing a classical bust at the entrance of the Vauxhall Pleasure Gardens. Savage's raffish life is grandly presented as a contest between two powerful patrons: unworldly

Poetry and Worldly Fortune, who are necessarily hostile to each other.

> Whom Phoebus favour'd, on whom Fortune frown'd
> Lies deep beneath this consecrated ground.
> Savage the name: – he was design'd by Fate,
> That err'd at his conception, to be great.
> And such he was, in boundless wit and pride;
> Title and heir his Mother's lust deny'd.

Within the tight, gavotte-like turns of mid-eighteenth-century occasional verse, the Epitaphist plays decorously on the idea of Savage's 'greatness'. Here was a great poet perhaps, but not a great social success. He was a man of great wit (in the sense of intelligence, rather than humour); but also great in his pride, arrogance and self-esteem – qualities which can blunt wit or make it blind. Then comes the scandalous, journalistic punch line: he should have been great in family title and financial inheritance too, but this was 'deny'd' him by his mother and – more outrageous yet – by his mother's 'lust'. This seems to be a libellous attack on the Countess of Macclesfield.

The Epitaphist now moves swiftly on to enlist sympathy for Savage. He suffered from poverty and dangerous misfortunes, yet he continued to write poetry. His mother cruelly withheld her support, but his Queen eventually saved him, and Heaven pitied him and forgave him, so that a greater justice eventually prevailed in his life.

> ... His life was Want, yet could his duteous Verse
> The Cruel's praise, that help withheld, rehearse.
> Danger extreme*, th'unhappy lawless knew,
> And woes he felt, as woes were all his due.
> Twice sov'reign Mercy found, a Queen* to save,
> From pitying Heaven, to end his cares, a grave.[4]

> * These want no Explanation.

It is remarkable that the Epitaphist assumes that all his readers will be familiar with the circumstances of Savage's trial, more than fifteen years before, and merely puts asterisks against the references to it, with a knowing footnote. His cause is still alive, even if the 'unhappy' poet himself is dead. Injustice, as much as poetry, has already granted him a kind of immortality.

Even though published in the *Gentleman's Magazine*, a largely pro-Savage paper, the Epitaph is by no means a panegyric. It accepts that Savage is a controversial figure, that the woes he felt were all his 'due', that he brought trouble on himself, that he was 'lawless' and that his 'cares' drove him to a premature grave. Nevertheless he remains a man of genius, a poet hounded by 'the Cruel' woman and suffering some ill-defined persecution and social injustice. Savage is not merely a case; he is already a cause.

The second document is an open letter to Edward Cave, the editor of the *Gentleman's Magazine* under his pseudonym Mr Urban, announcing a forthcoming biography of Savage. It appeared within three weeks of Savage's death in Bristol, and immediately demonstrates how topical the cause was. As the announcement explains, the anonymous writer will defend Savage's memory, and use his personal knowledge of the subject to produce an intimate portrait. It will be the work of a friend and confidante.

> Mr Urban: As your Collections show how often you have owed the Ornaments of your poetical Pages, to the Correspondence of the unfortunate and ingenious Mr Savage, I doubt not but you have so much regard to his Memory as to encourage any designs that may have a tendency to the Preservation of it from Insults or Calumnies, and therefore with some Degree of Assurance intreat you to inform the Publick, that his Life will speedily be published by a Person who was favoured with his Confidence, and received from himself an Account of most of the Transactions which he proposes to mention to the Time of his Retirement to Swansea in Wales.[5]

The letter adds that the *Life* will also give details of his imprisonment in Bristol, and use extracts from Savage's own private letters and those of his friends: 'materials still less liable to Objection'.

Great emphasis is laid on the speed at which this *Life* will be produced, and the accuracy of its sources. Other potential biographers are warned off the subject. The readers must also beware of any rival, romanticised versions which rely on speculation or fiction.

> It may be reasonably imagined that others may have the same Design, but as it is not credible that they can obtain the same Materials, it must be expected they will supply from Invention the want of Intelligence, and that under the Title of the *Life*

of Savage they will publish only a Novel filled with romantick Adventures, and imaginary Amours. You may therefore perhaps gratify the Lovers of Truth and Wit by giving me leave to inform them in your Magazine, that my Account will be published in 8vo by Mr Roberts in Warwick-Lane.[6]

This book is to be a true biography, quite different from the kind of 'novelized' lives which had become popular through the work of Daniel Defoe or Eliza Haywood, with their obsession with scandalous adventures and sexual exploits. The biography will be committed to an ideal of human truth, moral truth. It will be based on a distinction between fact and fiction. In short, the letter makes both a commercial claim to the literary market in Savage, and an aesthetic claim about the form of true biography. It adds, in a forthright manner, where the *Life* can be bought; though not yet the price.

This letter is written by the young Samuel Johnson, and is of historic importance in the development of English biography. It confidently asserts the value of the biographic form to a general public, the 'Lovers of Truth and Wit'; and aggressively declares war on the titillating fictional art of the Novel.

Samuel Johnson's publisher, Mr James Roberts of Warwick Lane off the Strand, saw the Savage story in different terms. As a publisher, Roberts specialised in tales of social scandal, runaway heiresses, adulterous skirmishes among the aristocracy, lost fortunes, orphaned sons, and careers of glittering crime. The Savage saga was easily adapted to this formula, and Roberts accordingly placed a long advertisement in the *London Evening Post* pointing out that the biography – though literary in appearance – could be safely relied on for its sensational contents. In this third document, Savage's life is seen as a labyrinth of deceit, injustice, passion and wrongdoing: in short, everything that might be expected of a poet's unstable existence in a materialistic society, redeemed only by the gracious interventions of royalty.

An account of the life of Mr Richard Savage, son of the late Earl Rivers. Who was, soon after he came into the world, bastardised by an act of Parliament, and deprived of the title and estate to which he was born; was committed by his mother, the Countess of Macclesfield, to a poor woman, to be bred up as her own son; came to the knowledge of his real mother, now alive, but abandoned by her, persecuted, and condemned for murder, and against all her endeavours, pardoned; made poet laureate to Queen Caroline, became very eminent for his writings, of which many are quoted in this Work, particularly the 'Bastard', the 'Wanderer', 'Volunteer Laureate', and 'Author to be Let'; went into Wales, to be supported by a subscription, promoted by Mr Pope, but at last died in Prison.[7]

This racy summary, with its neat and misleading telescoping of facts, conforms to the shape of what we might call an urban fairy tale. Savage is a kind of Frog Prince, placed under a cruel spell by his Wicked Mother, and saved from the jaws of death by the Good Queen, who transforms him back into his true self as an eminent poet. The premature death in prison, somehow under the auspices of Mr Pope (the most financially successful poet of the age), becomes a kind of moral to this tale. The poor Poet, whether saved or not, will always suffer for his Art. This is not so remote from the story actually told by Johnson; but it indicates what the public wanted to hear about Savage. His life will be an awful – and delicious – warning; and incidentally a very good read.

These are the reactions which people had to Richard Savage at the time of his death in 1743. They are already complicated and various. Savage had caught the popular imagination in a remarkable way. But most remarkable was the biographer who immediately entered the lists on his behalf. Who was this man?

Here again we are confronted with something peculiar in the nature of biography, and its layerings through time. If we assume that it was Dr Samuel Johnson (who received his doctorate from Trinity College, Dublin, in 1765), the man who subsequently made a household name in English literature through the work of James Boswell, we will understand little of the story that now begins to emerge. We have to deconstruct almost entirely that power-ful, domineering, confident, late-eighteenth-century figure whom Boswell created in his own biography. We have to recover a much more shadowy, fraught and uncertain personality: young Sam John-son, failed schoolmaster, provincial poet, and desperate Grub Street hack, who signed his letters in 1738 '*impransus*' – supperless.

It is worth considering here another fiction. What might an imaginary obituarist also have made of Johnson at this period? Suppose Samuel Johnson had also died at about forty years old, say in the summer of 1749 when he had been in London for just over ten years? This is Johnson more than a decade before he met Boswell. This is Johnson still virtually unknown, beyond a small circle of Fleet Street booksellers, when he has just published his first signed work, *The Vanity of Human Wishes*. This is the young Samuel Johnson that Savage would have recognised, but that we, looking backwards through history and Boswell's biography, might find difficult to imagine at all. This is how Death might have briefly framed his portrait at that date:

Mr Samuel Johnson: poet, playwright and sometime political journalist. News has just reached us in the London mails, of the untimely death of Mr Samuel Johnson, late of the city of Lichfield, at his house at Gough Square, Fleet Street, London, of a sudden Apoplexy.

He was the son of Michael Johnson, bookseller and stationer of Sadler Street and Market Square; and elder brother of Nathanial Johnson, who continued the family business until 1737 in this city. Mr Johnson's Learning and Eccentricities will be well remembered, which led him to abandon the useful paths of Pedagogy for the ephemeral pursuit of Letters in the capital city, where he found little Success. He was attached in various capacities to the *Gentleman's Magazine* of Mr Edward Cave, where he undertook extensive but anonymous Work, most notably the reporting of Parliamentary affairs in the scurrilous rubric of 'Debates in the Senate of Lilliput' which he continued for three or four years. He is believed to have published several anonymous Poems and political Pamphlets, of a generally Jacobite tenor and in Opposition to the late Ministry of Mr Walpole.

At the time of his Death, perhaps hastened by Poverty and Overwork, he was engaged in a delusory Scheme to compile by his singular efforts a General Dictionary of the English Language, an enterprise more rationally undertaken in France by a Committee of scholars labouring over many years. The tribulations and disappointments of his Life have been summarised in a recent poetical satire, 'The Vanity of Human Wishes', which some may take as his own Elegy.

Samuel Johnson was born in Lichfield on 18th September 1709, and taken by his Mother to London at the age of three years to be touched by her Gracious Majesty Queen Anne for the Evil, a Scrofula infection that marked him in a sad and monstrous Manner for the rest of his life. He was nearly blind in one Eye, and suffered from an unhappy series of nervous Spasms, which rendered him permanently unsuitable for the gracious departments of Society, and nullified many of his efforts to obtain Advancement. To these physiological Causes may be ascribed a melancholy of Temper, and irritable dogmatism of Address, which rendered him at times restless, willful, and barbarous. A brooding spirit of Opposition marked many of his proceedings; he felt the pain of Existence, and perhaps unduly resented the Comforts of Privilege, Fortune, or Power. Of his Learning, there can however be little Doubt.

He achieved Pre-eminence among his peers at the Lichfield Grammar School with remarkable celerity; and in October 1728 proceeded to Pembroke College, Oxford, with a reputation for Scholarship that was little short of prodigious; but after fourteen months was forced to withdraw owing to the Business-failings of his father, who died in 1731 leaving him no Patrimony. A period of lassitude and solitary Study now ensued, alternating with unsuccessful attempts to establish himself as a Schoolmaster at Market Bosworth and at Birmingham.

At last, in what might appear a strange fit of Optimism or of Despair, he married Mrs Elizabeth Jervis Porter, the widow of a Birmingham woollen-draper, the Mother of three children and a Woman over twenty years his senior, on 9 July 1735 at St Werburgh's church, Derby. This Union is said to have been the cause of great Solace to Johnson, and of great Merriment to his Friends. He invested his Wife's dowry of some £600 in the venture of a private School at Edial, Lichfield, which failed within two years, leaving him without Resource. He was therefore obliged to seek some other Means of Support, and having no Profession, became, by Necessity, an Author.

Removing precipitously to London in the spring of 1737, Mr Johnson sought Employment among the denizens of Grub Street, while attempting to finish 'Irene', a blank-verse Tragedy of the passions, incommodiously located in Constantinople at the time of the Turkish ascendancy. He is said to have been greatly attached to his heroine, Aspasia, who resists the heathen Blandishments of the Sultan Mahomet, confirming thereby her Virtue, her Religion, and eventually the Dictates of her Heart.

The insolence of Power, and the Temptations of the animal Passions, appear to have been a constant theme of Mr Johnson's meditations at this period of his Life, and may reflect upon his own unhappy Situation. But finding himself now no more successful as a Tragedian, than formerly as a Schoolmaster, he at length established a connection with the *Gentleman's Magazine* where he earned his Bread as a low writer of Translations, Reviews, Catalogues and Commentaries over the ensuing decade. Throughout these years he knew great Poverty, and his Union with Mrs Johnson is rumoured to have been at Times interrupted.

The spirit of Discontent, if not of Subversion, is revealed in his Imitation of Juvenal's Third Satire on Rome, which he published anonymously as 'London' in 1738; and his Pamphlets in prose and verse directed against the Ministry. In 1744 he published through Mr Dodsley a remarkable Apologia for the Life of the notorious Mr Richard Savage, the self-styled Volunteer Laureate and claimant to the Rivers title, a man renowned equally for his Poetry and his Profligacy.

Mr Johnson's familiarity with this Gentleman and his London haunts, at the very Nadir of his misfortunes, may indicate something of his own Circumstances. The Performance is executed with both Tenderness and Rigour, as if the Author was to some degree at War with his own Nature and Outlook in the judgement of his unhappy Friend. The Work, though cast in the ephemeral genre of commercial Biography, has received Praise in many quarters including the Approbation of Mr Henry Fielding (whose History of *Tom Jones: A Foundling* now lies before the World); and it may be counted among the most Successful and Diverting that Mr Johnson was destined to produce.

Disappointed in his literary Prospects, disheartened in his political Hopes, and perhaps embittered by his personal Affairs (but we make no Windows into the human Heart), Mr Johnson threw himself at last into the harmless drudgery of his English Dictionary, for which he undertook a contract in 1746, with a Chimerical fervour, and established himself on Credit at Gough Square with Mrs Johnson who steadily sought refuge from the World in Novels and Medicines. Turning once more to his favourite Juvenal, Mr Johnson now imitated the Disillusion of the Tenth Satire, in his poem 'The Vanity of Human Wishes', which he is believed to have composed while Walking in the country lanes of Hampstead in a delusory Attempt to escape the Toils of the City which had so fatally ensnared him.

The last concussion to his Hopes occurred this spring, when his long meditated Tragedy of *Irene* was mounted in Drury Lane by his Friend Mr David Garrick (one of the truly distinguished sons of Lichfield), to be received only with a Tepid expression of Politeness by the Town. The fatal Illness that now struck him down, at the age of Forty, may perhaps be assigned as much to Weariness and melancholy of Mind, as to premature Decay of his ungainly and damaged Body.

He remained throughout a devout and convinced Christian, and found that Solace in Heaven which he could not find in the World. Perhaps he composed an Elegy for himself, and for his Grub Street familiars such as Mr Savage, when he wrote in *The Vanity of Human Wishes*:

> Deign on the passing World to turn thine Eyes,
> And pause a while from Letters, to be wise;
> There mark what Ills the Scholar's Life assail,
> Toil, Envy, Want, the Patron and the Jail.[8]

CHAPTER 2

LOVE

When Johnson first came to London in 1737 he was twenty-seven years old; and Savage (as far as we can tell) was nearly forty. Johnson was young, unknown and untried; Savage was ageing, experienced and disreputable. We have to begin to imagine a relationship of mentor and pupil between the two men that is unlike almost anything in Johnson's later career, or in that part of it recorded by Boswell. Savage can be seen as a sort of urbane Mephistopheles, Johnson as a youthful Faust.

The friendship lasted at most only two years, but it seems to have been of great emotional intensity. When they eventually parted, in July 1739, Johnson says that he had 'Tears in his Eyes'. It is invariably said by Johnson's own biographers that the man who was weeping was Savage, not Johnson; thereby suggesting that Johnson was relatively unmoved. But this may not be the case. Johnson himself draws special attention to the moment of parting by making it one of the few places in his *Life of Savage* where he deliberately introduces himself as part of Savage's story. He emphasises the pathos of the moment with unusual explicitness.

Savage had resolved to abandon London for rural Wales to live frugally, and salvage his writing career. 'Full of these salutary Resolutions, he left London, in July 1739, having taken Leave with great Tenderness of his Friends, and parted from the Author of this Narrative with Tears in his Eyes."[1]

Tears in *whose* eyes? The sentence is curiously ambiguous, or deliberately so: the punctuation suggests Savage's eyes, but Johnson's dramatic introduction of himself in the final clause seems to claim the tears as his own. It is almost as if Johnson was impelled as a friend to bear witness to his own tears; but was embarrassed as a biographer to admit them in public. This embarrassment at the strength of his feelings for Savage, when he later looked back at it, provides us with a first clue to the whole story.

When Johnson came to correct the second edition of the *Life* in 1748, he noted carefully in the margin next to the 'Tears in his Eyes' an explanatory phrase: 'I had then a slight fever.' This seems to imply that Johnson was indeed recalling his own tears and emotion at losing Savage, but he felt awkward doing so, and subsequently wished to dismiss them as mere physical weakness, as temporary illness. But in this sense his whole intimacy with Savage may have been something of a young man's fever. It was hectic, intense, continually menaced by Savage's poverty and instability, and by Johnson's own struggles to establish himself professionally in London. Johnson seemed to conceive of their time together as something dreamlike, tidal like the River Thames; a friendship of arrivals and departures in the great city.

In his poem *London*, Johnson invests just such an imagined parting with a strange, solemn ritual of kissing the ground, bathing the whole moment in a bright silvery light, reflected from the shining water, of romantic intensity.

> While Thales waits the Wherry that contains
> Of dissipated Wealth the small Remains,
> On Thames's banks, in silent Thought we stood,
> Where Greenwich smiles upon the silver Flood:
> Struck with the Seat that gave Eliza birth,
> We kneel, and kiss the consecrated Earth...[2]

Nothing could be further from the atmosphere of Boswell's familiar tale of Johnson and young David Garrick riding to London to seek their fortunes in March 1737. Here, by contrast, is the touch of brisk heroic comedy like a picaresque adventure out of a Fielding novel. 'Both of them', says Boswell, 'used to talk pleasantly of it', and embellished it suitably as the years went by.

They were cheerful, poor, devil-may-care. Garrick would say that they had only one horse between them, and 'rode and tied' – that is, each one riding ahead in turn, tying up the horse to a tree or gate, and walking on till the other overtook and performed the next relay, as if they were gypsies. Johnson would add that his total finances were 'two-pence half-penny'. Garrick once mockingly challenged this in Boswell's hearing: 'Eh? what do you say? With two-pence half-penny in your pocket?' – Johnson: 'Why yes; when I came with two-pence half-penny in *my* pocket, and thou, Davy, with three half-pence in thine.' It became a favourite party piece, and passed into the Boswellian legend.

They took their 'precepts of economy' from an Irish painter, dined once a day at the Pine-Apple Coffee-house in New Street off the Strand for eight pence, and paid formal visits on 'clean-shirt-days' only. When Johnson first applied for literary work at a bookseller's in the Strand, the proprietor Mr Wilcox 'eyed his robust frame attentively' and then suggested he take a job as a vegetable porter in Covent Garden.[3]

But these picturesque details, lovingly gathered by Boswell, mask a much bleaker truth. Johnson was a failed schoolmaster, who had spent most of his wife's inheritance, and gone off to London with a teenage pupil in a desperate last attempt to recoup his fortunes. Garrick had a definite plan: to apply to Lincoln's Inn, and if that failed to stay with his actor-brother Peter. He was also due to inherit a legacy of a thousand pounds, sufficient to make him independent.

Johnson, by comparison, was adrift in the capital. He had the unfinished manuscript of his tragedy *Irene*, and an idea of applying to the *Gentleman's Magazine* for hack-work (it had been refused previously, in 1734). He also carried a kindly but useless letter of recommendation from his friend Gilbert Walmsley to the head-master of Colson's Academy, a fellow native of Lichfield. Omitting Johnson's personal circumstances, Walmsley wrote: 'Mr Johnson [is] to try his fate with a Tragedy, and to see to get himself employed in some translation, either from the Latin or the French. Johnson is a very good scholar and poet, and I have great hopes will turn out a fine tragedy-writer. If it should any way lie in your way, doubt not but you would be ready to recommend and assist your countryman.'[4]

This left out a good deal about the difficulties of Johnson's character and circumstances.

The young Johnson of Lichfield may have been 'a very good scholar and poet' potentially, but so far his professional achievements in either field had been minimal. At twenty-seven he had published nothing except some desultory essays in the *Birmingham Journal* and a pedestrian translation of Lobo's *Voyage to Abyssinia*. The translation had been dictated to his friend Edmund Hector, while Johnson lay in bed too depressed to go to his desk.[5]

His scholastic career was equally undistinguished. His failure to complete a degree at Pembroke College, Oxford, in December 1729 (because of his father's poverty, which had caused him endless humiliations) virtually destroyed his chances of a good grammar-school post or headmastership. Combined with his physical handicaps, this produced from 1730 onwards long periods of profound, chronic depression, with days of crushing slothful inactivity. At this time he told his school-friend, John Taylor of Ashbourne, that he 'strongly entertained thoughts of suicide'.[6]

Over the next six years, Johnson failed in half-a-dozen masterships in small schools scattered between Lichfield, Birmingham and Stourbridge; each time fleeing back to the houses of his friends – Walmsley, Hector, or John Taylor – for solace and domestic comforts. A final blow came in 1736, when an attempt to start his own school at Edial, two miles outside Lichfield, failed through lack of pupils renewing their fees. It was closed with the loss of several hundred pounds. This money was not his own, but belonged to his new wife.[7]

Johnson's difficulties were not merely, or even largely, financial or professional. They were profound problems of temperament and physical disability. These showed in depressive episodes, alternating with bullying aggression. His immediate appearance was outlandish: over six foot tall, looming in doorways, and shambling dangerously down streets (often muttering to himself). Closer up, he was a large, gaunt, bony young man of alarming, restless movement: quite unlike the noble, rolling, monumental, almost Buddha-like figure who emerges from the later descriptions of Boswell and portraits of Reynolds. He was partially blind in one eye, and heavily scarred round the throat with childhood scrofula. He suffered from frightening nervous spasms of the arms and shoulders, and uncontrollable facial twitches.

Boswell recorded these with great accuracy and tenderness in later life, when they had become almost endearing features. Yet even he notes that the painter Hogarth, on first spotting Johnson in Richardson's drawing-room, assumed he was a congenital idiot taken in for philanthropic reasons.[8]

In his late twenties Johnson was a figure of horrid fascination. Men were intimidated by him, women were both excited and repulsed, children were frightened in his presence and cruelly mocking behind his back. This disturbing, unfamiliar picture emerges from the confidential reports of several of the schools that rejected him.

The governors of Solihull, seven miles outside Birmingham, sent this reply to Gilbert Walmsley's recommendation of Johnson for the vacant headmastership in 1735: '... all agree that he is an excellent scholar, and upon that account deserves much better than to be schoolmaster of Solihull. But then he has the character of being a very haughty, ill-natured gent., and that he has such a way of distorting his face (which though he can't help) the gent. think it may affect some young lads; for these two reasons he is not approved on ...'[9] Boswell did not know of this report, or at any rate did not quote it.

A similar rejection came from the headmaster of Brewood Grammar School, fifteen miles west of Lichfield, in 1736. Johnson was refused the post of assistant master, 'from an apprehension that the paralytick affection ... might become the object of imitation or of ridicule, among his pupils'.[10] Boswell did have this report in his archives, but omitted it from his account of young Johnson, including it only as a retrospective footnote to his moving description of Johnson's death in 1784.

Less than a dozen letters have survived from this Lichfield period of Johnson's life, and so it has always remained obscure. But something of that 'haughty, ill-natured' manner appears in his earliest attempt to find a professional opening in London. Writing to Edward Cave of the *Gentleman's Magazine* in November 1734, he confidently recommends himself – an unknown, unemployed schoolmaster from Stafford – for the post of literary correspondent: 'Sir: As You appear no less sensible than Your Readers of the defects of your Poetical Article, You will not be displeased, if, in order to the improvement of it, I communicate to You the sentiments of a person, who will undertake on reasonable terms sometimes to fill a column.'[11]

We particularly catch young Johnson's voice in his bullish, and splendidly tactless, summary: 'By this method your Literary Article, for so it might be called, will, he thinks, be better recommended to the Publick, than by low Jests, awkward Buffoonery, or the dull scurrilities of either Party.'[12] The application met with a polite refusal.

Haughtiness covered not merely provincial gaucherie, but desperate loneliness and uncertainty. Johnson's frustrated intellectual brilliance hid extraordinary emotional immaturity. This, Boswell never seems to have grasped. For him, Johnson was a sage from boyhood, a wise owl from the egg. Yet the truth seems to be that, barricaded in his large monstrous body, Johnson had the tender, awkward emotions of an overgrown child.

He depended on his friends, and needed almost to be mothered by them. In 1735, he wrote one of his few revealing letters to Richard Congreve, a twenty-one-year-old undergraduate then at Oxford. Congreve had known him briefly at Lichfield and had written a summer letter vaguely suggesting a renewal of their 'old acquaintance'. Johnson, then twenty-six, replied with an awkward but surprisingly romantic enthusiasm. He imagines their friendship as a kind of Arcadia, from which he can flee from the hostile world.

Our former familiarity which you show in so agreeable a Light was embarrassed with no forms, and we were content to love without complimenting each other. It was such as well became our rural Retreats, shades unpolluted by Flattery and falsehood, thickets where interest and artifice never lay concealed! To such an acquaintance I again invite you . . .[13]

The way young Johnson already idealises friendship is striking. His instinct is to treat it as poetic and aphoristic. 'He may be justly said to be alone,' he tells Congreve, 'who has none to whom he imparts his thoughts.' Something intensely personal emerges in the description of the true friend: one with whom a man may converse 'without suspicion of being ridicul'd or betray'd'.[14] This secret longing for companionship prepares us for Savage's tremendous impact on his life.

The actual news that Johnson conveys to Congreve is oddly muted: 'little has happened to me recently', he remarks, and he will not dwell on 'past disappointments'. The only thing worthy of note is the Edial scheme, 'a private boarding-school for Young Gentlemen whom I shall endeavour to instruct in a method more rational than those commonly practised'. It is what he fails to tell his Arcadian friend that is most remarkable: that in less than a fortnight he is due to be married. Indeed his future wife, Elizabeth Porter, gets no mention at all. Johnson appears too embarrassed, too uncertain of himself, to mention his strongest feelings.

Yet these strong feelings certainly existed, especially in sexual matters. Johnson's profound emotional frustration throughout the early part of his life, both in Lichfield and in London, forms a part of his literary personality that has rarely been recognised. Just as it is difficult to imagine Johnson young, so it seems impossible to imagine Johnson in love. Thanks largely to Boswell, the very phrase sounds faintly ludicrous. But Boswell, whose *Journals* reveal how fascinated, amused and tortured by sex he was all his own life, could never really bear to envisage his sage in equivalent throes of lust or passion. Having first met Johnson at the age of fifty-four (Boswell then being a mere twenty-three), he always projected a venerable father-figure, a moral counsellor, detached from passion. So, perhaps understandably, he could never really accept the vulnerable, tender and romantic side of 'the Great Cham', in his far-distant youth. This has subtly affected our view of Johnson's whole biography ever since.

Boswell always deflects the question of Johnson's sexual feelings by treating them whimsically, if not farcically. He admits that Johnson was attracted by women: 'Johnson had, from his early youth, been sensible to the influence of female charms'; but he typically diffuses this by archly remarking on the 'facility and elegance' with which Johnson could 'warble the amorous lay'.[15]

This deflating humour is deployed whenever he writes about the women who, throughout Johnson's life, were the serious objects of his interests, hopes and passions. There were more than is usually thought: apart from his wife Elizabeth Porter, there was the adored Molly Aston; Hill Boothby (intended as Johnson's second wife); Hester Thrale (the confidante who replaced a second wife); the understanding Elizabeth Desmoulins (the young widowed daughter of his doctor); the admired Elizabeth Carter; and half-a-dozen young women writers and actresses, whom Boswell often simply omits from his account.[16]

His treatment of Johnson's strange, passionate and deeply unhappy marriage to Elizabeth Porter as a sentimental farce of 'connubial felicity' is wholly characteristic.[17] Nowhere does he seriously consider the impact of Johnson's sexual frustrations on his beginnings as a writer and poet. Modern biographers tend to take the same line. Even James Clifford writes: 'Johnson could never give himself up wholeheartedly to romance, whether in life or in literature.'[18]

Yet the women who knew young Johnson best, either directly or through family gossip and reminiscence, take a very different attitude. Among them are Lucy Porter (Johnson's stepdaughter), Anna Seward and Hester Thrale: almost invariably cited by Boswell as 'unreliable' witnesses.

Anna Seward (1747–1809), who became the poet known as 'the Swan of Lichfield', was not born when Johnson left for London. But she became an invaluable source for local memories and hearsay about him, especially through her grandfather (who had taught Johnson), her mother (who knew Elizabeth Porter) and the Walmsley family, about all of whom she wrote extensively. Boswell delights in disproving her stories on innumerable points. Yet Anna frequently throws revealing light on young Johnson's emotions. One of her most suggestive formulations is this: 'Johnson was always fancying himself in love with some princess or other.'[19]

Johnson first fell in love some time in his middle teens. His princess was Ann Hector, the sister of his school-friend, Edmund Hector, at Stourbridge. It is probably for her that he wrote his first poem: 'On a Daffodil: The First Flower that the Author had seen that Year', which refers to a smiling nymph, Cleora. A distinguished modern biographer, Walter Jackson Bate, remarks that 'when we think of the later Johnson, the very title is hilarious'.[20] Yet this seems a curiously revealing admission. For the poem does not appear particularly absurd for a sixteen-year-old:

> But while I sing, the nimble moments fly,
>   See! Sol's bright chariot seeks the western main,
> And ah! behold the shriveling blossoms die,
>   So late admir'd and prais'd, alas! in vain!
>
> With grief this emblem of mankind I see,
>   Like one awaken'd from a pleasing dream,
> Cleora's self, fair flower, shall fade like thee,
>   Alike must fall the Poet and his theme.[21]

When Boswell discovered this romance, he used another characteristic form of deflection: he omitted it from the Lichfield years, and retold it retrospectively as a reminiscence of Johnson's in his sixty-seventh year. It was displaced, and thus disarmed. Yet what Johnson says is moving and significant. 'She was the first woman with whom I was in love. It dropt out of my head imperceptibly; but she and I shall always have a kindness for each other.' When he talked of Ann Hector that night, 'he seemed to have had his affection revived; for he said, "If I had married her, it might have been as happy for me." '22

Later at Stourbridge, just before going up to Oxford, he fell more seriously in love with Olivia Lloyd, the beautiful and well-educated daughter of a rich Quaker family of ironmasters and philanthropists. Olivia was two years older than him, well-read in Greek and Latin classics (which she later taught to her nephews), amusing and quick, and renowned for her looks. She was known locally as 'the pretty Birmingham Quakeress'.23 Johnson fantasised about her throughout his university years, and she was one of the dreams he had to abandon bitterly along with his degree.

Olivia was the first in a line of pretty, vivacious bluestockings whom Johnson quietly worshipped (and also helped professionally) in London. Boswell takes a single sentence to describe the affair: 'he was much enamoured of Olivia Lloyd ... to whom he wrote a copy of verses, which I have not been able to recover.'24

Edmund Hector recalled acting as a go-between in this situation: 'some Young Ladies in Lichfield had a mind to act *The Distressed Mother*, for whom [Johnson] wrote the Epilogue and gave it me to convey privately to them.' Johnson's agonies of self-consciousness about his monstrous appearance are glimpsed in that 'privately'.

Other poems possibly connected with Olivia Lloyd include a series of translations from Horace, normally the most urbane, ironic and detached of poets. But Johnson selects passages that are surprisingly moody, bleak and romantic:

> But being counsell'd to go home
> And see my mistress face no more
> Confus'd about the streets I roam
> And stop'd unwilling at her door.
> Then to the inclement skies expos'd I sat
> And sigh'd and wept at her relentless gate.25

Johnson must have chosen these particular stanzas (from Horace's Eleventh Epode) because they reflected something in his own situation, his eternal longings for *la princesse lointaine*. As a picture of the lover unrequited, the man shut out, the roamer through the dark windswept streets, they also prepared him for Savage.

There are several other love-poems and poetical flirtations (mostly collected by Edmund Hector) which date from this sad post-Oxford period: 'To a Young Lady on her Birthday', 'An Ode on a Lady Leaving her Place of Abode', and a verse to the eighteen-year-old Dorothy Hickman, 'Playing on the Spinet'. Dorothy was the daughter of another friend at Stourbridge, George Hickman, and she married soon after in 1734.

The pattern of longing, frustration and self-laceration (however formalised in drawing-room 'impromptus') is common throughout these poems. As he wrote of Dorothy Hickman, 'We bless the Tyrant, and we hug the Chain.'[26]

Young Johnson's daydreams were not only confined to suitable girls. His princess might also be some tempting, racy actress. At about the time he first met Elizabeth Porter he also 'was in love with' a Junoesque young actress who visited Lichfield with a local repertory company, playing Flora, the romantic lead in Colley Cibber's suggestive farce, *Hob: or the Country Wake*.[27] David Garrick seems to have known something about this infatuation, and remarked that Johnson (possibly because of his eyesight) did not have a delicate ('*elegans*') taste in the female form, and could also appreciate brazen and 'vulgar' sexual talents.[28] Boswell once again safely confined this episode to Johnson's reminiscences forty years later.

Anna Seward seems to have been right about Johnson's 'princess' syndrome, and the pattern that emerges is not unlike the classic fairy-tale of Beauty and the Beast. Johnson's marriage does not really seem to have altered this, and throughout Johnson's early London years there is evidence that it continues. It made Johnson both peculiarly sympathetic, and perhaps even vulnerable, to Savage's own much wilder emotional fantasies.

Johnson's strange romance with Elizabeth Porter began in 1734. His good friend Harry Porter, a mercer at Edgbaston, had been taken ill, and Johnson rode out frequently from Lichfield to attend Harry's sick-bed. Johnson became a friend of the whole family in their distress: two young sons Jervis and Joseph; an eighteen-year-old daughter, Lucy; and Mrs Elizabeth Porter, then aged forty-five.[29]

Boswell, and all Johnson's subsequent biographers except Anna Seward, failed to draw the obvious conclusion. If Johnson had any interest other than pure friendship, it was evidently in the princess, the eighteen-year-old Lucy, to whom he had been attracted since his schooldays.[30] Her mother Elizabeth, who was nearly twice his age and devoted to her ailing husband, was not initially the object of his dreams.

A formal introduction to Lucy, as with other girls, had later been made by Edmund Hector, who bought his clothes from Harry Porter.[31] This was probably in 1732, when Lucy was a blossoming sixteen and Johnson twenty-three. She vividly recalled Johnson from those early visits, with a physical revulsion that is expressive. This is Beauty describing the Beast, as reported years later to Boswell. Both maintain the comfortable fiction that Johnson was only ever interested in Lucy's mother. But this is not what emerges, and it is not what Anna Seward thought either: 'the rustic prettiness, and artless manners of her daughter, the present Mrs Lucy Porter, had won Johnson's youthful heart.'[32]

In pictorial terms, these early meetings resulted in perhaps the most unforgettable image of Johnson in his twenties that we have. Boswell records:

> Miss Porter told me, that when he was first introduced to her mother, [Johnson's] appearance was very forbidding: he was then lean and lank, so that his immense structure of bones was hideously striking to the eye, and the scars of the scrophula were deeply visible. He also wore his hair, which was straight and stiff, and separated behind: and he often had, seemingly, convulsive starts and odd gesticulations, which tended to excite at once surprize and ridicule.[33]

This, with its touch of horrified exaggeration, is almost worthy of Hogarth. The detail of the hair, 'stiff and straight', worn without a wig, and yet combed self-consciously behind, is curiously disturbing; and perhaps there is a grotesque hint, through Lucy's eyes, of the suitor. Lucy recalls her mother's extraordinary reaction: 'this is the most sensible man that I ever saw in my life.'

Anna Seward was quoting a Lichfield tradition that Johnson was first in love with Lucy. She goes on to suggest, by way of proof, that Johnson's poem 'On a Sprig of Myrtle' was written for Lucy, and given to her around 1733. Boswell ridicules this, and is able to show conclusively that the poem was written before they met, in 1731, and at the special request of a quite different friend of Edmund Hector's – a Mr Morgan – who 'waited upon a lady' in the neighbourhood. At Boswell's urgings, Hector even produced an original manuscript dated 1731. There biographers have left the matter.[34]

No one has considered that Johnson may *later* have given the same poem, or a version of it, to Lucy Porter as well, exactly as Anna Seward claims. The poem is about the 'ambiguity' of love, as summed up in the emblem of the myrtle which can mean many things in lover's lore:

> The Myrtle crowns the happy Lovers heads,
> Th' unhappy Lovers Graves the Myrtle spreads;
> Oh! then the Meaning of thy Gift impart,
> And cure the throbbings of an anxious Heart . . .[35]

Anna Seward's account of its presentation to Lucy, written privately to Boswell, is particularly insistent:

> I *know* those verses were addressed to Lucy Porter, when he was enamoured of her in his boyish days, two or three years before he had seen her mother, his future wife. He wrote them at my grandfather's, and gave them to Lucy in the presence of my mother, to whom she showed them on the instant. She used to repeat them to me, when I asked her for *the Verses Dr Johnson gave her on a Sprig of Myrtle, which he had stolen or begged from her bosom.* We all know honest Lucy Porter to have been incapable of the mean vanity of applying to herself a compliment not *intended* for her.[36]

It seems unlikely that Anna Seward was muddled about the particular poem, or that she should be completely wrong about the general direction of Johnson's feelings.

At all events, when Harry Porter suddenly died and was buried on 5th September 1734, the situation evidently changed. Elizabeth was now a widow, with a small family fortune of £600, a lively interest in books and a desire for solace. Johnson and she clearly enjoyed each other's company; both were to some degree eccentric. Physical passion emerged on both sides, and Johnson would later insist, 'with much gravity', that it was 'a love-marriage' for both of them.[37]

Mrs Porter was a vivacious woman with a well-rounded figure, a mass of blonde hair and a large maternal bosom. She dressed well, used make-up, lived quite expensively and liked to talk and tipple in the evenings. Johnson, starved for love and intelligent conversation, childlike and shy in his affection, punished for his physical ugliness, was slowly captivated over the next eighteen months. He must have given up any hope he may have had for children of his own. He abandoned, at least temporarily, his dream of the princess.

Instead, it was agreed as part of the marriage contract that Mrs Porter would invest her money in the school at Edial. When the forthcoming wedding was announced, all the Porter relations were appalled; her older son Jervis (then training for the Navy) refused ever to see his mother again, while the younger, Joseph, was unreconciled for many years.[38] Only Lucy stood by her mother and tenderly accepted her outlandish stepfather.

Lucy Porter never married subsequently. Her sweet nature, her shyness and her loyalty to Johnson became proverbial.[39] He later told Mrs Thrale how he would always get Lucy on his side when he had an argument with his wife.[40] She also became the one person who could manage his old mother at Lichfield, and eventually ran the bookshop, the accounts, and the whole household there when Johnson had left for London. Lucy ultimately became like a beloved younger sister to him: a confidante in all matters, financial and emotional, and in some ways closer to him than his wife.

Elizabeth Porter was, after all, much nearer to his mother's generation; and in the London years one can sometimes glimpse Johnson confiding to Lucy behind the backs of the two elder women simultaneously. With Lucy, he is familiar, teasing, self-revealing in a way that appears nowhere else in his early life; and certainly not in the few known letters to Elizabeth Porter. His manner can be quite startling.

When Lucy's rich uncle, Joseph Porter, died in 1749, and Lucy wrote to Johnson about family business using a black wax on her letter seal, he replied: 'You frighted me, you little Gipsy, with your black wafer, for I had forgot you were in mourning and was afraid your letter had brought me ill news of my mother, whose death is one of the few calamities on which I think with horror. I long to know how she does, and how you all do. Your poor Mamma is come home but very weak yet I hope she will grow better, else she shall go into the country. She is now upstairs and knows not of my writing.'[41]

It is only a glimpse, but it is expressive of much: the tenderness, the confidentiality, the sense of Johnson and Lucy coping together with two elderly mothers who can cause such anxiety and heartache. Sarah Johnson was then eighty, and Elizabeth Porter sixty. It is an obvious question to ask, from all this, how far Johnson had actually married not a princess, but a mother-figure.

There are many anecdotes of Johnson and Elizabeth together – from Garrick, from John Taylor, from Mrs Desmoulins, from Hawkins – nearly all of them in a vein of high, and sometimes cruel, sexual comedy, which encouraged Boswell to dismiss the whole question of Johnson's romantic nature.[42] It comes across as a grotesque liaison – 'tumultuous and awkward' – viewed through a biographical keyhole. Taylor put it most bluntly of all: 'She was the plague of Johnson's life, was abominably drunken and despicable . . .'[43]

In later life, Johnson would endlessly, loyally and guiltily profess his undying affection for his 'Tetty'. There are huge contradictions in the evidence. But it seems that one of the reasons that Johnson left Lichfield for London in 1737, besides the search for a regular income, was to escape both his wife and his mother. And perhaps to dream, once again, of a princess.

All this begins to suggest a young Johnson quite different from Boswell's sage, with his dry epigrammatic resignation about marital infelicity – second marriage is 'the triumph of hope over experience', and so on. Indeed, the purely external facts of finance and domesticity suggest a clear pattern of romantic disenchantment during the first decade or so of the marriage.

Once Johnson had used up the bulk of Elizabeth's £600 dowry on the failed school at Edial, he contrived to live apart from her for steadily increasing periods of time. Edial failed in the autumn of 1736, and Johnson left for London the following March, remaining away for six or even eight months, much longer than a professional reconnaissance of the capital could possibly have required.

This was the first significant absence, but others soon followed. Having brought Elizabeth back to London at the end of 1737, he established her in relatively comfortable West End lodgings at Castle Street, off Cavendish Square. But by winter 1738 Johnson was again drifting away, using separate rooms off Fleet Street, or at least spending many nights away. Boswell denies this, but Hawkins seems definite on the point and speaks of a 'temporary separation'.[44] Modern biographers concur: 'Everything we can piece together about Johnson's own way of living, at least by the winter of 1738–39, indicates not merely that he was living elsewhere, probably in or near Fleet Street, but also that he sometimes even roamed the streets without settled lodging.'[45]

This separation coincides with his greatest period of intimacy with Savage. It is also the first time that Johnson began to earn an independent income from his literary work: editorial wages from the *Gentleman's Magazine*, ten guineas for the publication of his poem *London* (May 1738), and £49.7s.0d. for a translation of Sarpi's *Council of Trent*, paid in instalments up till April 1739.[46] Johnson, always the most generous of men, probably used most of this money to support Elizabeth at Castle Street and, if there was spare, to help Savage who was renowned for his relentless borrowing from any friend in sight.

Johnson was now suspended between unhappy, dutiful domesticity and the roving, bohemian poet's life in the city, allowing him the freedom which he craved. Curious glimpses of this life of garrets, taverns, journalists and prostitutes appeared years later, and only mildly disguised, in his *Rambler* essays.[47] Hawkins comments severely on the decline of his 'domestic virtues', and on the effect of Savage's loose morals and his acquaintance with 'the vices of the town', during these hectic months. He remarks that Johnson's reflections on this time later gave him great 'uneasiness'.[48]

When Savage finally left London, after the tearful parting of July 1739, Johnson almost immediately left the city too. He abandoned Elizabeth in Castle Street. Though his official reason was a possible schoolmastership in Appleby, Leicestershire, this third separation also lasted about six months, until April 1740. 'Abandon' does not seem too strong a word. During this time Johnson fell in love with a woman of his own age, the dashing, high-spirited Molly Aston.

Molly was the second daughter of Sir Thomas Aston, and Johnson had admired her from afar at Lichfield ever since his return from Oxford. He called her 'a beauty and a scholar, a wit and a whig'; she was probably the most entrancing of all his princesses. When Mrs Thrale once asked him what had been the happiest period of his whole life, he replied without hesitation that it had been a single evening spent with Molly. 'That indeed (said he) was not happiness, it was rapture; but the thoughts of it sweetened the whole year.'[49]

Molly was just three years older than him: tall, elegant, well-read and brilliantly amusing. She was rich, clever and slightly daunting; many men were frightened of her and women tended to be jealous. Anna Seward, who confirms Johnson's passion for her, called her 'handsome but haughty'.[50] She had a high, slightly beaky profile;

an impatient mass of auburn hair that she brushed back hard; and she did not suffer fools gladly.

Johnson loved her for all this, and respected her opinions. Her remarks on Pope and Gray appeared, years later, in his *Lives of the Poets*, a sort of delayed lover's tribute from him. He once deferred to her on a question of economics.[51] When he had heard her one evening speaking in a whiggish way about political freedom (an attitude he normally detested), he gallantly deflected his disagreement into a Latin epigram about her beauty, '*Pulchra Maria*'. Her beauty allowed him no freedom, since he was her slave. (It was translated, long after, by Mrs Thrale (who had become his confidante in all these matters of the heart):

> Persuasions to freedom fall oddly from you,
> If freedom we seek, fair Maria, Adieu![52]

Another cycle of six poems, 'To Stella', which Johnson finally published anonymously (perhaps because of his wife) in the *Gentleman's Magazine* in 1747, also seems to be associated with Molly Aston. One of Molly's sisters had married George Walmsley and another sister Johnson's rumbustious friend Henry Hervey Aston. Johnson visited Molly at both their houses in Lichfield, and perhaps also at Hervey's town house in London. It was Harry Hervey who transcribed the 'Stella' group in their original form, during the period of their greatest intimacy, between 1737 and 1743.[53] It has been cautiously suggested that Johnson wrote them for Harry himself to send to some unnamed 'attractive girl in her teens'; perhaps even the Aston sister whom Harry married. But even if this were so, Johnson's private inspiration still seems to have been Molly herself.[54]

The titles of the poems trace a delicate, oblique, drawing-room romance: 'To Miss – On her Playing Upon the Harpsichord'; 'To Miss – On her Giving the Author a Gold and Silk Net-Work Purse'; 'Stella in Mourning'; 'An Evening Ode: To Stella'; and, above all, 'The Winter's Walk', which obviously relates to that difficult winter of 1739–40, when Johnson's heart was balanced – as he puts it in the poem – between 'rapture' and 'despair'.

If it seems strange to imagine Johnson in such romantic throes, yet the poems have a more than drawing-room passion, and indeed strike a recognisably Johnsonian note of pain and longing. This is especially true of the close of 'The Winter's Walk'. Beginning with a bleak, rather Thomson-like description of the chill Staffordshire landscape, 'the naked hill, the leafless grove', it moves inwards to the 'stern winter' in the poet's own heart:

> Enliv'ning hope, and fond desire,
>   Resign the heart to spleen and care,
> Scarce frighted love maintains his fire,
>   And rapture saddens to despair.
>
> In groundless hope, and causeless fear,
>   Unhappy man! behold thy doom,
> Still changing with the changeful year,
>   The slave of sunshine and of gloom.
>
> Tir'd with vain joys, and false alarms,
>   With mental and corporeal strife,
> Snatch me, my Stella, to thy arms,
>   And screen me from the ills of life.[55]

How far can we really take these verses as an expression of personal emotion? Perhaps the very fact that they exist (and are so rarely quoted) itself suggests something not usually recognised about Johnson's sensibility: his gloomy longings for physical tenderness in a world of 'ills'. Hawkins did not believe him 'susceptible of amorous emotion', but accepts there was one 'romantic passion' in his early youth; and admits that Molly Aston was the one 'danger' and that Johnson always spoke of her with 'rapture'.[56]

Boswell mockingly dismisses the 'Stella' poems as a serious expression of Johnson's feelings.[57] He argues that since in old age Johnson could 'condescend to trifle in *namby-pamby* rhymes, to please Mrs Thrale and her daughter', so in earlier years he may have jokingly composed such pieces.[58] But this reveals Boswell's own limitations of portraiture. It is precisely to Mrs Thrale, and not to Boswell, that Johnson spoke openly about Molly Aston.

Hester Thrale gives us a penetrating female view of Johnson's psychology. From the time she met him in 1765, she entered more deeply into his confidence than any other woman in his life. Her *Anecdotes* (1786) provide a continual revelation into the hidden side of his emotional nature: his tears, his guilts, his regrets, and his sudden storms of feeling. Such glimpses appear in numerous tiny incidents, like the time that Johnson came fretfully back from seeing Hester's son to school, suddenly immersed in memories of his own adolescence. '"Make your boy tell you his dreams: the first corruption that entered my heart was communicated in a dream." "What was it, Sir?" said I. "*Do* not ask me," replied he, with much violence, and walked away in apparent agitation.'[59]

Mrs Thrale knew about the tensions in Johnson's marriage, and affirms Elizabeth's knowledge and jealousy of Molly Aston. Johnson's own romantic feelings are lightly, but clearly indicated in a story he told Mrs Thrale of meeting a Gypsy fortune-teller while out walking in the country with his wife. The Gypsy read his palm, and in so doing reduced Elizabeth to tears. 'Your heart is divided, Sir, between a Betty and a Molly: Betty loves you best, but you take most delight in Molly's company: when I turned about to laugh, I saw my wife was crying.' Johnson added gallantly, 'Pretty charmer! she had no reason.' But the significant thing is that he told such a story to Mrs Thrale at all. He was admitting deep and divided feelings, even long afterwards.[60]

It was only Elizabeth's sudden injury (a torn tendon), and financial desperation, which finally brought him back to London and his marriage in 1740. There was also a chance to get *Irene* staged. These considerations shape the rest of the much-tested relationship: Elizabeth confined more and more to bed, drinking, reading and taking opium pain-killers; Johnson working hard, supporting and indulging her like an invalid, but emotionally withdrawn. The bedroom is no longer shared.[61]

The tone of the letter written at the end of January 1740, in which Johnson promises to return to Elizabeth, expresses a great deal. He is penitent, affectionate and guilty: 'You have already suffered more than I can bear to reflect upon, and I hope more than either of us shall suffer again. One part at least I have often flattered myself we shall avoid for the future our troubles will surely never separate us more.'

He continues contritely: 'I still promise myself many happy years from your tenderness and affection, which I sometimes hope our misfortunes have not yet deprived me of.'

But there is some uncertainty about her resentment: 'I hope You do not think so unkindly of me as to imagine that I can be at rest while I believe my dear Tetty in pain.'

Moreover there is a defensiveness about his own dalliance with Molly Aston, which surely hides resignation at the fact that his princess had once again eluded him: 'Be assured, my dear Girl, that I have seen nobody in these rambles upon which I have been forced, that has not contributed to confirm my esteem and affection for thee . . .' But he ends with a gallant flourish: 'I am, my charming Love, Yours, Sam Johnson.'[62]

It is interesting that Boswell slides over this whole separation, does not quote from the letter, and once again only refers to the friendship with Molly Aston retrospectively, at a much later date, in 1776: 'the lady of whom Johnson used to speak with the warmest admiration . . . who was afterwards married to Captain Brodie of the navy.'[63]

From then on the marriage slowly petrified. Elizabeth was increasingly ill, or drunk. She at first took some part in Johnson's journalistic work, reading and researching for him, but this soon tailed off. Her dowry was spent, her family relations (except Lucy in Lichfield) alienated from her, her husband sunk in hack-work. Some time in the mid-1740s she began to visit the country village of Hampstead for her health, and by 1748 she had almost permanent lodgings there. Johnson visited her on some evenings and at weekends.

She did not manage to attend the first night of *Irene*, Johnson's final bid as a dramatic poet, in February 1749. Perhaps this was a relief to both of them. Garrick's vicious caricature of her dates from this final stage of the marriage: 'very fat, with a bosom of more than ordinary protuberance, with swelled cheeks, of a florid red, produced by thick painting, and increased by the liberal use of cordials; flaring and fantastic in her dress, and affected both in her speech and her general behaviour.'[64] Yet it is the emotional disappointment of the entire marriage which is partly reflected in this sad parody of Johnson's longed-for princess.

At Hampstead, Elizabeth was attended on by a young widow, Mrs Desmoulins, an old friend of the Lichfield circle, whom Johnson had brought south to be her companion. In old age she was cross-questioned by Boswell about the relations between husband and wife. What he discovered was omitted from his biography, and filed separately under the Latin heading *Tacenda* – to be held back in silence.

What Mrs Desmoulins said was this. Elizabeth drank heavily, using the excuse that she was not well; was usually in bed asleep when Johnson appeared; and had refused for years to have sexual relations with him. Johnson would retire to a separate bedroom, and when in bed would call in Mrs Desmoulins to talk with him. Presently she would lie on the bed, on top of the sheets but with her head on the pillow next to his. He would then cuddle and fondle her in an amorous way, before sending her abruptly out of the room.

To Boswell's further, insistent questions and demands for detail (he was expert in every physical nuance of such encounters), Mrs Desmoulins would only reply that Johnson 'never did anything that was beyond the limits of decency'.[65] Boswell never established what young Mrs Desmoulins had thought those limits were; but the picture – tender, tragic, ludicrous – is clear enough.

It was at exactly this period, walking alone in the lanes of Hampstead outside his wife's lodgings, that Johnson composed his greatest poem, *The Vanity of Human Wishes*. And it was now, as I have suggested, that his fictional biography might have ended, at the age of forty, in an apoplexy brought on by hard work, lack of recognition, frustration and misery.

It is against the background of this marriage, this longing for companionship, and this frustrated 'dream of princesses', that Johnson's friendship with Savage has to be reconsidered.

CHAPTER 3

NIGHT

There has always been one vivid, popular legend of Johnson's unlikely friendship. It is enshrined in a particular anecdote that was passed lovingly around Johnson's later circle: each one heard, embroidered and retold a different version of it. The account describes how Johnson and Savage walked round the squares of London all one night, being too poor to afford either food or lodging but sustained by the passionate intimacy of their conversation.

This story, in its various renditions, became symbolic of the Augustan writer's life in Grub Street, just as the story of Thomas Chatterton's death in a Holborn garret became symbolic of the romantic poet for the later eighteenth century. It passed quickly into treasured anecdote, and remains to this day the one clear image of young Johnson in London. A recent American scholar summarises it with relish: 'Those who know nothing else of his early life can envision in Hogarthian detail Johnson in his ill-fitting great-coat and Savage dressed like a decayed dandy, wandering the street for want of a lodging and inveighing against fortune and the Prime Minister.'[1]

It is easy to see why the story appealed. It is indeed like a Hogarth illustration to Johnson's famous line, from his poem *London*, 'Slow rises worth, by Poverty depressed'. The link between poverty and genius, between poetry and lack of recognition, is axiomatic for the young writer coming to try his fortune in the great city.

We can instantly imagine the scene: the cobbled streets, the stinking rubbish, the tavern signs, the shuttered house-fronts; the moonlight and the dark alleys; the slumbering beggars, the footpads and the Night Watch; and the two central figures striding along, bent in conversation, convivial and ill-matched. Here is the huge, bony Johnson with his flapping horse-coat and dirty tie-wig, swinging the famous cudgel with which he once kept four muggers at bay until the Night Watch came up to rescue him; and here the small, elegant Savage with his black silk court-dress (remarked on at his trial), his moth-eaten cloak, his tasselled sword and his split shoes, which well-wishers were always trying to replace.

It is a night scene: these friends are outcasts from society, without money and without lodgings, talking of poetry and politics and reforming the world, while the wealthy complacent city slumbers in oblivion. They are in a sense its better conscience, ever wakeful; or its uneasy dream of oppression and injustice. It is a romantic, Quixotic, heroic or mock-heroic picture, depending on one's point of view. But how true is it?

There are in fact four separate accounts of these night-wanderings. They are given by Sir John Hawkins, Johnson's early biographer; by his young friend the Irish playwright, Arthur Murphy; by his later companion in the celebrated Club, the painter Sir Joshua Reynolds; and by Boswell. All depend on hearsay, for none of them actually knew Johnson at the time, or had ever seen him together with Savage. Indeed an extraordinary fact at once emerges: no one, at any time, or in any place, ever left a first-hand account of seeing Johnson and Savage together. It was, from the start, an invisible friendship.

The episode of their night-walks exists as a kind of composite memory rather than as a specific event which anyone witnessed. All the accounts must have had Johnson as their ultimate source, but the circumstances are never quite the same. To show how the story developed, it is interesting to unwrap each version and examine its layered contents. We begin with Boswell, and work backwards until we finally reach Johnson's original account, dating from 1743.

Boswell was writing forty years later, and paints a general picture without describing a specific time or location in London. He emphasises the stoicism of the two friends whose imaginations could rise above the grim material facts of their poverty. 'It is melancholy to reflect, that Johnson and Savage were sometimes in such extreme indigence, that they could not pay for a lodging; so that they have wandered together whole nights in the streets. Yet in these almost incredible scenes of distress, we may suppose that Savage mentioned many of the anecdotes with which Johnson afterwards enriched the Life of his unhappy companion, and those of other Poets.'[2]

Boswell seems to admit tacitly that there may be some picturesque exaggeration in Johnson's fond recollections of these 'almost incredible scenes of distress'. (Indeed the degree of Johnson's poverty will bear further examination.) He likes to suppose that their talk was literary and anecdotal. He shrewdly imagines Johnson as collecting biographical 'anecdotes' from Savage, for the later *Lives of the Poets*; much as he in turn, many years later, would quiz Johnson for his own *Life*. His version of the night-walk is poetic: a handing-on of tales and traditions.

Uncharacteristically Boswell adds no visual details: nothing of dress, weather or season – a summer amble under the stars would presumably be very different from a winter tramp in rain or frost. But he does suggest, rather uneasily, that the two friends might sometimes have had enough money for other pursuits of the night, specifically drinking and whoring. 'I am afraid, however, that by associating with Savage, who was habituated to the dissipation and licentiousness of the town, Johnson, though his good principles remained steady, did not entirely preserve [his] conduct ... but was imperceptibly led into some indulgencies which occasioned much distress to his virtuous mind.'[3]

This is merely a hint, but a hint from Boswell on such a subject – *experto crede* – is much; and deserves to be borne in mind. So too does the rich London low-life material which Johnson subsequently incorporated into his *Rambler* essays, including a two-part biography of a country girl who becomes a prostitute, 'The Story of Misella'. She ends her life in an appalling series of late-night taverns and infested night-cellars, which Johnson describes with bitter conviction:

Thus driven again into the Streets, I lived upon the least that could support me, and at Night accommodated myself under Penthouses as well as I could ... In this abject state I have now passed four Years, the drudge of Extortion and the sport of

Drunkenness; sometimes the Property of one man, and some-times the common Prey of accidental Lewdness; at one time tricked up for sale by the Mistress of a Brothel, at another begging in the Streets to be relieved of Hunger by wickedness; without any hope in the Day but of finding some whom Folly or Excess may expose to my Allurements, and without any reflections at Night but such as Guilt and Terror impress upon me.

If those who pass their days in Plenty and Security could visit for an Hour the dismal Receptacles to which the Prostitute retires from her nocturnal Excursions, and see the Wretches that lie crowded together, mad with Intemperance, ghastly with Famine, nauseous with Filth, and noisome with Disease; it would not be easy for any degree of Abhorrence to harden them against Compassion, or to repress the Desire which they must immedi-ately feel to rescue such numbers of Human Beings from a state so dreadful.[4]

Sir Joshua Reynolds's account has a very different atmosphere. President of the Royal Academy, an elegant, easygoing man of the world, Reynolds had been fascinated with Savage's story ever since he had first read Johnson's *Life* in the 1750s. He had then shared with Johnson an acute dislike of aristocratic pretensions, and at a supper party in the presence of the Duchess of Argyll, the two pretended to be manual labourers, and loudly discussed the hourly wage-rate: 'How much do you think you and I could get in a week, if we were to *work as hard* as we could?'[5]

Reynolds had first read of Savage on returning from his painter's apprenticeship in Rome, casually picking up the book in a drawing-room in Devonshire. He began to read it 'while he was standing with his arm leaning against a chimney-piece. It seized his attention so strongly, that, not being able to lay down the book till he had finished it, when he attempted to move, he found his arm totally benumbed.'[6]

This is a painter's anecdote, mental attention represented by physical posture, with a certain flattering exaggeration of pose. Reynolds evidently questioned Johnson subsequently about his night-walks with Savage, and produced a witty *bravura* version, which would have told well in the Club. He supplies an exact location, a brisk amusing style, a conversational theme and a dra-matic flourish at the end. All is high style and insouciance, a brilliant Society sketch:

[Johnson] told Sir Joshua Reynolds, that one night in particular, when Savage and he walked round St James's Square for want of a lodging, they were not at all depressed by their situation; but in high spirits and brimful of patriotism, traversed the square for several hours, inveighed against the minister, and 'resolved they would *stand by their country*.'[7]

The touch of heroic absurdity – two down-and-outs resolving to save the nation – is designed for indulgent laughter. But Reynolds, if he reports Johnson accurately, tells us two surprising things. The first is that the night-walks did not take place in the fabled zone of Grub Street but in the new, fashionable squares of the West End. The second is that their talk was not literary but *political*. They talked daring opposition politics against the corruption of the Whigs and the Prime Minister, Sir Robert Walpole; and they praised 'patriotism', a specifically eighteenth-century usage, implying a radical politics which reviled the 'German' monarchy of the Hanoverians. Both this geography and this ideology throw a significant light on the young Johnson and his friend.

The compact geography of eighteenth-century London meant that the city could be crossed on foot in two hours, from the Tower in the south-east to Tyburn in the north-west. It represented a well-defined grid-map of power, professions and social classes. The central axis, running east–west parallel to the River Thames, was the broad boulevard of the Strand. Originally, as the name implies, the Strand was a riverside thoroughfare open to the water, with warehouses, shops, town houses, quaysides, and open unwalled shingle along its length. There was no regular Embankment, and no bridge across the river at this point. A painting by Canaletto, made from the terrace of Somerset House looking east in the 1740s, shows a broken vista of houses, balustrades and riverside steps going beyond St Paul's to the single London Bridge at Southwark in the East End.

The river was itself a thoroughfare as busy as the Strand, packed with skiffs, wherries, sailing barges and every conceivable kind and size of water-taxi, which passengers hailed at scores of stairs, landing-stages and pontoons. This constant flow of human traffic, east–west along the Strand and the Thames, by day and night, represented the shuttle of power and business activity within the capital.

So, to the east of the Strand, from Ludgate to the Tower and Spitalfields, lay commercial London: banking, broking, shipping, publishing, manufacturing, and the slums. This was the original, historical site of Grub Street, a narrow road of printers, taverns and lodging-houses roughly where the Barbican and the Museum of the City of London now stands.[8] It was where Edward Cave had established his *Gentleman's Magazine*, in rooms actually above the old medieval arch of St John's Gate, in Clerkenwell, which young Johnson 'beheld with reverence' when he first arrived in London. It was where a young writer began when he came to seek his fortune, and where an old one ended if he had failed to find it. It was the kingdom of Alexander Pope's Dunces. It was the East End of hope, and of despair.

But this is not where Johnson and Savage walked all night: they had gone 'up West' to the London of political power, wealth and social privilege. They were walking in enemy territory, the land to be conquered, and they came like spies in the night, their very presence a provocation.

To the west of the Strand, then, lay the smart coffee-houses of Charing Cross, the ministries of Westminster and Whitehall, Parliament and the Court, the royal parks and the elegant new squares of what became Mayfair. St James's Square, only laid out in the 1720s, was the home of dukes and dandies, next to the clubs of St James's and the royal palace itself. To talk of ministerial corruption and 'patriotism' here was like blowing a trumpet under the walls of Jericho. It was an heroic gesture, a defiant pose, which a painter like Reynolds would not forget.

Moreover, such a night-incursion into the domain of wealth and privilege was not a casual expedition. Reynolds may not have known this, but for Savage it was almost a ritual, repeated many times previously and solemnly enshrined in his own writings. In taking his young protégé Johnson into these familiar haunts, he was guiding him ceremonially, as Virgil guides Dante, through a purgatorial topography where much is to be learned by the angry young provincial, familiar only with book-learning:

> The Moon, descending, saw us now pursue
> The various Talk: – the City near in view!
> Here from *still Life* (he cries) avert thy Sight,
> And mark what *Deeds* adorn, or shame the Night![9]

This is from the key poetic document of Savage's career, the long visionary poem *The Wanderer* (1729), part meditation and part confession. Here, in its third canto, Savage describes such a night-pilgrimage through London. The young poet is guided by the Virgilian figure of 'the Hermit', a sage who has retired from the fret and folly of city life, to read poetry and philosophy in a cave and contemplate the wild beauty of Nature. This is one of Savage's recurring fantasies of himself, as Johnson eventually came to understand.

The Hermit points out the glittering, delusive dissipations of the West End, as Savage must have instructed Johnson during their own nocturnal pacings round the squares of Mayfair:

> Yon Mansion, made by beaming Tapers gay,
> Drowns the dim Night, and counterfeits the Day.
> From lumin'd windows glancing on the Eye,
> Around, athwart, the frisking Shadows fly.
> There Midnight *Riot* spreads illusive Joys,
> And Fortune, Health, and dearer Time destroys.[10]

Against this glimpse of shadow play of aristocratic revelry the Hermit points out the solitary light from a garret window, which signals the 'patriot' poet hard at work, perhaps at the other end of the Strand, somewhere near Grub Street. For him, true wealth is not a handsome building, a property speculation, but an intellectual construction, a mental tower of learning and independent intelligence:

> A feeble Taper, from yon lonesome Room,
> Scatt'ring thin rays, just glimmers through the Gloom.
> There sits the sapient *BARD* in museful Mood,
> And glows impassion'd for his Country's Good!
> All the bright *Spirits* of the *Just*, combin'd,
> Inform, refine, and prompt his tow'ring Mind![11]

One may suspect, like Boswell, that Savage's poetry was more improving than his conduct on such occasions. His Hermit, to say the least, is an idealisation. For it was on just such a night-walk, ten years before, that Savage had been involved in a brawl in a whorehouse, and killed a man and injured a woman, five minutes from St James's Square in Charing Cross. As Johnson later observed, 'The reigning Error of his Life was, that he mistook the Love for the Practice of Virtue'.[12]

When Johnson himself came to describe such night-walks in his own poem *London* (May 1738), he was much less dreamy and elevated. Indeed he was bitingly realistic, and we see again the big man with the cudgel. He seems to make some unmistakable reference to Savage's less poetical exploits:

> Prepare for Death, if here at Night you roam,
> And sign your Will before you sup from Home.
> Some fiery Fop, with new Commission vain,
> Who sleeps on Brambles till he kills his Man;
> Some frolick Drunkard, reeling from a Feast,
> Provokes a Broil, and stabs you for a Jest.[13]

The irony here may be deeper than it first appears. Because this may be *Savage himself* speaking. There is considerable evidence that this passage, and indeed much of the poem, is a dramatic monologue written partly in Savage's own voice. The whole of *London* may be partly Johnson's attempt to render, in verse, the impact of Savage's long conversations through the night. In this sense the poem could be considered as Johnson's first version of Savage's biography.

Certainly it seems true that Johnson first discovered in their night-walks the new form of intimate life-writing. It was to be like an extended conversation in the dark, taking ordinary facts and anecdotes, and pursuing them towards the shadowy and mysterious regions of a life, at the edge of the unknown or unknowable.

Johnson's early impressions of these night-walks continue to be modified, in a complex way, by the other friends who recollected them. Arthur Murphy, a genial Irish playwright nearly twenty years Johnson's junior, turned them into a piece of delightful comedy. Moving them even deeper into the West End, to the edge of Hyde Park, he added picturesque details of time and money, and with his playful turns of phrase seems to conjure up the witty outlines of a sketch that might have been written long after by Peacock or G. B. Shaw. (It should be read, perhaps, in a light Dublin brogue.)

> Johnson has been often heard to relate, that he and Savage walked round Grosvenor Square till four in the morning; in the course of their conversation reforming the world, dethroning princes, establishing new forms of government, and giving laws to the several states of Europe, till, fatigued at length with their legislative office, they began to feel the want of refreshment; but could not muster up more than fourpence halfpenny.[14]

The 'fourpence halfpenny' is, of course, a spurious comic exactitude. Yet there is something about Murphy's whole scenario, with its gracious absurdities, that carries a curious literary conviction. Why is this?

It is, surely, that Murphy has captured or suggested a premonition of the high, elegant, philosophic comedy of Johnson's *Rasselas* (1759). The destitute Savage talking to Johnson about giving laws to Europe is not unlike the deluded Astronomer telling Prince Imlac that he has been secretly assigned the universal regulation of the weather. '. . . The sun has listened to my dictates, and passed from tropic to tropic by my direction; the clouds, at my call, have poured their waters, and the Nile has overflowed at my command; I have restrained the rage of the Dog Star, and mitigated the fervours of the Crab. The winds alone, of all the elemental powers, have hitherto refused my authority . . .'[15]

These confidences, too, are delivered in the dark, in the Astronomer's turret, during a midnight storm. It was perhaps Savage who first gave Johnson the theme for *Rasselas*: that 'dangerous prevalence of the imagination' which Imlac discovers in the most interesting of human minds. Among those is the Poet himself, who must be acquainted with 'all the modes of life', who must commit his claims 'to the justice of posterity' and who must write 'as the interpreter of nature, and the legislator of mankind'.[16]

Of all the versions of the night-walks which we have, it is that by Sir John Hawkins, with his direct knowledge of young Johnson from the mid-1740s, which most sharply emphasises the subversive political nature of their talks. Boswell consistently derides Hawkins's accounts; not merely because he is the chief rival biographer, an amateur and musicologist, and so gratifyingly full of factual errors and 'solemn inexactitudes'. For Hawkins, himself a lonely and awkward personality, gives an altogether rougher, darker, more emotionally unstable picture of the young writer finding his path than Boswell's hero-worship will allow.

Hawkins's youthful Johnson is never a comfortable figure, never a natural Tory clubman. He is anxious, self-doubting and obsessive. His politics, like his whole personality, are fierce and to some degree disruptive. Boswell could never be easy with this. Hawkins sees immediate common political ground between the two outcasts. 'They had both felt the pangs of poverty, and the want of patronage: Savage had let loose his resentment against the possessors of wealth, in a collection of poems printed about the year 1727, and Johnson was ripe for an avowal of the same sentiments.'[17]

They both shared, according to Hawkins, 'the vulgar opinion, that the world is divided into two classes, of men of merit without riches, and men of wealth without merit'. Hawkins also says that Savage's 'principles of patriotism' – the semi-subversive Opposition to the Whig Government and the Hanoverian Crown – shaped Johnson's political outlook during their talks, and may even have made him run the risk of Jacobite treason. 'They both saw with the same eye, or believed they saw, that the then Minister meditated the ruin of this country; that Excise Laws, standing Armies, and penal Statutes, were the mean by which he [Walpole] meant to effect it; and, at the risk of their liberty, they were bent to oppose his measures . . .'[18]

Hawkins's evident disapproval of this youthful radicalism makes it all the more convincing as evidence. It is exactly these political themes that Johnson does go on to address in his earliest, anonymous poetry and prose, up to the age of thirty-five. In the satire *London*, it takes the form of a general charge of political corruption against those in power:

> Here let those reign, whom Pensions can incite
> To vote a Patriot black, a Courtier white;
> Explain their Country's dear-bought Rights away,
> And plead for Pirates in the Face of Day . . .[19]

In the pamphlet *Marmor Norfolciense* (1739) – viz. 'The Stone of Norfolk' – it becomes a specific attack on the Prime Minister, Sir Robert Walpole (whose estates lay in that county), and Hanoverian rule. As a recent critic, Thomas Kaminski, has observed, here 'we find a Johnson unknown to the readers of Boswell – a rabid, harsh opponent of the ruling government, a critic not only of a party but of the King'.[20] And in the Latin pastiche 'prophesy', attached to the pamphlet, which Johnson translated as the poem 'To Posterity', we meet a baleful vision of complete national subversion, the land overrun by alien redcoat soldiers, and the entire British population ready for rebellion:

> Whene'er this Stone, now hid beneath the Lake,
> The Horse shall trample, or the Plough shall break,
> Then, O my Country! shalt thou groan distrest,
> Grief swell thine Eyes, and Terror chill thy Breast.

Thy Streets with Violence of Woe shall sound,
Loud as the Billows bursting on the Ground.
Then thro' thy Fields shall scarlet Reptiles stray,
And Rapine and Pollution mark their Way . . .
Then o'er the World shall Discord stretch her Wings,
Kings change their Laws, and Kingdoms change their Kings.[21]

So Hawkins's night-walk is that of romantic, political malcontents. The two men are penurious, angry, to some degree sinister. The walk has a wintry atmosphere, chill and discomforting, with even a hint of cloak and dagger. Like Boswell, like Reynolds, like Murphy, Hawkins also says he is telling the story directly as Johnson described it; only as something that happened frequently, perhaps over many months.

> Johnson has told me, that whole nights have been spent by him and Savage in conversations of this kind, not under the hospitable roof of a tavern, where warmth might have invigorated their spirits, and wine dispelled their care; but in a perambulation round the squares of Westminster, St James's in particular, when all the money they could both raise was less than sufficient to purchase for them the shelter and sordid comforts of a night cellar. Of the result of their conversations little can now be known, save, that they gave rise to those principles of patriotism, that both, for some years after, avowed.[22]

Hawkins's suspicions would have been further darkened had he known – or had he suspected that Johnson knew – that Savage, many years previously, had actually been arrested and questioned on a charge of treasonable, Jacobite publication; and that for some months he was the subject of Secret Service reports.[23] Whether young Johnson knew this then, or later, will soon become a leading question about their friendship.

For Johnson himself these night-conversations in London with Savage were a transforming experience. They shaped his idea of the city itself, his politics, and his whole notion of the writer's task and situation. That Savage appeared both poor and outcast must have struck him as bitterly ironic and yet curiously glamorous. Here was a brilliant, strange and enchanting man, who had known all the leading writers of the day – Sir Richard Steele, Colley Cibber, Alexander Pope, James Thomson – and moved in circles close to Parliament and the Court. Yet he was reduced to the back streets, he voiced subversive politics, and he befriended someone as obscure and socially inept (not to say monstrous) as Johnson himself.

Savage needed company and talk, needed them with something approaching desperation, to act out his own life and his extensive fantasies. This soon became clear to Johnson. In this too there was at once a common bond. Both men dreaded solitude, and Savage had found a remedy with which Johnson instantly identified. Talk held off the terrors and depressions of loneliness.

'His Method of Life particularly qualified him for Conversation, of which he knew how to practise all the Graces,' wrote Johnson appreciatively. 'His Language was vivacious and elegant, and equally happy upon grave or humorous Subjects. He was generally censured for not knowing when to retire, but that was not the Defect of his Judgment, but of his Fortune; when he left his Company he was frequently to spend the remaining Part of the Night in the Street, or at least was abandoned to gloomy Reflections, which it is not strange that he delayed as long as he could . . .'[24] This could be Johnson writing of himself. One can begin to see how sympathetically two such men might meet, as Cave's offices emptied at Clerkenwell, or the taverns closed along the Strand.

So when Johnson came to write Savage's *Life* in 1743, he put Savage's night-walking at the heart of the story of his literary career. He did it so powerfully that he created a legend, almost an eighteenth-century archetype, of the Outcast Poet moving through an infernal cityscape, the 'City of Dreadful Night', in which his eye alone witnesses the horror, filth and misery that the rich and powerful have created as they slumber, uncaring.

To achieve this, Johnson does something extraordinary. He completely withdraws himself from the story. He never makes a single mention of himself as Savage's night-time companion. The two Hogarthian figures, joined in their companionable talk, who appear again and again in the memoirs, never once appear in Johnson's original account. Savage is essentially, and one might say symbolically, alone.

Johnson places this description or evocation of the Outcast Poet at a pivotal moment in his own narrative. It is set in 1737, immediately after the publication of Savage's poem 'Of Public Spirit' (including an extract in the *Gentleman's Magazine*), and at the time that Johnson himself first arrived in the city and became aware of Savage's work (though this fact is studiously omitted).[25]

The theme of Savage's poem is also dramatically relevant. It considers how far the State is responsible for the poor, incapacitated or underprivileged in society; and in particular whether the Whig policy of expatriation – forcible emigration to the new colonies in North America and Africa – can be morally justified. Is this 'outcasting' of men from their native homes and families, a true expression of 'Public Spirit'?

Rising above his own situation, like the true poet, Savage touches on this general issue of social justice, which Johnson summarises with angry force:

> The Politician, when he considers Men driven into other Countries for Shelter, and obliged to retire to Forests and Deserts, and pass their Lives and fix their Posterity in the remotest Corners of the World, to avoid those Hardships which they suffer or fear in their native Place, may very properly enquire why the Legislature does not provide a Remedy for these Miseries, rather than encourage an Escape from them. He may conclude, that the Flight of every honest Man is a Loss to the Community . . .[26]

But Savage, here presented by Johnson as the spokesman for the oppressed, goes much further than this. He attacks the whole notion of colonisation itself.

In historical terms of the early eighteenth century this is a truly radical position. Savage runs directly counter to the prevailing maritime, trading and enterprise culture of commercial exploitation, which Walpole's administration notoriously represented, with support for such institutions as the South Sea Company and the East India Company. Again, Johnson's summary is forceful and angry: 'Savage has not forgotten . . . to censure those Crimes which have been generally committed by the Discoverers of new Regions, and to expose the enormous Wickedness of making War upon barbarous Nations because they cannot resist, and of invading Countries because they are fruitful; of extending Navigation only to propagate Vice, and of visiting distant Lands only to lay them waste.'[27] Ever afterwards, this anti-Imperialist stance became Johnson's own.

In his poem Savage is specific about colonial exploitation. To illustrate this, Johnson does something new in literary biography. He quotes extensively from the poetry and begins to integrate these quotations into the texture of his prose narrative by placing them in careful footnotes. These quotations are, technically, a new biographical device, because they bring us an impression of Savage's own voice, of Savage actually talking to the reader (and of how he talked to Johnson). It is the biographer's answer to the novelist's most powerful mode of verisimilitude: direct speech.

The quotations perform the role of 'authentic' monologue, a mode which would normally imply that very fictionalisation which Johnson had dismissed as a legitimate means of historical truth. By taking them from Savage's own poetry, Johnson gives them textual authenticity: these are his own words, they are not invented, but they strike us in his own voice, they are what he actually said. Moreover, by using extracts, Johnson effectively reanimates Savage's work.

Savage's lines paradoxically work much better as fragments of contemporary reported speech than as more formal and extended passages of mid-eighteenth-century poetry. That is, compared to the best of Pope or Thomson they are weak; but compared to some of the diffuse, first-person narratives of Defoe or Eliza Haywood they are vividly alive. As a critic, Johnson knew that 'Of Public Spirit' was a slapdash performance – 'not sufficiently polished in the Language, or enlivened in the Imagery, or digested in the Plan'.[28] But as a biographer he knew it was deeply expressive, and conveyed one aspect of Savage's fantastic idealising power with great intensity.

Savage's two main targets are the East India trade in silks, spices, hardwoods and other luxury goods; and the West African trade in black slaves. Both produce their own kinds of oppression, and make outcasts of men powerless within their system. In India he sees this primarily as a cultural oppression, in which the indigenous populations are simply subdued by the Western traders, who care nothing about native laws, customs or religions. He calls on the colonisers to be more respectful, more just, more generous:

> Do you the neighb'ring, blameless Indian aid,
> Culture what he neglects, not his invade;
> Dare not, oh! dare not, with ambitious View,
> Force or demand Subjection, never due.[29]

In Africa, he recognises with horror a trade in human bodies that is both indefensible in itself and cruel and hypocritical in its operation. The great Whig merchants, so much of whose personal wealth, houses, estates and even servants are drawn directly or indirectly from this trade, defend themselves with the cry that 'while they enslave, they civilize'.[30]

The black servant – especially as coach-driver, table-waiter or personal valet – was a familiar feature of eighteenth-century London smart society. Johnson himself later took on a black manservant, Frank Barber, originally as a wild and illiterate teenager, who promptly ran away to sea. But this was one of Johnson's spiritual reparations: he took infinite trouble to trace him, buy him out of the service, educate him, provide for him and his family, and eventually made him an inheritor in his will, so he became virtually an adopted son, ending his days in ease in Hampshire, corresponding genially with Boswell. Savage saw this enslavement with acute revulsion, which suggests at some level a personal identification:

> Why must I Afric's sable Children see
> Vended for Slaves, though form'd by Nature free,
> The nameless Tortures cruel Minds invent,
> Those to subject, whom Nature equal meant?[31]

The clue to this identification may lie in the word 'cruel', which Johnson discovered had an almost talismanic significance for Savage's personal mythology. But the political implications for Savage of such colonial and imperial attitudes were frankly apocalyptic. The imperial London through which they walked, like Cassandras in the night, might be destroyed by its own unjustly subject peoples. The wheel of fortune and of power would turn round; the outcasts would occupy the inner seats of power:

> Revolving Empire you and yours may doom;
> Rome all subdued, yet *Vandals* vanquish'd Rome:
> Yes, Empire may revolve, give them the Day,
> And Yoke may Yoke, and Blood may Blood repay.[32]

These parallels with the decline and fall of Rome were particularly significant to Johnson, because they were to lead him to the satires of the second-century Roman poet Juvenal, as a new model for his own poetic persona in *London*.

Savage and Juvenal were always closely connected in Johnson's mind as critics of a corrupt, materialist, urban society. Savage roamed through London as Juvenal once roamed through Rome; and Johnson followed both.

With the publication of his poem 'Of Public Spirit' in June 1737,

Johnson is able to present Savage as he first perceived him. He is the spokesman for the outcast, the oppressed, the 'sons of Misery'.[33] He is even the spokesman for the daughters of misery, the prostitutes of the city, the 'beauteous Wretches' who the 'nightly Streets annoy, / Live but themselves and others to destroy'.[34] Savage stands out against social injustice. 'He has asserted the natural Equality of Mankind, and endeavoured to suppress that Pride which inclines Men to imagine that Right is the Consequence of Power.'[35] He writes with 'Tenderness'.[36]

It is against this heroic moral background that Johnson carefully places his portrait of the Outcast Poet. In biographical terms it is a close-up, or a montage of street scenes, animated and visualised. It is written with great force and anger, with almost poetic power.

The first paragraph enacts Savage's progress through the dark labyrinth of streets in a single, unwinding sentence. Its keynote is one of pathos:

> He lodged as much by Accident as he dined and passed the Night, sometimes in mean Houses, which are set open at Night to any casual Wanderers, sometimes in Cellars among the Riot and Filth of the meanest and most profligate of the Rabble; and sometimes, when he had no Money to support even the Expences of these Receptacles, walked about the Streets till he was weary, and lay down in the Summer upon a Bulk, or in the Winter with his Associates in Poverty, among the Ashes of a Glass-house.[37]

Clearly this is not the experience of one bohemian summer night out in the West End. This is a dreadful, Dantesque repetition, at all seasons, and at many locations over London: alleys behind the Strand, off Covent Garden, beyond the Fleet Ditch, behind St Paul's, in Clerkenwell, off Smithfield, out in Spitalfields.

The alternative forms of lodging open to Savage mark the stages of a humiliating decline from poverty to absolute indigence. The 'mean House' would be a penny-a-night public lodging or spike, with stinking dormitories of wooden beds. The 'Cellar' would be a single, dark, basement dossing-room of sacks and straw heaps, fouled with urine and vomit, populated by drunks, diseased and ageing prostitutes, lunatics, tramps and psychopaths (the very same in which Johnson finds 'Misella').

The 'Bulk' was a low, wooden stall attached to a shop-front on which fresh market produce was displayed by day and left to rot at night: old vegetables at Covent Garden, old fish at Billingsgate, old meat at Smithfield. The 'Glass-house' was a small factory (like a bakery or kiln) where carriage-glass, window-panes, water jugs, wine-glasses, decorative buttons, cane-tops and other fancy ornaments were melted and cast in fast-burning coal-fired ovens, found all over the East End, with their brick chimneys billowing smoke and their backyards full of warm grey ash and clinker.

Here even a complete down-and-out could keep warm (just as the modern tramp sleeps on a ventilation-grille), though rising as ash-grey as a ghost in the morning. Thus Johnson charts Savage's decline in the infernal city night; falling as low, if not lower, than those whose rights he 'asserted' as a poet.

The ashes of the Glass-house (like the ashes of the grave) may have had a particularly emotive overtone for the eighteenth-century reader. Glassware of all kinds, as opposed to metal or wood, was the province of the rich, and the expression of luxury and refinement. Even the clinker, which smelted into fantastic shapes and vivid oxidised colours, might be prized. It is an expressive irony that Savage's one-time editor and publisher, the wealthy Aaron Hill, once planned to construct a 300-foot-square rockery in his splendid Richmond garden, composed of blue stones, seashells bought from London toyshops and 'chosen clinkers, from the glass-houses'. The clinkers were to be carefully 'picked out of the cinder heaps, and brought in boats' up the Thames from the East End. On the top of this rockery Hill planned to build an elaborate Chinese summerhouse as an allegorical 'Temple of Happiness'.[38]

Johnson never identifies himself as an 'associate in Poverty' with Savage, among those ashes. Yet he writes with an immediacy that suggests familiarity – if not first-hand knowledge – of such 'Receptacles' of the London night. He is rhetorically present, giving plain and moving testimony.

In the second paragraph Johnson stands back. Pathos turns to anger, plain testimony to high irony. This contrapuntal shift of keys or tones becomes one of Johnson's most subtle methods of interpreting Savage's life through narrative. He repeats the stations of Savage's humiliation, word for word, object for object. But now he sets them into literary perspective with a note of bitter elegy. His phrases are shaped, given a rhythm and mounting climax of outrage. The Tramp is revealed as the Poet, and the 'casual Wanderer' becomes again the author of his greatest poem. Johnson for the first time reveals how passionately he feels about his friend, and how profoundly he identifies with Savage's outcast situation.

> In this Manner were passed those Days and those Nights, which Nature had enabled him to have employed in elevated Speculations, useful Studies, or pleasing Conversation. On a Bulk, in a Cellar, or in a Glass-house among Thieves and Beggars, was to be found the Author of the *Wanderer*, the Man of exalted Sentiments, extensive Views and curious Observations, the Man whose Remarks on Life might have assisted the Statesman, whose Ideas of Virtue might have enlightened the Moralist, whose Eloquence might have influenced Senates, and whose Delicacy might have polished Courts.[39]

The noble cadences into which Johnson finally lifts this passage, suggest that for his young listener Savage's night-talk in the London streets sometimes approached the condition of poetry. It is a public poetry, which should have concerned the 'Moralist', the 'Statesman', the men in power at Parliament ('Senates') and at Court. In this sense Savage fulfilled the Augustan concept of the poet as potential 'legislator', put forward in Sir Philip Sidney's *Arcadia* and reiterated by Imlac in *Rasselas*. But because of Savage's outcast state, his poverty and humiliating sufferings, it is poetry which is not heard, not acknowledged, by those in power: 'Of Public Spirit' sells exactly seventy-two copies.[40] Savage is, for young Johnson, the poet who has no place, no social position, no influence on affairs, and literally no home.

Johnson is in effect making a Romantic claim for him. Savage is the Poet as Outcast, the poet as '*unacknowledged* legislator'. This was to be exactly the claim that, fifty years later, the anarchist philosopher William Godwin would make for all poets in *Political Justice* (1792); and his son-in-law Shelley would make with openly revolutionary intent in *A Philosophical View of Reform* (1820) and *A Defence of Poetry* (1821). Johnson had identified in Savage a new poetical archetype. He had, astonishingly, glimpsed in the back streets the first stirrings of the new Romantic age.

One further incident becomes part of Johnson's heroic account of Savage's night-existence in the great city. Johnson wrote: 'Savage was ... so touched with the Discovery of his real Mother, that it was his frequent Practice to walk in the dark Evenings for several Hours before her Door, in Hopes of seeing her as she might come by Accident to the Window, or cross her Apartment with a Candle in her Hand."[41]

This haunting image of the figure shut out from the lit window, of the man in the edge of shadows and the beloved woman with her candle, also becomes an archetype of the Romantic outsider and can be traced down through popular fiction, even to its Victorian apotheosis in the figure of Heathcliff outside Cathy's window in *Wuthering Heights*.

However, there may be another interpretation of this incident. Savage may not be a figure of pathos but of terror; not patiently waiting, but violently seeking entry; not a poetic outcast, but a pathological intruder.

CHAPTER 4

MOTHER

So much for the influential story of the night-walks, as it has come down to us. But how in practice did Johnson set about the task of transforming his private feelings into a public and commercially acceptable biography? His conversations with Savage had not been interviews. He had made no notes. He knew very little of Savage's early life or contacts. Savage's supposed mother, Lady Macclesfield (by now the seventy-year-old widow, Mrs Brett), was unapproachable. His early patrons, Sir Richard Steele, the essayist, and Anne Oldfield, the actress, were dead. Among his few close literary friends, James Thomson had become something of a recluse at Richmond, and Alexander Pope was mortally ill at Twickenham.

Johnson was not interested in what a modern biographer would call 'research'. He did not even attempt to investigate the circumstances of Savage's birth, or walk over to St Andrew's, Holborn, to examine Savage's baptismal register. (Years later it was Boswell who meticulously did all this.) He relied almost solely on the books, papers and magazine articles which Edward Cave could supply from the *Gentleman's Magazine* archives.

In September 1743 Johnson was working in haste, in poverty, and under the very Grub Street conditions that Savage himself had so often experienced. An undated note to Cave, from Johnson's rooms in Castle Street, gives a vivid glimpse of the harassed young biographer preparing his materials and estimating his rate of production against his financial reserves.

... *The Life of Savage* I am ready to go upon, and in great Primer and Pica Notes reckon on sending in half an Sheet a day, but the money for that shall likewise lie in your hands till it is done. With the [Parliamentary] Debates shall I not have business enough? – If I had but good Pens. – Towards Mr Savage's Life what more have you got? I would willingly have [the text of] his Trial etc, and know whether his Defence be at Bristol; and would have his Collection of Poems [1726] on account of the Preface. – The Plain Dealer [articles] – All the Magazines that have anything of his or relating to him.

Johnson's postscript to this letter is expressive. He has no candles, and Cave's printer's boy 'found me writing this, almost in the dark'. Cave had also asked for a preliminary epitaph on Savage, to be printed in the forthcoming issue. But Johnson has been ill, and is late producing it. 'I had no notion of having any thing for the [Savage] Inscription, I hope You don't think I kept it to extort a price. I could think on Nothing till today. If You could spare me another Guinea ... I should take it very kindly tonight, but if You do not shall not think it an injury. – I am almost well again.'[1]

Because of these conditions, it is invariably thought that Johnson wrote the biography very fast, 'at white heat', and largely from memory. It is taken as a sort of spontaneous effusion of friendship; and its surprising romanticism, and many errors and omissions, are easily explained away on these grounds. Boswell was partly responsible for this conventional view, for though he greatly admired the 'strong and affecting' narrative, he thought its evident 'partiality' might reasonably be excused by haste of composition. During their tour of the Hebrides, thirty years later, he reported Johnson as saying that he wrote 'forty-eight of the printed octavo pages at a sitting, but then I sat up all night'.[2]

If true, this would have been about a quarter of the book in a twenty-four-hour period, and the whole *Life* in less than a week. In fact Johnson took about three months compiling and expanding the biography, between mid-September and 14th December 1743, when he signed a receipt for fifteen guineas for passing the completed manuscript to Cave. By Johnson's standards this was a leisurely and reflective pace of production.[3]

It is clear from the typographical evidence of the book's printing that the epic all-night sitting refers to a single period of *rewriting*, later in January 1744. Working against a printer's deadline, Johnson recast the final section with new materials about Savage's death, and the last forty-eight pages were reset.[4] This rewriting session further delayed the book's publication until February 1744, some five months after he had started. It is characteristic of the unusual care which Johnson lavished on the whole manuscript, and which forced Cave – who was acting as his editor – to delay what had been originally intended as a piece of instant, topical journalism by the publisher Roberts.

Nor did Johnson compose haphazardly, from memory or a loose collection of personal reminiscences. Many things that he said subsequently about biography might suggest this. Johnson had later insisted to Boswell that true biographical knowledge could only grow out of close companionship: 'nobody can write the life of a man, but those who have eat and drunk and lived in social intercourse with him.'[5] Reflecting on the biographical process, in *The Rambler*, no. 60, Johnson also emphasised the need for intimacy, in an aphorism that became famous. '. . . More knowledge may be gained of a man's real character by a short conversation with one of his servants, than from a formal and studied narrative, begun with his pedigree and ended with his funeral.'[6]

Savage of course had never had a servant, and the absence of a domestic ménage of any kind, except for those temporarily borrowed (and quickly alienated) from other households such as Lord Tyrconnel's, posed its own peculiar mystery round his unusual solitude, which Johnson had to penetrate.

The value of personal witness, of small impressions and trivial incidents, of recent memories and vivid anecdotes, however fleeting and partial they might be, was defended by Johnson as essential to biography. '. . . Most accounts of particular persons are barren and useless. If a Life be delayed till interest and envy are at an end, we may hope for impartiality, but we must expect little intelligence; for the incidents that give excellence to biography are of a volatile and evanescent kind, such as soon escape the memory, and are rarely transmitted by tradition.'[7]

This might have been written with his *Life of Savage* specifically in mind; and such 'volatile' impressions, recalling their friendship with rueful tenderness, streamed easily from Johnson's pen once he began to write. Savage's innocent, almost childlike vanity as an author produces one such typical incident. 'He could not easily leave off when he had once begun to mention himself or his Works, nor ever read his Verses without stealing his Eyes from the Page, to discover in the Faces of his Audience, how they were affected with any favourite Passage.'[8]

Yet Johnson has removed himself from this moment, just as he did in the great description of the night-walking. His personal presence, as Savage's friend, is absorbed in the anonymity of 'the Faces of his Audience'. The witness, the friend, is absent. This remains true almost throughout the *Life*: though intensely personal and partial, its narrative voice appears distanced and carefully withdrawn. This makes Johnson's attitude, and the level of his irony, peculiarly difficult to judge.

Indeed Johnson based the opening section of his story on something quite different from the personal impressions and interviews with friends that a modern biographer might expect. In fact what he did was so unexpected that it was overlooked by many commentators (though not by Boswell). For the first half of Savage's life, up to the trial for murder of 1727 at least, Johnson simply used a previous biography.

This was a twenty-nine-page booklet, issued anonymously by the 'bookseller J. Roberts' in December 1727, entitled *The Life of Mr Richard Savage ... Who was Condemned ... the last Sessions at the Old Bailey, For Murder ... With some very remarkable Circumstances relating to the Birth and Education, of that Gentleman, which were never before made publick*. Johnson followed its storyline paragraph by paragraph, adding his own commentary and occasional new facts or corrections.

The booklet is a defence of Savage, intended to save him from the gallows. It was published, significantly, by the same James Roberts who commissioned Johnson's work. Johnson assumed its information was taken direct from Savage, during a series of interviews in the condemned cells at Newgate Prison. But a contemporary letter from Savage in Newgate suggests this was not strictly so, and he certainly contradicted some of the booklet's facts later.

So Johnson, far from using original sources or research, was basing the first section of his biography on a partial and secondary source, the 'Newgate' booklet, whose proclaimed aim was to exculpate Richard Savage from his crimes.

For the second part of Savage's *Life*, from 1728 onwards, Johnson would work in another way. Not only would he use his own impressions, often brilliantly perceptive and blackly humorous. He would incorporate no less than forty pages of quotations from Savage's poetry and letters (some twenty per cent of the entire text).[9] But for the crucial beginning of the biography, dealing with Savage's mysterious childhood and shadowy early career to the age of thirty, Johnson very largely accepted the 'Newgate' version of 1727. He postponed any serious attempt at psychological enquiry or historical research until later. He opened for the defence, with the materials on hand.

Why did Johnson do this? Laziness, or deadline pressure, are hardly sufficient explanations. Johnson took his time and he wrote *con amore* of a friend who had meant something vital in his own escape to London and launching of a literary career. He was well aware, too, of the perils of biographical bias. He recalled in *The Rambler* his own situation in 1743: 'If the biographer writes from personal knowledge, and makes haste to gratify the public curiosity, there is danger lest his interest, his fear, his gratitude, or his tenderness, overpower his fidelity, and tempt him to conceal, if not to invent.'[10] Perhaps he believed in retrospect that he had been, to some degree, overpowered by the Savage legend as set forth in the 'Newgate' booklet.

What I think happened was this. Johnson was caught up in its romantic drama. He responded overwhelmingly to the picture it presented of Savage as a man on trial for his life, a victim of society, and particularly as a victim of one woman's cruelty. For this is the central argument of the 'Newgate' version, and one that Johnson amplifies with passion, and even something close to fury, in his own *Life*.

While relying on the bare outlines of the 'Newgate' version, Johnson transforms the first thirty years of Savage's life into an extraordinary and emotional piece of story-telling. It is highly compressed, occupying only a quarter of the overall biography, and astonishingly sketchy with facts and dates. Yet it grips the reader from the first moment with its drama and pathetic images of rejection and persecution.

Richard Savage is introduced as a tragic outcast from eighteenth-century society, not merely disowned by his supposed mother, Lady Macclesfield, but 'with an implacable and restless Cruelty' pursued and persecuted by her 'from the first Hour of his Life to the last'.[11]

Johnson never seriously questioned 'Newgate's' assertion that Savage was the illegitimate child of Lady Macclesfield. He did not even bother to examine the documentary evidence, or question those who might have seen it, like Aaron Hill or Lady Macclesfield's nephew, Lord Tyrconnel. His view of Savage's wayward character and misfortunes is grounded on the supposed injustice he suffered throughout his life when that claim was consistently denied, for whatever motives, by Lady Macclesfield.

He accepted Savage as a rejected child, flung out from his rightful place in society, and presented this with all the pathos at his command. 'Born with a legal Claim to Honour and to Riches, he was in two Months illegitimated by the Parliament, and disowned by his Mother, doomed to Poverty and Obscurity, and launched upon the Ocean of Life, only that he might be swallowed by its Quicksands, or dashed upon its Rocks.'[12]

The image of the child launched helplessly upon the waters, like young Moses in his basket of reeds, is powerfully emotive. It indicts not merely the mother but society as a whole (represented by Parliament). Johnson was later to develop this social indictment with great effect.

He pursues this interpretation to far greater lengths, and with even greater biographic daring, or recklessness, in his portrait of Lady Macclesfield herself. Here again he accepts the 'Newgate' version of the facts without question, and without investigation, and he intensifies it to an extraordinary degree. No attempt is made to give the objective details of her life, her family circumstances, her social connections or even her age. She is presented simply as a type of the worthless aristocratic woman: capricious, voluptuous, vindictive and relentlessly cruel. Johnson is so roused by this image that he openly courts a charge of libel.

This Mother is still alive, and may perhaps even yet, though her Malice was so often defeated, enjoy the Pleasure of reflecting, that the Life which she often endeavoured to destroy, was at least shortened by her maternal Offices; that though she could not transport her Son to the Plantations, bury him in the Shop of a Mechanick, or hasten the Hand of the publick Executioner, she has yet had the Satisfaction of imbittering all his Hours, and forcing him into Exigencies, that hurried on his Death.[13]

It can be suggested that this figure is a fictional rather than a biographic creation. Johnson seems to have built on Savage's fantasies in *The Bastard* and *The Wanderer* and unconsciously added something of his own. Throughout the *Life* he identifies strongly with Savage's obsessive anger and feelings of rejection by a powerful woman. There is an undercurrent of vengefulness, if not of misogyny, in his portrait of Lady Macclesfield which seems uncharacteristic of the later Johnson and which we can only explain by his own romantic disappointments, surely aggravated by his physical grotesqueness and sexual awkwardness as a young man. At no moment is he prepared to consider events from Lady Macclesfield's point of view: she is always Savage's persecutor, a figure of 'motiveless malignity', torturing him for her sport. Again and again he calls her 'unnatural', like Lady Macbeth; and describes her as 'outragious and implacable', as if she was the force of destiny itself.[14]

At the time Johnson wrote, in 1743, the real Lady Macclesfield was a rich, sad and reclusive widow in her late seventies, living alone in a small house in Old Bond Street. She had lost her title through divorce, and was known by the name of her second husband (by then deceased) as Mrs Anne Brett. Her whole life had been shaken by domestic unhappiness and public scandals.

Born in Shropshire in 1668, the daughter of Sir Richard Mason, a Clerk Comptroller in the royal household, with a house in Whitehall, she had made an early and disastrous marriage to a young Whig firebrand, Viscount Brandon, when she was only fifteen. Brandon was a violent and dangerous character who had killed a boy in the London streets when drunk, and was later twice imprisoned in the Tower for treason.

The marriage broke down in the first few weeks, and by the age of seventeen she was separated and living with her sister Lady Brownlow at Beaufort House, where she remained for the next twelve years, fearful of her husband's rages. She none the less pleaded on her knees before the King, in order to obtain Brandon's pardon after the Rye House plot, when he had been implicated in an assassination attempt on James II.

In 1694 her husband inherited the title of Lord Macclesfield, though no reconciliation and no children were forthcoming. Two years later Lady Macclesfield, now approaching her thirtieth birthday and desperate for affection, fell in love with Richard Savage, the Fourth Earl Rivers. It was another disastrous choice. Rivers was well known as a gambler, rake and political intriguer, and was renowned for his amours. He kept a large establishment, with gardens, at Rivers House, Great Queen Street, in the parish of Holborn. Lady Macclesfield bore him two illegitimate children, a girl and a boy, in rapid succession and great secrecy. Lord Macclesfield, hearing rumours of this but unable to establish proof, began divorce proceedings in the House of Lords on 15th January 1698.

Throughout, Lady Macclesfield protested her innocence, concealed the affair with Rivers and took immense precautions to cover up the illegitimate births. Later evidence shows that the boy was born in private rooms at Fox Court, Holborn, with both parents using pseudonyms, and Lady Macclesfield even wearing a mask throughout her labour in order to disguise her identity from the midwife.[15]

The birth of the son was registered at St Andrew's, Holborn, on 16th January 1697, with Earl Rivers signing himself as godfather, under the name of Captain John Smith. The child was christened Richard Smith. Lord Macclesfield was never able to establish these facts, and the name of Earl Rivers was never mentioned in the House of Lords. None the less a divorce was granted in March 1698, and Lady Macclesfield's personal fortune was returned to her as part of the settlement. She subsequently married Colonel Henry Brett, in 1700, and bore him a legitimate daughter to whom she was greatly attached. Through Brett's contacts in Drury Lane (he was a director of the Theatre Committee), she moved for a time in literary circles, and made a friend of the dramatist Colley Cibber. But on the Colonel's sudden death in 1724, she largely retired from social life, devoted herself to her daughter, and died a recluse at the age of eighty.[16]

She always insisted to Brett (who of course knew all the details of the divorce) that both her illegitimate children had died as babies and there is considerable documentary evidence for this claim (see Appendix). She had a reputation as an attractive, kind, and perhaps foolish woman; and as a notably loving mother (as even Savage was forced to admit on occasions). Nothing we know of her from external evidence supports the picture drawn by Johnson.

The one real mystery about her behaviour (as Boswell pointed out after extensive investigation) is why she never sued for libel, either on the publication of the 'Newgate' booklet in 1727 or of Johnson's own *Life* in 1744. But one can imagine that after the scandalous House of Lords divorce case in 1698, she had had

enough of litigation. It even seems possible that she may have felt
sorry for Savage, at least in the early years, regarding him as a
talented but deluded young man rather than a criminal impostor. But
again, by identifying so completely with Savage's claims, Johnson
excludes this interpretation.

Whatever the truth of the affair, the salient feature of this part
of the biography is that Johnson did not attempt to unearth it
through research. Boswell, although he thought that 'the world
must vibrate in a state of uncertainty' as to the final facts, saw this
very clearly.[17] It is one of the reasons he so distrusted Savage's
influence over Johnson's mind and heart, and regarded the whole
friendship as an aberration. For him, Johnson's powers of judgement
were temporarily seduced by Savage. Yet one may feel, equally,
that for the first time Johnson had found a story that enabled him
to give full literary expression to his passionate nature, his intense
human sympathies, and his rage against social injustice.

Limiting himself to the 'Newgate' materials, and committed to
his romantic, and indeed melodramatic version of Savage's early
life, Johnson narrates it as a fable of the Outcast Poet, persecuted
and spurned by a malign mother, brought up in poverty and obscur-
ity, and finding temporary succour from a series of generous but
frequently disreputable benefactors. Whatever picturesque details
he can add, he takes on trust from Savage's personal reminiscences
(though the versions frequently changed).

This is the account that Johnson gives. Born in January 1698
(not 1697 as the registration shows), inexplicably rejected by his
mother, Savage was brought up somewhere in London by an
anonymous nurse and a godmother called Mrs Lloyd who died
when he was aged ten. (Savage later said, 'As for ... the mean
nurse, she is quite a fictitious character'.[18]) Defrauded of a £6,000
legacy from Earl Rivers, who died in 1712, Savage was farmed out
to a small grammar school near St Albans, under his nurse's name
(the 'fictitious' one), still not knowing his true identity. Next there
was an attempt to ship him 'secretly' to the American colonies, a
plot which Savage somehow eluded; and then he was apprenticed
to a shoemaker in Holborn, 'a Scheme for burying him in poverty
and obscurity'. All these machinations were contrived 'at a Distance'
by Lady Macclesfield, through her own mother Lady Mason, with-
out Savage being aware of their source. His godmother, Mrs Lloyd,
never told Savage of his true birth.[19] (The godmother actually regis-
tered on 'Richard Smith's' birth certificate was Dorothy Ousley,

wife of Earl Rivers's agent, of whom Savage makes no mention.)

On the death of his nurse (again, the 'fictitious' one), Savage 'went to her House, opened her Boxes, and examined her Papers, among which he found some Letters written to her by the Lady Mason, which informed him of his Birth, and the Reasons for which it was concealed'.[20] Johnson cannot date this crucial event, if it ever occurred, but it would have been around 1715 when, as we shall see, Savage first began using Earl Rivers's family name. Savage later frequently referred to these letters, and claimed to have sent them to Aaron Hill (his future editor); and they would of course be decisive in establishing his birth. But neither Johnson nor any other witness subsequently saw them; and even Aaron Hill is studiously vague about their contents, and gives no explanation of Lady Macclesfield's 'reasons' for concealing, far less for persecuting, Savage. They are perhaps the key document that a biographer would normally have pursued.

Instead, Johnson moves rapidly on to the start of Savage's roaming, struggling life in the streets of London. Refused all recognition by Lady Macclesfield ('she avoided him with the most vigilant Precaution'), he loiters outside her house in Old Bond Street during the 'dark Evenings', and continues this practice on and off for several years. This is the image – taken directly from 'Newgate' – which so moved Johnson; though he omits to mention at this point why Savage eventually, and abruptly, stopped his vigil. Unable to obtain money from her, Savage was therefore (in Johnson's famous explanation of the literary motive) 'obliged to seek some other Means of Support, and having no Profession, became, by Necessity, an Author'.[21]

Haunting the literary coffee-houses, like Button's off Covent Garden, Savage picked up topical subjects and began to write with remarkable facility: first producing political doggerel on Jacobite themes, and then adaptations of popular Spanish plays, much in vogue at that period. The speed with which he learned to master these subjects struck Johnson as one of the proofs of Savage's genius.[22]

About 1719 he was befriended by the essayist Sir Richard Steele, an habitué of Button's, and employed as an amanuensis. Johnson gives an amusing account of this tutelage in hack-work, including the exemplary Grub Street tale of a pamphlet composed by the two of them over an expensive dinner in a tavern. When the dinner and the pamphlet were finished, 'Sir Richard told him, that he was without Money, and that the Pamphlet must be sold before the Dinner could be paid for; and Savage was therefore obliged to go and offer their new Production to Sale for two Guineas, which with some Difficulty he obtained.'[23]

Steele was Savage's first patron who, according to Johnson, accepted the story of his illegitimacy and proclaimed 'that *the Inhumanity of his Mother had given him a Right to find every good Man his Father*'.[24] This statement was taken purely from 'Newgate', and no corroboration can now be found in Steele's extensive correspondence. Johnson also says that Steele offered Savage the hand of his own illegitimate daughter in marriage, together with a dowry of a thousand pounds; but that the offer was withdrawn after a quarrel between the two men.[25] Unknown to Johnson, Savage later gave other versions of the proposal and the quarrel,[26] and again there is no supporting evidence, least of all as to how the notoriously impecunious Steele could ever have raised such an enormous sum of money, the equivalent of a professional income over ten years. Indeed, shortly after, Steele retired in straitened circumstances to Wales; just as Savage was to do some twenty years later.

Johnson now shows other patrons, from the theatrical world, apparently crowding forward to help Savage. Among these were the ageing tragic actor Robert Wilks and the fashionable comedienne Mrs Anne Oldfield. They too accepted his claims, though no explanation is offered as to why they should have done so. Certainly Savage had established a theatrical connection and was now working on his *Tragedy of Sir Thomas Overbury*, a story of political intrigue and betrayed friendship, which was staged at Drury Lane in 1723.

Departing from his 'Newgate' source, Johnson even hints at a romance between Savage and Mrs Oldfield: 'in his *Wanderer*, he ... celebrates her not for her Virtue, but her Beauty.' He makes the startling statement that the actress actually supported him until her death in 1730. She was 'so much pleased with his Conversation, and touched with his Misfortunes, that she allowed him a settled Pension of fifty Pounds a Year, which was during her Life regularly paid'.[27] He adds that when she died, Savage expressed his feelings 'by wearing Mourning as for a Mother'.

Johnson can only have had this information direct from Savage, and he is careful to explain that Savage always denied a specifically sexual relationship, though the denial was couched in a somewhat teasing way: 'it is proper to mention what Mr Savage often declared in the strongest Terms, that he never saw her alone, or in any other Place than behind the Scenes.'[28]

Here for once we can make some assessment of the kind of emotional fantasies that Savage embroidered in Johnson's company. For not only did Savage later go back on the story of the £50 allowance, in a letter of 1739 which Johnson never saw;[29] but a theatrical contemporary and close friend of Mrs Oldfield described the relationship in a different but far more convincing way. Cibber's son, the young Theophilus Cibber, was the producer of Savage's play at Drury Lane and knew him intimately in these early years. Cibber denied both the romance and the allowance – 'there was no foundation for them'; and painted exactly the awkward, demanding kind of connection that Savage always seemed to have established with his supporters, especially if they were women.

Theophilus Cibber's explanation runs as follows: 'That Savage's misfortunes pleaded for pity, and had the desired effect on Mrs Oldfield is certain: – But she so much disliked the man, and disapproved his conduct, that she never admitted him to her conversation, nor suffered him to enter her house. She, indeed, often relieved him with such donations, as spoke her generous disposition. – But this was on the solicitation of friends, who frequently set his calamities before her in the most piteous light . . .' Annotating Johnson's *Life* in 1753, Cibber added that Savage's veracity was not 'greatly to be depended on', and that in this as in other matters the 'good-natured' Johnson had 'suffered his better understanding to be misled'.[30]

Despite the romantic tale of the actress and her allowance, Johnson continues to picture Savage in an extreme state of poverty and obscurity throughout this period. The conditions under which he composed his *Tragedy* in 1723 are an epitome of the Grub Street way of life. 'During a considerable Part of the Time, in which he was employed upon this Performance, he was without Lodging, and often without Meat; nor had he any other Conveniences for Study than the Fields or the Streets allowed him, there he used to walk and form his Speeches, and afterwards step into a Shop, beg for a few Moments the Use of the Pen and Ink, and write down what he had composed upon Paper which he had picked up by Accident.'[31]

All these humiliations and deprivations, with which young Johnson so clearly identified, are squarely laid at the door of Lady Macclesfield in a passage of unparalleled ferocity. '. . . if they deserve Death who destroy a Child in its Birth, what Pains can be severe enough for her who forbears to destroy him only to inflict sharper Miseries upon him; who prolongs his Life only to make it miserable; and who exposes him without Care and without Pity, to the Malice of Oppression, the Caprices of Chance, and the Temptations of Poverty; who rejoices to see him overwhelmed with Calamities; and when his own Industry, or the Charity of others, has enabled him to rise for a short Time above his Miseries, plunges him again into his former Distress?'[32] By this point in the biography, Johnson's powerful image of the Outcast Poet as an innocent victim of society is firmly established.

However, if we consider what Johnson omitted, or never discovered, or left without comment or challenge, and what we now know of this part of Savage's career, then an entirely different figure begins to emerge. Savage is still in some sense a Romantic Outcast. But he is also dangerous, unstable, ambitious, irascible. He manipulates, persecutes and campaigns for his own recognition. He is far stranger, far more extreme, in every way than Johnson portrayed him. As the evidence comes in, we have to ask if Johnson was misled, or was misleading, in the romantic and pathetic biography he sets out to tell.

Here is the story of what Johnson does *not* say. There is no documentary evidence for Savage's birthright, except for his own statements and anecdotes, which often vary in detail. But his first authenticated appearance in that role, at the age of eighteen, is nevertheless striking for another reason. In November 1715 he was arrested on a charge of political subversion, in the aftermath of the Jacobite rising in Scotland. The *Weekly Packet* reported that 'Mr Savage, natural son to the late Earl Rivers' was accused of 'having a treasonable pamphlet in his possession'. This was his own doggerel poem 'An Ironical Panagerick on his pretended Majesty George'. He escaped by impeaching 'one of Mr Berington the Printer's Men'.[33] For the next eighteen months he was the subject of Secret Service reports by a government agent, Robert Girling, who was tracking subversion among a group of young men associated with Gray's Inn.

Johnson prefers not to quote from any of this treasonable work. But the 'Jacobite poems' of 1715–17 got Savage into the Gray's Inn circle of young wits and university rebels in London; together with *The Convocation* (1717), a verse pamphlet in satyric support of the supposedly heretical and Jacobite Bishop of Bangor. The

'Newgate' pamphlet comments on this: 'he grew himself ashamed of this Piece, and contributed all he could to suppress the Edition.'[34]

Why Savage was so keen to obliterate this less innocent record of his activities, appears in Girling's report of 1717, now filed in the Home Office archives. Savage had been identified as a political troublemaker, and a major prosecution was evidently being considered. Johnson cannot have known of the Secret Service dossier, but his hasty dismissal of these political writings – 'probably lost among the innumerable Pamphlets' – suggests a willingness to let sleeping dogs lie safely. His own Jacobite sympathies, revealed in the night-walking period, also make this plausible.[35]

Robert Girling's report, which incidentally makes no reference to the Earl Rivers connection, reads in part: '. . . the said Savage was about a Year & a half or two Years ago Pardoned for Publishing, & being the Author of Several Treasonable & Seditious Pamphlets, but since that has writ a great Many More than he did before, and as he himself told me had Corrected Several pamphlets for one Weston who was Clarke of Gray's Inn, all this I am ready to make Oath of . . .'[36]

Savage escaped prosecution because of the General Amnesty ordered by the new king, George I, in 1717. But fresh light is thrown on his character by this episode – not least by his 'impeachment' of a printer, to save his own skin; and it explains some of the nervous political opportunism which so troubled Johnson in his later attempts to obtain patronage from a Whig government that he always affected to detest.

Savage's worldly education, and rise from obscurity, continued in ways – and with an alacrity – further unrecorded by Johnson in his account of persecuted Genius. Between 1716 and 1718, Savage enjoyed the patronage of his first, significant benefactress (long before Mrs Oldfield). This was a certain Mrs Lucy Rodd Price, who acted semi-legally as a Councillor at Law and held an eccentric *salon* of youthful wits and poets in her rooms at Gray's Inn. She had been separated from her husband, on grounds of adultery, twenty-five years previously.[37]

Mrs Price knew Spanish, had good theatrical connections, and adopted handsome and likely young authors as her protégés in the London literary world. There is no evidence that she accepted Savage's claims, but she certainly adopted him in the motherly fashion he craved and provided him with both the subjects, and the working translations, of his first plays which were plagiarised from

Calderon's *Woman's a Riddle* (1716) and *Love in a Veil* (acted at Drury Lane in 1718).

Soon after this – when Savage had moved up, as it were, into the orbit of Sir Richard Steele – he quarrelled bitterly with Lucy Rodd Price. This pattern of motherly (and fatherly) 'betrayals' is repeated again and again in Savage's relations with his patrons, and clearly reflects what he imagined – and perhaps came to believe – was the primary, unforgivable betrayal by Lady Macclesfield. In many cases there is an element of sexual ambiguity (were the maternal Mrs Rodd Price, or the glamorous Mrs Oldfield, really his lovers?). This ambiguity may even stretch at times to the male patrons. Numerous contemporaries refer to Savage as strangely 'fascinating'; and without some subliminal psychological attraction such as this, it is genuinely difficult to account for Savage's extra-ordinary (if temporary) influence over so many different kinds and classes of people: aristocrats, intellectuals, players, tavern cronies and (at the last) a simple jail-keeper.

How far Johnson himself was conscious of this pattern, and its implications, will slowly emerge. But by placing the primary figure of the mother so strongly in his opening narrative, his biographical inventions and shortcomings seem to rise towards a larger, more inward psychological truth. The mother relationship, however we interpret its frustrations and fantasies, is crucial to Savage's idea of himself and his possible place in the world. And when Johnson picks out such a tiny detail as Savage at Mrs Oldfield's death, wearing 'Mourning as for a Mother', one can already believe that he is conscious of a great deal.

Savage's impact on literary London continued to be sharper, and more skilfully managed, however, than Johnson suggests. In 1719 he succeeded in obtaining a valuable half-page entry in Jacob's widely-read *Poetical Register*, a two-volume biographical dictionary of major British writers. Savage was one of the youngest in the entire collection. He was evidently allowed to dictate the entry, which for the first time publicly states his claims – 'This Gentleman is a Natural Son of the late Earl Rivers, by the Countess of Maccles-field' – and gives a brief but colourful account of his neglected childhood. It lists his work (naturally omitting the 'Jacobite Poems'), and comments admiringly: 'Under all these Misfortunes, this Gentleman having a Genius for *Dramatic Studies*, gave us Two Plays between the Age of Nineteen and Twenty-One.'[38]

One can imagine Savage perusing this publication with care as well as pride, for the second volume happens to contain a complete summary of the Sir Thomas Overbury story and was very likely the inspiration for his third play. The elements that might have attracted Savage leap from the page: Thomas Overbury (1581–1613) was a poet, the author of a long, amorous lament, *A Wife*, and the victim of a notorious Court intrigue. A close friend of Sir Robert Carr, Earl of Somerset, he assured his own downfall by advising Carr not to marry the beautiful but vindictive divorcee, Lady Frances Howard, Countess of Essex. Hearing of this advice, the Countess worked steadily to destroy the friendship, and by Machiavellian plotting finally persuaded Carr to have Overbury imprisoned in the Tower and foully murdered by the administration of a poisoned clyster.[39] It is additionally significant, perhaps, that when Savage's *Tragedy* was finally produced at Drury Lane in 1723, he took the unusual step of playing the title role himself.

As author, Savage earned £100 in profits, his first lucrative achievement, which came back to haunt him at the end of his life with further dreams of theatrical triumph (just as young Johnson dreamed of *Irene*). But the success was not one based on dramatic quality. The play is a clumsy, sub-Shakespearian, historical melodrama; much of the text had to be amended by its young actor-producer Theophilus Cibber (and also, as it turns out, by Aaron Hill); and it was only staged during the unpopular, 'novice' season of midsummer when the serious theatre-going audience had left London for their country houses.

The success was one inspired by scandal. The Brett family connection with the elder Cibber, and with Drury Lane itself, was common knowledge. Yet here was the claimant Savage, not only being produced by Cibber's son, and supported by the Drury Lane veteran Robert Wilks, but actually playing the tragic lead in a brazen gesture of self-advertising which broke all the rules of gentlemanly decorum.

Johnson, who affected to despise the whole unmanly race of actors except Garrick ('contemptuous, insolent, petulant, selfish'), just as he secretly adored the actresses ('the silk stockings and white bosoms of your actresses excite my amorous propensities'), extenuated Savage's behaviour as best he could.[40] He records Savage's financial profits but dismisses his abilities as a thespian: 'the Theatre being a Province for which Nature seemed not to have designed him.' He adds that Savage later regretted the shameful publicity of the whole episode. 'He was himself so much ashamed of having been reduced to appear as a Player, that he always blotted out his Name from the List, when a Copy of his Tragedy was to be shown to his Friends.'[41] The gesture of deletion, an attempt to 'blot out' a small but inconvenient piece of his past (and thereby only calling attention to it), is itself revealing. But the act of self-promotion was wholly characteristic of Savage's career by this time.

Even as early as 1720, there is unexpected evidence that he was fast becoming a fashionable and scandalous figure, in growing demand by smart booksellers. At this date Savage contributed eleven erotic songs to an anthology of flute and harpsichord music published in Covent Garden. A manuscript copy exists in the Bodleian Library and was previously unknown to all biographers, apparently including Johnson.[42] Although the lyrics are conventional, several are curiously violent statements of sexual passion:

> See! From my arms Seymora flies!
> I love! I rage! grow mad! despair!
> Flames sparkle fiercely in her Eyes,
> As lightning flashes through the Air ...
>
> Love kindles up a fond desire
> I burn! my raving Brain's o' fire
> To curst Ixion's wheel I'm bound:
> The giddy motion whirls me round and round! ...[43]

The classical image of 'Ixion's wheel', applied to the dizzy, relentless spin of sexual passion, seems a typical piece of Savage's bravura. If the tropes of fire and madness are the commonplace of smart Augustan drawing-room recitals (for which the anthology was destined), the energy of the phrasing is none the less unusual. Mr Hemming, the composer of the accompanying music, 'vivace for the flute', noticed this, and set long *glissandos* on words like 'rage', 'burn' and 'flash' to bring out their suggestive voracity. 'Rage' in the second line is scored with thirty-seven semi-quavers; 'flashes' in the fourth line is scored with fifty-five: a gasping orgasm of sound.

The anthology was published privately by the fashionable instrument-maker and music printer, John Jones, of the Golden Harp, New Street, Covent Garden. It was intended as an elegant piece of publicity for his shop among his wealthy clientele: 'Ladies and Gentlemen ... Be pleased to accept my Humble Thanks ... I have taken all the Care I could to have [the following Compositions] done by the best Hands, and hope they will prove so Entertaining as to engage your favours again, the next Year . . .'

To choose Savage as his major contributor (eleven songs out of twenty by various hands) for such commercial publicity strongly indicates that the young man was already something of a name, or a notoriety, in the West End. Indeed Jones makes a deliberate feature of Savage's contributions by marking them with an asterisk on the contents page: 'NB the Songs marked thus * the Words by Rich: Savage Gent: Son of the late Earl Rivers.' The others are anonymous.

Several of Savage's songs also seem to have veiled or oblique references to his mother. One refers to the despair of 'Alexis', a literary pseudonym which recurs in later *Plain Dealer* articles about Savage. Another harps on Clorinda, 'cruel as she's fair'. A third song – 'To a Young Lady on seeing Her look out o' the Window' – seems to play openly with the well-known anecdote of Savage standing for hours in the darkened street outside his mother's house hoping to catch a glimpse of her at the window in the moonlight:

> Thus when bright Luna looks from high
> Her lustre we admire,
> And thus the Windows of the sky
> Reflect celestial fire . . .[44]

If Johnson did know of these songs, he kept discreetly silent.

Savage used all the work published during this period, up to his *Tragedy of Sir Thomas Overbury* in 1723, to make more and more open claims upon his mother, and to publicise his story throughout London. Johnson never refers to this campaign, which even before Savage had met Aaron Hill has an air of menace, if not yet of blackmail. The dedication to *Love in a Veil* (1718) already has this kind of opportunism, though it still pointedly omits Lady Macclesfield's actual name:

> It is my Misfortune to stand in such a Relation to the late Earl Rivers, by the Countess of ——, as neither of us can be proud of Owning; but that is the smallest part of my Unhappiness, since I am one of those *Sons of Sorrow*, to whom he left nothing, to alleviate the *Sin* of my *Birth*.[45]

After the *succès de scandale* of *Sir Thomas Overbury*, other approaches became more daring. In 1723 Savage discovered that

Bessy Savage, one of the recognised illegitimate offspring of Earl Rivers, was expecting a child. Bessy had made a good marriage to a minor member of the aristocracy, Frederick Nassau-de-Zulestein, third Earl of Rocheford. Her child was to be christened Richard Savage de Zulestein. Savage duly claimed to be Bessy's brother (though her mother was an earlier mistress than Lady Macclesfield) and published: 'To the Right Honourable Bessy Countess of Rochford (Daughter of the late Earl Rivers) when with Child'.[46]

Savage used this occasion to paint a harrowing picture of his own miserable situation in contrast to Bessy's. The poem has many curiously effective lines, playing with the wintry imagery of disinheritance, and is a miniature prelude to *The Wanderer*.

> Hail Rivers! Hallow'd Shade! descend from Rest!
> Descend and smile, to see thy Rochford blest!
> Weep not the Scenes through which my Life must run,
> Though Fate, fleet-footed, scents thy languid Son!
> The Bar that, dark'ning, cross'd my crested Claim,
> Yields at Her Charms, and brightens in their Flame:
> That Blood, which, honour'd in thy Rochford reigns,
> In cold, unwilling Wand'rings trac'd my Veins!
> Want's wint'ry Realm froze hard around my View!
> And *Scorn's* keen Blasts a cutting Anguish blew![47]

Despite the provocative reference to the heraldic 'bar sinister', which is placed diagonally across a family coat of arms in the case of illegitimacy, the poem was surprisingly well-received, and Bessy proved a supporter and a subscriber to his later work. Johnson ignored this notable poetic development of the Outcast theme, perhaps because Savage's campaign with the Rochefords appeared too calculating.

For the first time, Savage also began to exploit the tortured psychology of the rejected 'bastard', cruelly deprived of maternal affections. He suggests that his misery, as an unrecognised son, might almost be a form of madness. This pathological note will recur:

> To such sad Weight my gath'ring Griefs were wrought,
> Life seem'd not Life, but when convuls'd with Thought!
> Decreed beneath a Mother's Frown to pine,
> Madness were ease to Mis'ry form'd like Mine![48]

By the following year Savage's story had become well enough known in literary circles to appear lightly disguised in a popular novel by Eliza Haywood, *Memoirs of a Certain Island Adjacent to the Kingdom of Utopia* (1724). Mrs Haywood, a handsome and raffish figure in her thirties, had established herself as a Society gossip and editor of a titbits magazine, *The Female Spectator*. A female rival of Defoe's, she became famous in the 1720s for a number of scandalous *romans-à-clef* (the 'key' always being provided in a tantalising index at the back) which hovered between lush, sentimental fiction and rumour-mongering biography. This was exactly the genre that Johnson was attempting to dethrone.

Though financially successful, Mrs Haywood's own notorious *amours* gradually undermined her reputation, and she ended up being pilloried in Pope's *Dunciad* as little better than a literary whore:

> See in the circle next, Eliza placed;
> Two babes of love close clinging to her waist . . .
> Pearls on her neck, and roses in her hair,
> And her fore-buttocks to the navel bare.[49]

Throughout the *Life*, Johnson studiously omits all reference to Eliza Haywood, perhaps regarding her as a dangerously tainted source. Yet he may also have been trying to protect Savage's reputation, for his involvement in the Haywood circle raises a number of murky speculations. Savage definitely courted Eliza's attentions, first by publishing poems in praise of her early books: 'On her Novel called *Love in Excess*' in 1720, and 'On her Novel called *The Rash Resolve*' in 1723. The first refers to her literary 'Wonders', the second to her womanly 'Softness' and 'sweet Genius'.[50]

When the novel *Utopia* appeared in 1724, it contained a ten-page section entitled 'The History of Masonia, Count Merville and Count Riverius' which gives a highly romanticised account of the Rivers affair and Lady Macclesfield's ('Masonia's') attempts to disown her illegitimate children, complete with much breathy – and clearly invented – dialogue.[51] Masonia's behaviour is described as 'guilty', and 'the most unheard-of and unnatural Barbarity'. Both children are said to have survived (the boy is keyed as 'Mr S——e'); a fairy godmother appears as 'Mrs Floyd'; a mysterious 'Gentleman' acts as young Savage's guardian (otherwise unknown); and the melodramatic story of kidnapping Savage for the American plantations (never before mentioned) makes its first appearance.

How far Savage provided these materials for Mrs Haywood, or himself later incorporated them into the versions of his life, must remain problematic. Did he inspire the novel, or rather draw inspiration from it? We simply cannot tell: but the small error over Mrs Lloyd's name, the large error over the daughter's survival (her death is well documented – see Appendix), and the spectacular arrival of the 'kidnapping' tale, suggest some fascinating combination of fact and fiction. No wonder if Johnson was chary.

However, Mrs Haywood also drew a mischievous portrait of the adult Savage, the 'Ingenious Riverius'.[52] He is a tender, melancholy youth, loudly proclaiming his 'Misfortunes' but gifted by Apollo with 'the Spirit of Poetry'. He is also venal, naïve and easily misled. He has become sexually involved with an evil poetess, 'Gloatitia', and uses her favours to advance his worldly ambitions. 'Gloatitia' is keyed as Martha Sansom, a young writer in Aaron Hill's circle, to whom Savage certainly addressed several admiring poems. Eliza's disgust at this connection suggests jealousy, and for a moment we have a glimpse of a whole network of romantic intrigue surrounding Savage, though it is impossible to establish exactly what this was about. Johnson's silence over this aspect can only be one of genuine ignorance or tactful propriety.

Mrs Haywood accepts Savage's claims, but she embroiders them so lavishly that it is clearly the scandal rather than the truth that interests her. Moreover though she praises him as a poet, she sees his hunger for publicity and supporters as a psychological and even moral flaw. He emerges from the novel as a chameleon figure, a literary changeling, restless, ambitious, without scruples. All this seems curiously astute. She summarises his essential opportunism through the affair with Gloatitia; and reveals too her own emotional involvement, like so many others.

Not inconsiderable are the number of Friends which his Genius this way has gain'd him – and had he not been unhappily introduced to the acquaintance of a vile Woman, a Pretender to that Art [of Poetry], he might have deserv'd many more than he has found; but led by her Insinuations, and perhaps instigated by a belief, that complying with her Humour might be some advantage to his Fortune, he has been swayed not only to mean Actions, but such also as are unjust and wicked.[53]

It is not known what Savage's reactions were to the publication of *An Island Adjacent to Utopia*; a piece of publicity at which he must have connived or initially encouraged. It attacks Lady Macclesfield on his behalf, but also throws an unwelcome light on his own character and behaviour. Perhaps he was prepared to pay the price, for the time being, until he moved into more elevated circles. Certainly he republished the poems in Eliza Haywood's praise two years afterwards. It was only in 1730 that he turned on her, as on other Grub Street friends, with sudden venom.

If Johnson did deliberately draw a veil over this whole episode, it may also have been because he was uneasy at some of the methods Savage first employed against his mother. Johnson knew that Savage, some time around this period, had actually trespassed in Lady Macclesfield's house in Old Bond Street, and so frightened her that she refused to consider any private interventions on his behalf. Johnson only refers to this incident much later in his story, during the course of the trial of 1727. He says that it 'was omitted in the order of the Time' of his narrative, so as to explain the reports of Lady Macclesfield's vindictive behaviour at that later date.

But it is clearly vital to our understanding of Savage's increasingly aggressive campaign against her at this juncture, when wealth and recognition seemed within his grasp. Far from mooning romantically outside her house at night, like Endymion in his 'window' song, Savage had actually broken in and gone up to her bedroom like MacHeath in *The Beggar's Opera*.

However indulgently we interpret this incident (and Johnson is magnificently indulgent), it shows Savage in a curiously menacing light. Restored to its proper context, in the early years, it vividly demonstrates the kind of terrorising and persecution to which Lady Macclesfield would be subjected by Savage. Whether he was really her son or not, he emerges from it as a more sinister and ambiguous figure; and Lady Macclesfield as a less callous and commanding one. Indeed, the roles of persecutor and victim are already almost reversed:

Mr Savage, when he had discovered his Birth, had an incessant Desire to speak to his Mother, who always avoided him in publick, and refused him Admission into her House. One Evening walking, as it was his Custom, in the Street that she inhabited, he saw the Door of her House by Accident open; he entered it, and finding none in the Passage, to hinder him, went up Stairs to salute her. She discovered him before he could enter her Chamber, alarmed the Family with the most distressful Outcries, and when she had by her Screams gathered them about her, ordered them to drive out of the House that Villain, who had forced himself in upon her, and endeavoured to murder her.

Here we have Savage as a different kind of night-walker. He is an 'incessant' and perhaps obsessive prowler, and he finishes up standing at the bedroom door of a screaming, terrified, middle-aged woman. Johnson extricates him as best he can, no doubt giving the intruder's own explanation. He insists that the house door was 'accidentally' open, and that Lady Macclesfield was hysterical with anger. 'Savage, who had attempted with the most submissive Tenderness to soften her Rage, hearing her utter so detestable an Accusation, thought it prudent to retire, and, I believe, never attempted afterwards to speak to her.'[54] But the incident leaves its mark.

In 1724 Savage's position was transformed when he was publicly taken up by the eccentric dilettante, business speculator and man of letters, Aaron Hill (1685–1750). Hill speculated in everything – epic poems, English vineyards, Scottish pine trees, and the York Building Company (through which Savage once reported he had earned 'an hundred thousand pounds').[55] He financed theatrical productions, and any young poet who took his fancy – including John Dyer, James Thomson, Martha Sansom and Richard Savage. In 1724, observing the new vogue for coffee-house periodicals, he launched a bi-weekly magazine, *The Plain Dealer*, to popularise his various projects, and formed a dandified circle of writers known as the 'Hillarian group', to promote in its pages.

Something of his peculiar charm is caught in the titles of his ceaseless flow of occasional poems: 'On a Bee, that was swallowed by a Lady, in a Glass of Wine'; or 'On the Broad-brimmed Hats, which were brought over by the French, about the time of the Treaty of Utrecht'; or 'To a Lady, who put herself in a Bad Way, by taking spirit of Nitre by spoonfuls, instead of a Few Drops'; or 'Blowing Kisses at the Playhouse'; or 'On hearing a *very* dull Sermon'.[56] Johnson says that Savage received 'great Assistance on many Occasions' from Hill, and that he never mentioned him in conversation 'but with the utmost Tenderness and Regard'.[57]

The truth is that Hill was a sort of Svengali-figure in Savage's life over a period of almost ten years. The relationship was often stormy; but it led to many of the most important contacts in

Savage's career: with the Hillarian group, with Pope, with Thomson and eventually with Lord Tyrconnel. Above all, it led to a persistent public campaign to extort recognition and money from Lady Macclesfield and her relations.

Savage wrote several poems to Hill (as also to his wife, 'the Excellent Miranda'), of which 'The Friend' (1726) represents Savage in his most gushing – and therefore most dangerous and demanding – mode of high-blown sentiment. Johnson described it as showing 'the utmost Ardour of Affection'.[58]

> O Lov'd Hillarius, thou by Heav'n design'd
> To charm, to mend, and to excel Mankind!
> To thee my Hopes, Fears, Joys, and Sorrows tend,
> Thou Brother, Father, nearer yet! – Thou Friend!
> Thou dearer far (Oh, what can equal thee?)
> Than int'rest, Kindred, Love, or Fame, to me.[59]

Johnson says that Aaron Hill only began seriously to involve himself with Savage on the production of *Sir Thomas Overbury* in 1723, for which he wrote both the verse Prologue and Epilogue. Ironically, in view of later events, Hill praised Savage for *not* writing autobiographically about his own personal history:

> He swims, unyielding, against Fortune's Stream,
> Nor to his private Sufferings stoops his Theme.[60]

But Savage had begun to seek Hill's favours as early as 1721. A dozen letters from Hill to Savage, from this date to 1726, have come to light.[61] Though Savage's side of this correspondence remains unknown, a clear picture of his advance into the Hillarian circle emerges. From 1722 his address is given as Button's Coffee-house, where he appears to be arranging meetings and writing poetry. There is no suggestion that he is penniless, or cannot afford this fashionable location. But he may of course have been putting on a brave front for Hill.

From the start Hill is in the role of mentor and adviser, and much of the correspondence concerns Savage's headstrong schemes and quarrelsome behaviour. There are tantalising references to the affair with Martha Sansom (known in Hill's poetical manner as 'Clio'), and to the row with Sir Richard Steele. Hill is continually urging Savage not to prejudice his claims (which he promises to take up) by his persistent arrogance and aggressive behaviour. Hill demonstrates great patience and unusual affection for his young tyro, but is often very outspoken about his manners. We have the sense of Aaron Hill 'grooming' Savage for greater things.

One letter of May 1723 gives the flavour of Hill's witty, mocking school of charm.

> I received an odd sort of letter from you; the first paragraph of which is to complain of a gentleman's *envy, ignorance*, want of common *good sense*, and common honesty, and a good deal to the same purpose, or rather to no purpose at all ... I daresay of all the numerous company who were present at the Argument, only Mr Savage thought Mr Savage in the right ... Let me intreat you, be your own Friend, and change or mortify this over-rampant something, which your enemies call Vanity.[62]

The following spring, Hill decided that his gifted but troublesome protégé was ready (indeed it appears chafing) to be exhibited before the world, and he ran a sensational series of three long articles on Savage's story in his magazine. These appeared in *The Plain Dealer* during May, June and November 1724. They were a semi-libellous concoction of investigative journalism, topical poetry, correspondence and editorial 'issue' raising: what duty do parents owe to children, what support does society owe to its men of genius?

There can be no doubt that Savage was closely involved with these articles. In fact, it appears from a letter of August 1724 that not only was he rashly boasting of Hill's help, but he was ungraciously demanding that the campaign be stopped up. Hill's reaction in this letter expresses much: his fondness for Savage, his alarm and growing irritation at his behaviour, and the distinct sense of Machiavellian cloak-and-dagger which shrouds the whole affair.

> What motive, but my Affection and regard to your merit, can I have to pretend that I value you? What interest could I have in flattering you? ... I had newly heard from all hands the silly story of your insisting publically on having the *Plain Dealer* paper printed without alteration; and I found too, that you had not kept the promise you made me, of telling nobody that we had been together that day, when I walked in the Fields with you. It was upon this last occasion I recommended to you that Italian maxim, of *a locked breast and an open face* ... the *Plain Dealer*, to recommend your Subscription, and the poems that I promised you,

you have a claim to expect, because I did promise them. I will discharge that promise as much to your advantage as I can. But I will now make you another: that if ever you send me such another letter as this was, it shall put an end to our Acquaintance and Correspondence forever.[63]

Johnson must have seen the *Plain Dealer* file, since he quotes from it in the *Life*, but he gives no indication that it was a serial campaign, or that Savage's case was now taken up by the Hillarian group as a fashionable cause. Even the names of Eliza Haywood, Martha Sansom and John Dyer fail to appear in his account; or the various poems they began to exchange with each other on the subject.

The substance of the campaign was as follows. In the May issue Hill published a long, fictional dialogue between 'Mr Plain Dealer and Major Steadfast' on the subject of bad parents and orphaned men of genius. He added one of Savage's poems to John Dyer which makes plangent reference to his outcast condition:

> Fall'n as I am, by no kind Fortune rais'd,
> Depress'd, Obscur'd, Unpitied, and Unprais'd . . .[64]

In the June issue, carefully increasing the public pressure, Hill published a long essay signed 'Amintas', describing the early history of Savage's life and misfortunes (including the romantic version of his walking at night outside his mother's house). It describes her 'cold indifference' to her son, but without actually naming her. The essay was followed by a despairing, 32-line 'Lament' – 'Hopeless, abandoned, aimless, and oppress'd' – signed by Savage.

Finally in November (though originally planned for August) Savage contributed an open letter about his case, claiming to have the set of 'convincing Original letters' which proved his birthright; and promising or threatening to publish a volume of poetry which would further promote his cause. This became the *Miscellaneous Poems* of 1726, with a startling Preface which greatly impressed Johnson.

The 'convincing Original letters' never materialised at this or at any other time. It is remarkable that Aaron Hill claimed to have seen them, as he stated in a slightly guarded editorial comment at the end of the issue: 'the Proofs [Mr Savage] sent me, are too *strong*, to be easily mistaken'.[65] But he never quoted a single word from them.

Savage's poetical 'Lament' published in the June issue is also crucial to his story at this moment. It is a significant development of the Romantic side of his legend. Characteristically Johnson published the verses in full, as a footnote to his *Life*. He calls them 'affecting Lines', and adds with emphasis that 'they had a very powerful Effect upon all but his Mother, whom by making her Cruelty more publick, they only hardened in her Aversion'.[66]

What he does not mention is that Hill actually sent them privately to Lady Macclesfield, to test her reactions, before publishing them in the magazine. It seems again close to a form of blackmail: pay up, or we publish. But apparently he received no reply.

The poem casts Savage in his full, historic posture as the rejected, unacknowledged genius. It is pictorial in its treatment, calling up the popular broadsheet cartoons of the Poor Poet. He lies flung across his bed, 'in wild Disorder'. His rejection is driving him close to madness. His Cruel Mother haunts him with all the romantic force of a Cruel Lover. He addresses her in short, passionate gasps, as if he were dying of unrequited love. The imagery of cold, of wintry exposure, of urban bleakness, of being *shut out* from house and heart, dominates the quick panting lines of the opening:

> Hopeless, abandoned, aimless, and oppress'd,
> Lost to Delight, and, ev'ry Way distress'd;
> Cross his cold Bed, in wild Disorder, thrown,
> Thus sigh'd Alexis, friendless, and alone –
>   Why do I breathe? – What joy can Being give?
> When she, who gave me Life, forgets I live!
> Feels not these wintry blasts; – nor heeds my Smart;
> But shuts me from the Shelter of her Heart!
> Saw me expos'd to Want! to Shame! to Scorn!
> To Ills! – which make it *Misery*, to be *born*!
> Cast me, regardless, on the World's bleak Wild;
> And bade me be a Wretch, while yet a Child![67]

The directness of this, together with its deliberate melodrama, is, as Johnson said, extraordinarily powerful. Indeed it is very rare to find this kind of emotional display, coupled with unrestrained autobiography, in Augustan verse. It seems like a premonition of Romanticism, and the verse of Sensibility.

But the poem does not remain in this purely confessional mode. In its central passage, it moves to a philosophical position, which touches on the great eighteenth-century debate associated with the

Third Earl of Shaftesbury, on the naturalness of human affections and impulses to good.

Shaftesbury (1671–1713) had retired from London to write moral philosophy, working in an isolated brick belvedere especially constructed in the middle of the fields on his remote Dorset estate. The fruits of these pastoral labours were his *Characteristics of Men* (1711) in which he challenged the cruel Hobbesian notion of a brutish world dominated by self-interest and low, animal passions. Instead he proposed the innate existence of 'disinterested' affections, and a 'moral sense' which held all mankind in harmonious, familial relationships.

From this had arisen the idea that the justice of human society depended ultimately on the natural virtues of conscience, altruism and affective feeling. If human beings do not love and bond together by virtuous instinct, then all social hierarchy is really a form of artificial submission and suppression. The just society reflects and embodies the natural virtues of the happy family. But if family affections are hollow – and especially the affections between parents and children – then the whole rational, customary superstructure of the Augustan world is equally hollow, unnatural and fundamentally false. Consequently, if the love of a mother for her child fails, then the entire social fabric is called into question. Something like this is clearly implied in the following lines:

> Where can he hope for Pity, Peace, or Rest,
> Who moves no Softness in a Mother's Breast?
> Custom, Law, Reason, *all*! my Cause forsake,
> And *Nature sleeps*, to keep my Woes *awake*![68]

Johnson was much concerned by this idea, a metaphysical doubt about the sources of Good in the world. How could one be sure that Evil had not, secretly, got the upper hand? Savage's plight seemed to suggest a fracture, a chink, in Shaftesbury's cosmology of benevolence. Maybe there were powers that tortured and persecuted us, purely for their own pleasure?

Years later Johnson would still be wrestling with this terrible possibility (of which his own physical disabilities continually reminded him). The world looked a different, far colder place to those who were poor, handicapped, disadvantaged, disinherited or unloved. In his monumental review of Soames Jenyns's *A Free Enquiry into the Nature and Origins of Evil* (1757) he would consider with horror the idea that there might be 'some beings above us, *who may deceive, torment, or destroy us for the ends only of their own pleasure or utility'.*[69]

The very existence of the Cruel Mother (itself a moral paradox) which defied 'Nature, Custom, Law and Reason' might suggest that this could be true in a philosophical sense. This is one of the profound unconscious motives that must have compelled Johnson to speak for Savage, against Lady Macclesfield; to believe him, and to defend him. 'Life must be seen before it can be known.'[70]

The 'Lament' has one further, surprising twist. It suggested that Lady Macclesfield is, in all other respects except towards her son, well-known as a kindly and generous woman. Was this intended as bitter irony, or as a calculated appeal to her better feelings? Was it a kind of sentimental blackmail, or a diplomatic olive branch? It is difficult to tell:

> Yet has this sweet Neglecter of my woes,
> The softest, tend'rest Breast, that *Pity* knows!
> Her Eyes shed Mercy, wheresoe'er they shine;
> And her Soul *melts* at ev'ry Woe – but *mine*.[71]

The overall impact of the poem must have been devastating in the tight, gossipy world of London Society. It was even claimed that it reached the hands of Queen Caroline herself. Whatever else, Savage's case was no longer obscure, thanks to Aaron Hill's *Plain Dealer*.

It is all the more remarkable, therefore, that Savage subsequently told Johnson that although he had signed the poem it was not his own work. 'Mr Savage afterwards declared' that it had been written for him by Hill.[72] And indeed it was later reprinted in Hill's posthumous *Works* (1753) under the explicit title: 'Verses made for Mr S—v—ge; and sent to my Lady M—ls—d, his Mother'.

Johnson makes no comment on this shift of ground, which reminds us uneasily of Savage previously deleting his name from the list of players in *Sir Thomas Overbury*. What was the truth? Had Savage grown 'ashamed' of his part in the publicity campaign, on later reflection? Or had Aaron Hill brilliantly taken over, almost reinvented his voice and persona as the Outcast Poet, the rejected child of Genius?

Or was the poem in some sense a joint composition, with Hill cleverly developing the pathetic hints from Savage's earlier fragments of verse-autobiography? This seems the most likely solution. Hill, with his talent for publicity and projects, had in effect shown Savage how to capitalise poetically on his situation. He had shown him how to develop his obscure biography into a fashionable cause, and Savage would soon build on this with the dazzling and outrageous poem of *The Bastard* (1727–8).

We know that Hill had already offered to correct and improve *Sir Thomas Overbury*. Savage had even written him a poem about this: 'Verses sent to Aaron Hill, Esq; with *The Tragedy of Sir Thomas Overbury*, expecting him to correct it'.[73] What he expected from Hill's guiding, worldly-wise hand is eloquently phrased. It was sharper, more vigorous verse, leading (like the Philosopher's Stone) to fame and money:

> This Hero, clogg'd with drossy Lines,
>   By thee new vigour tries;
> As thy correcting Hand refines,
>   Bright Scenes around him rise.
>
> Thy touch brings the wish'd Stone to pass,
>   So sought, so long foretold;
> It turns polluted Lead, or Brass,
>   At once to purest Gold.[74]

Some sort of 'correcting' and refinement of the 'Lament' must surely have taken place to produce the striking poetic breakthrough. Hill had edited, or ghosted, Savage, and given him the new voice which would launch the legend of his rejection. Savage's blanket denial of authorship to Johnson was surely disingenuous. How else can one explain the similarity between a line from the poem he acknowledged (to John Dyer) in the May issue of *The Plain Dealer*: 'Depress'd, Obscur'd, Unpitied, and Unprais'd' with a line from the poem he disavowed from the June issue: 'Hopeless, abandoned, aimless and oppress'd'?

But Johnson refused to see this, or to consider the implications. He wanted to believe that Savage had found his own poetic voice through suffering, and not through journalistic myth-making.

CHAPTER 5

BARD

Something now happened to Savage which moved his life in a new
direction and altered his poetic ambitions. He met the young Scot-
tish poet James Thomson (1700–48) and gained entry into the most
influential literary circle of the day. Concentrating on his tale of
the Outcast, Johnson simply omits this new development. Yet it
throws a singularly revealing light on the complexities of Savage's
actual career and his rapid turns of fortune.

James Thomson arrived in London on the coach from Edinburgh,
in February 1725. He was aged twenty-four, penniless, well-
educated, but unknown: one more literary novice seeking his for-
tune in the great metropolis. Yet the plump, round-eyed, affable
Thomson was independent-minded and extremely astute. He had
poems prepared and introductory letters in his pocket. Like Johnson
a decade later, he settled in furnished rooms above a tradesman's
shop, off the Strand. He gave his postal address as Forest's Coffee-
house, Charing Cross.[1] His official plan was to train for the ministry,
but his 'secret design', as he told his friend Cranstoun, was to join
up with his literary fellow-countryman David Mallet and make his
name as a poet.

In the next eight weeks Thomson made a strategic survey of the
theatrical and poetical world of the capital, much as the young

Johnson must have done. What he found confirms the shadowy outlines of many figures we have already glimpsed.

The theatre was dominated by the actor-managers Wilks, Colley Cibber and his son Theophilus. But the actresses Mrs Booth and Anne Oldfield were the most exciting discovery. This is what a young poet came to see on his arrival in London. Mrs Booth was stunning in her portrayal of Ophelia's madness in *Hamlet*, but she also danced 'so deliciously' on stage, with such 'melting lascivious motions, airs and postures', that she threatened to throw young Thomson's 'material part' into an erection. Above all there was Anne Oldfield. 'Mrs Oldfield has a smiling jolly face, acts very well in comedy but best of all, I suppose, in bed. She twines her body, and leers with her eyes most bewitchingly.'[2]

The literary scene was duller: 'I might say Wit's at a very low ebb here.' There was Alexander Pope, but even he seemed to be putting all his efforts into translations of the classics. 'Pope indeed subsists on Homer's stock, or else he might become as destitute as his neighbours.' The Grub Street world of coffee-houses and taverns was bustling with writers, but they all seemed futile and undistinguished. Only one caught Thomson's eye, and that was largely because of his arrogance, and his obsessive habit of repeating his own verses in public. This was none other than Richard Savage.

> The scribbling rhyming generation (lord deliver us!) buzz and swarm here like insects on a summer's day, and are as noxious: so that every coffee-house shop and stall in Town crawl with their maggots. One vengeful hornet (Savage, if you'll indulge me a pun at his name) so plagued and stung me yesterday, with everlasting repetition, as provokes me to this rude – perhaps – complaint ... For my part I renounce the tunefull starving trade.[3]

This glimpse of Savage by a contemporary is interesting on many counts. His vanity and aggression, like his publicity-seeking, provoked the shy and gentle Thomson. It was evidently impossible for any new writer to be in London for more than a few weeks without encountering him (and this fact also bears on Johnson's swift meeting in 1737). Equally, one notices how quickly Savage must also have found out Thomson, the unknown young poet, and homed in on him like 'a hornet'. The provocation was perhaps deliberate on Savage's part, an intuitive search for unrecognised talent like his own. More than this, and again like Johnson, Savage soon turned Thomson into one of his most faithful and indulgent friends.

Initially the shrewd, fastidious young Scotsman was repelled by Grub Street. His description of its pullulating 'insects and maggots' gives a new meaning to the term itself. But he did not renounce the 'tunefull, starving' trade of poetry, choosing instead a prudent course of advancement. Mallet helped him obtain the post of tutor to the son of Lord Binning, and during the course of the summer he was introduced to a number of influential figures including Pope, the playwright John Gay and even the Prime Minister, Robert Walpole. This was exactly the kind of advancement that Savage sought.

By the autumn of 1725 Thomson was starting to write the early fragments of the descriptive poem that became 'Winter', the first of his great blank-verse sequence, *The Seasons*.[4] Another letter to Cranstoun, of October 1725, shows the poem in the process of creation, as Thomson recalls the delights of the Scottish countryside from the dark streets of London: 'Now, I imagine you seized with a fine romantic kind of a melancholy, on the fading of the Year. Now I figure you wandering philosophical, and pensive, amidst the brown, wither'd groves; while the leaves rustle under your feet . . . Nature delights me in every form, I am just now painting her in her most lugubrious dress; for my own amusement, describing winter as it presents itself.'[5]

This vision of the rural world, as an alternative to the city, was not new in itself. The classical tradition of the pastoral was as old as Virgil, and already had a long English tradition running through Spenser's *Shepheards Calender* (1579) to Pope's own youthful *Windsor Forest* (1713). But in Thomson's 'Winter' it would produce a new truth of feeling through its very harshness and 'romantic' melancholy (Thomson's own term), and gradually create a revolution in the settled urbanities of Augustan poetry. One of the first to respond to this was Savage.

David Mallet sent a prepublication copy of 'Winter' to Aaron Hill, and in April 1726 a first meeting between Thomson and Hill was arranged, at which Savage was present. Thanking Hill for his hospitality afterwards, and praising the 'downright Inspiration of your Society', Thomson added: 'It gives me an additional Pleasure, to reflect how justly pleased, too, Mr Savage was.'[6]

By August, Savage was in regular correspondence with both Mallet and Thomson, and feeling his way into the circle of younger poets and their new aesthetic of Nature-writing. He had himself made a startling move away from the city, by renting spacious lodgings in Richmond, then a small, fashionable, country retreat ten miles up-river by ferry from Whitehall Stairs, 'for the benefit of the Air, and the Convenience of his Studies'.[7] This was deliberately close to Alexander Pope's residence, across the Thames, at Twickenham. For Savage was also seeking an introduction to the man he regarded as 'the Monarch of the tuneful Train'.[8]

In this way Savage began a curious double-life, with one foot comfortably in the country and the other retained in London where he still lived like the starving poet of his legend. This pattern, which appears to continue over the next decade, suggests reserves of money at which his friends never seemed to guess. Johnson certainly makes no reference to it at this time; and only years later in his *Life of Thomson* (1781) did he touch upon the growth of these influential friendships. One can only assume that Savage never told him of these early 'rural retirements', in which he acted out the role of the literary gentleman working away quietly at a major poem. It was at Twickenham or Richmond that he first conceived the idea for *The Wanderer*, in a descriptive-philosophic mode strongly influenced by Thomson and Mallet.

In August Savage wrote to Mallet, in a new discreet style of avuncular compliments and literary talk which emphasises this surprising new persona. For once there is not a word of Lady Macclesfield, or persecution, or lonely poverty in the London streets: 'Dear Sir, I had long before now acknowledged your two last, had I not been fatigued and unsettled; for I am truly sensible of yr many undeserved favours which I owe your Friendship ... Your verses to Mr Thomson are correctly wrote, finely imagined, and in a word very generous and like yourself.'[9]

The letter goes on to describe his relaxed and sociable life at Richmond. The chance survival of this document, in papers belonging to the Thomson circle, suggests how easily whole areas of Savage's existence must have disappeared from the historical record. Without such a piece of evidence this side of Savage's life before 1727 would have remained as unknown and unsuspected as it did to Johnson.

Here is Savage working concentratedly on his new, long poem, and asking Mallet modestly for literary advice: 'I have set my whole Thoughts on my Poem call'd "The Misfortunes of Humane Life", but find it very difficult to please myself. I wish I could be favoured with some of your Thoughts on that subject.'[10] The reference is to the first draft of *The Wanderer*, in which Savage is struggling to transpose sections of his autobiography and dreams into the new mode of Nature-description. The imagery of the cold, wintry life of the Outcast is to become a sustained allegoric vision of the winter landscape, inhabited by his alter ego the Hermit.

Despite his long hours of solitary work, Savage is also regularly playing host to a highly select group of literary figures. These people are not journalistic hacks or fashionable promoters, but substantial intellectuals who come for the pleasure of his conversation, his endless fund of stories and scandalous anecdotes and his concern for the new poetry. They include Dr Edward Young (1683–1765) a poet-parson from south London and future author of the famous *Night Thoughts* (1745) upon which Savage may have had some influence. There is John Dennis (1675–1734), the most distinguished critic of the age, author of *The Grounds of Criticism in Poetry* (1704), a difficult and cantankerous man who would never suffer fools gladly and whose visits are a guarantee of serious intent. Above all, there is Alexander Pope (1688–1744), who is just beginning his work on *The Dunciad*, and for whom Savage would supply many of the inside details about the dunces of Grub Street.

Savage seems to have achieved a surprising degree of acceptance from these writers, as he is evidently proud to inform Mallet: 'Since my rural retirement I have been visited by Dr Young, who mentions you often with an affectionate and uncommon ardour. Mr Pope has thrice done me the favour of a Visit also, and entertained me very handsomely at his House. Mr Dennis has also been with me, and staid three days.'[11]

Thomson refers to Savage showing him early parts of *The Wanderer* in manuscript; and to them laughing together at some recent correspondence with Hill, who was spending September touring Scotland 'in his own Coach and six'.[12] All three poets had reason to cultivate Hill's friendship: he was printing Mallet's poetry in *The Plain Dealer*, supporting Savage's *Miscellaneous Poems*, and giving praise and publicity to Thomson's 'Winter' (which in July 1726 ran to a second edition).

They may never have been simultaneously under one roof at Richmond (all three complain of each other's failures to answer letters quickly enough). There does, however, seem to have been a conscious grouping of poetic efforts and a detailed exchange of ideas and verse passages. The formation of the circle was certainly noticed at the time, since the *British Journal* in October 1726 ran a series of satirical articles attacking what it called 'The Brotherhood of Sublime-Obscure', in which Thomson, Mallet, Savage and John Dyer were singled out.[13]

Thomson's 'Winter', already published to great acclaim, was the standard bearer of the new style. The agreed aim was to develop a genre of long, meditative, Nature poems capable of carrying deep personal feeling and observation, but also with a unified dramatic structure and philosophy.

Thomson, who had begun by thinking of 'Winter' as a series of atmospheric fragments, was now working on 'Summer' and had conceived the quartet structure of the four *Seasons*. It was Mallet who had advised this shift from 'detached pieces' to a full, 'connected' sequence. David Mallet in turn was working on *The Excursion*, upon which Thomson also advised him. Savage was working on *The Wanderer*, and sought comments from both the other two. All three showed each other manuscript sections from their work in progress.

Thomson in particular gave detailed criticism of individual lines and passages from all three poems, and in doing so developed something close to an aesthetic of 'the Sublime'. The term itself was taken from essays by the critic Dennis, and becomes historically significant in the development of Romanticism.[14]

What did Thomson mean by the 'Sublime', and why was it of similar importance to Savage? The engendering impulse seems to have been a new intensity of emotional response, both to the natural world and to the human heart. Thomson wanted the 'ancient Simplicity of Expression' renewed, and a recognition of extremes and extravagance. Quoting two lines of *The Excursion*, he bursts out: 'This is Poetry! this is arousing Fancy! Enthusiasm! Rapturous Terror!' Picking out a single, bare, monolithic image from Mallet – 'The rough Rock rises bleak, and chills the Sight' – he writes appreciatively: 'This is a very full, natural, dismal, Picture. It rises even abrupt in the Poem, and that too with some Surprize. I am not only chilled, but shiver at the Sight.'[15]

From Savage's *The Wanderer*, Thomson fastens on a passage of psychological extravagance, which he says Savage composed with immense and ingenious effort. The passage is indeed almost surreal in effect. It makes an extended comparison between the east wind, the pain of toothache, and the fragility of human comfort. Thomson mentions it in the context of his own difficulties with composing a simile for the sun in 'Summer'. 'I have racked my Brain about the common Blessing of the Sun, as much as ever S[avage] did his in that elaborate Description of the Tooth-Ache.'

The section, from Canto I of *The Wanderer*, shows how Savage was deliberately extending his own private imagery of winter, chill, and pain. From the streets he moves to the countryside, and the universal condition of man. Its 'sublimity' perhaps consists in its poetic violence and obsessional logic. It connects a minute physiological occurrence inside a man's mouth, miraculously well-observed, to a whole exterior landscape of rawness and vulnerability:

> Now veers the Wind full East, and keen, and sore,
> Its cutting Influence aches in ev'ry Pore!
> How weak thy Fabrick, Man! – A Puff, thus blown,
> Staggers thy Strength, and echoes to thy Groan.
> A Tooth's minutest Nerve let Anguish seize,
> Swift kindred Fibres catch! (so frail our Ease!)
> Pinch'd, pierc'd, and torn, enflam'd, and unassuag'd,
> They smart, and swell, and throb, and shoot enrag'd!
> From Nerve to Nerve fierce flies th'exulting Pain!
> – And are we of this mighty Fabrick vain?[16]

This passage became famous in the group, and Thomson notes with wry amusement that it much 'disconcerted' the pious and conservative Edward Young. In the end it is quite unlike anything written by the genial, well-balanced and essentially realistic Thomson in *The Seasons*. Savage's winter is an interior one. His convulsed and frozen landscapes are spiritual and autobiographical.

Moreover Savage's supposedly pastoral world is haunted by terrible figures, whose 'sublime' aspect has nothing in common with the 'rapturous Terror' of Thomson's earthly storms or Mallet's wild border landscapes. These figures are inward, psychological ones whom Savage presents with his own completely original form of bardic 'Extravagance', drawing on modes of 'Gothick' imagery not yet in vogue and perhaps influenced by the new flamboyant styles of staging Shakespearian tragedy he had witnessed at Drury Lane. Such a figure is 'Suicide', a vengeful female apparition who rises unbidden from the winter sunlight, displaying the decorated costume and formalised gestures of a theatrical tragedy queen. For all her staginess, 'Suicide' is a figure of genuine horror, and evidently comes from the depth of Savage's private demonology of moral terror and despair:

Here the lone Hour, a Blank of Life, displays,
Till now bad Thoughts a Fiend more active raise;
A Fiend in evil Moments ever nigh!
Death in her Hand, and Frenzy in her Eye!
Her Eye all red, and sunk! – A Robe she wore,
With Life's Calamities embroider'd o'er . . .
She dreams, starts, rises, stalks from Place to Place,
With restless, thoughtful, interrupted Pace;
Now eyes the Sun, and curses ev'ry Ray,
Now the green Ground, where Colour fades away.
Dim Spectres dance! Again her Eye she rears;
Then from the blood-shot Ball wipes purpled Tears;
Then presses hard her Brow, with Mischief fraught,
Her Brow half bursts with Agony of Thought!
From me (she cries) pale Wretch thy Comfort claim,
Born of *Despair*, and *Suicide* my name![17]

Psychologically, this is a glimpse of something new and hitherto unsuspected in Savage's character: his deep fear of depression and solitude – the 'Blank' of the 'lone Hour'. But Johnson recognised it instantly, and placed this passage with great force later in his narrative.

Thomson's own realisation of his fellow-poet's strangeness, his inner deserts and demons, grew rapidly that summer of 1726. We catch it in a letter to Mallet, who had complained of Savage's unreliability as a correspondent, in the rapid exchange of verse and criticism. Thomson ironically defends Savage as being too much of a genius for such a prosaic virtue. In fact he is extremely rude about him, and his 'writh'd' poetry; but behind the exasperation and mockery lies a growing affection.

How can you be so unreasonable as to expect regularity from S[avage]? As well you might hope for Poetry from a satchel of rhymes, writh'd lines, and hard words. What in the name of Inconsistency has he to do with being punctual? Would you bring the wild Ass from the range of the desert: he who cries, bray, bray, and laughs at the letter-writing throng? Why he has given me as many promises of a letter, this summer, as he has writ lines, nay repeated lines; and yet, 'tis well known, it never entered his head, but when he promised, to perform – if then.[18]

Thomson also adds that Savage was considering applying for the poet laureateship.

How had Savage financed his new life as gentleman-bard of
Richmond, living in his rural retirement and entertaining influential
literary guests? The change in his situation was, after all, dramatic.
Three years previously, at the time of writing *Sir Thomas Overbury*,
he is described by Johnson as being too poor even to purchase his
own ink and paper. But from summer 1726 until at least November
1727 he is wealthy enough to afford both town and country lodg-
ings, one at Westminster and the other at Richmond, to commute
between the two and to write at leisure. Johnson became aware of
these facts from the transcripts of the 1727 trial, which referred to
both of Savage's addresses and his ostentatious prosperity. How-
ever, Johnson enquires no further.

The answer seems to lie in the controversial publication history
of Savage's *Miscellaneous Poems* of 1726. The collection is not what
it seems. To begin with, it is a group anthology of the Hillarian
circle of poets, of which Savage was the editor but not the major
contributor. Others included Aaron Hill himself, Martha Sansom,
John Dyer and David Mallet. Thomson was also invited to contrib-
ute, but declined the honour. Mallet had likewise refused, but found
two of his poems included by Savage none the less.[19]

In literary terms, the volume consisted of much complimentary
and mutually flirtatious verse, together with a common debating
theme about the nature of 'true greatness' and the advantages and
disadvantages of aristocratic privilege.[20] This theme appears notably
in a linked exchange of poems between Savage, Dyer and 'Clio'
(Martha Sansom).

In one of these – 'The Picture: To Mr Dyer, when in the Country'
– Savage hints that his role as gentleman-poet is merely the prelude
to greater things: he dreams of social advancement and perhaps
political activity in the affairs of state. By gaining power and recog-
nition, he will be able to act on behalf of the poor and oppressed.
Yet his overwhelming aim is personal glory:

> Think not light Poetry, my Life's chief Care,
> The Muse's Mansion is at best but Air!
> Not sounding *Verse* can give great Souls their Aim,
> *Action* alone commands substantial Fame.
> Though with clip'd Wings I still lie flutt'ring here,
> I'd soar sublime and strike the Topmost Sphere . . .
> Thus to Enquiry prompt th' imperfect Mind,
> Thus clear dim'd Truth, and bid her bless Mankind.

From the pierc'd Orphan thus draw Shafts of Grief,
Arm Want with Patience, and teach Wealth Relief.[21]

Savage's whole contribution consisted of fourteen poems, yet most of these remained occasional and complimentary pieces, like 'The Friend: Addressed to Aaron Hill Esq'. No drafts of the early *Wanderer* appear. The most distinguished poem in the volume was undoubtedly John Dyer's 'Grongar Hill', a topographical poem in the new style, which eventually became a favourite among editors.

One could say that initially the collection had the appearance of an elegant 'benefit' volume for Savage, following on from Hill's campaign in *The Plain Dealer*. This impression was reinforced by the distinguished prepublication list of subscribers, who no doubt thought (like most of the contributors) that they were supporting a piece of harmless and rather stylish literary philanthropy. Notable catches were John Savage Esq., the direct legitimate heir to Earl Rivers (a nephew); and Bessy Rivers, the Countess of Rocheford, whom Savage claimed as his sister. The Duke of Rutland subscribed for no fewer than ten copies, since Savage had written him a poem about his wife the Duchess's recovery from smallpox the previous year: one of Savage's most nimble pieces of opportunism.

Among other subscribers were a high proportion of well-heeled, well-intentioned and often elderly female members of the aristocracy: the Dowager Countess of Warwick, the Countess of Strafford, the Lady Viscountess Cheyney, the Lady Viscountess Castlemaine, Lady Gower, Lady Lechmere, and so on.[22] Johnson listed all these, 'who so generously contributed to his Relief', in a polite footnote. The *Miscellany* was dedicated by Savage to Lady Wortley Montagu, a fashionable young authoress (one of the original 'Blue Stockings'), who promptly sent a few guineas herself. But here Johnson was moved to remark that this dedication flattered her 'without Reserve, and, to confess the Truth, with very little Art'.[23]

When this apparently decorous production appeared in February 1726, Savage's editorial additions had transformed its character to an outrageous degree. It is not clear if Aaron Hill was involved in this, but it seems likely. Not only had Savage signed all his fourteen poems 'Son of the late Earl Rivers', but he had supplied a long Preface in which he attacked Lady Macclesfield with relentless and brilliant satire; and reprinted the *Plain Dealer* articles. From a 'benefit' volume by the Hillarian group, the book had been transformed into a personal jeremiad, scathing, witty and merciless.

Demand for it immediately became clamorous, and 70 guineas' worth of subscriptions appeared at Button's Coffee-house, 'probably produced', as Johnson calmly remarks, by this 'uncommon Strain of Humour'.[24]

Savage had finally manoeuvred himself, with Aaron Hill's aid, into a position of negotiation with Lady Macclesfield. It seemed almost indistinguishable from blackmail. He would suppress the Preface, if she would make amends in financial terms. Johnson makes no mention of this, or what followed, but his 'Newgate' source is guardedly explicit. This was the method by which Savage finally, though briefly, obtained his gentlemanly income.

The 'Newgate' authors described the successful extortion process as follows:

[Mr Savage] had also wrote a long Preface [to the *Miscellaneous Poems*], giving some Account of his Mother's unparalleled ill-treatment of him; but was prevailed on through the Imposition of some very considerable Persons to cancel it; and about that Time he had a Pension of 50 Pounds a year settled upon him. I will not venture to say whether this Allowance came directly from *her*, or, if so, upon what Motives she was induced to grant it him; but choose to leave the Reader to guess at it. This is the first time that he may properly be said to have enjoyed any Certainty in Life.[25]

Johnson's omission of these secret negotiations, and their successful financial outcome, though clearly stated in his primary biographical source, comes close to a whitewashing of Savage. He could not include them because they contradicted his image of Lady Macclesfield as a relentless persecutor of his friend. They suggested, in fact, the reverse: that since 1724, with Hill's help, Savage had steadily turned the tables and become *her* publicly pursuing demon.

The original edition of *Miscellaneous Poems* was indeed withdrawn, to be reissued in July 1726 with the offending Preface and the *Plain Dealer* articles removed. Subsequent correspondence from Aaron Hill in the 1730s shows that the 'considerable Person' who intervened, and induced Lady Macclesfield to produce the £50 pension as hush-money, was her young nephew, the Whig noble and landowner, Lord Tyrconnel. Savage eventually dedicated his long Richmond poem, *The Wanderer*, to Tyrconnel, who was to play an increasingly important role as his patron.[26]

The Preface itself is one of the most remarkable pieces of prose that Savage ever wrote. It gives a vivid insight into his personality, with its extraordinary mixture of pathos, wit and malice. Johnson faithfully printed it in its entirety but confined his comments to its uncommon humour, and its 'Gaiety of Imagination'. The Preface is certainly witty, but in the obsessive, almost surreal way which is already becoming evident in Savage's poetry. It is six pages long, and amounts to an *apologia* for his whole life and a stinging attack on Lady Macclesfield and everything she stands for in the society of privilege. It opens, in high decorous style, with a tag from Virgil, 'Crudelis Mater magis, an Puer improbus Ille?' – 'a cruel Mother: but crueller than that Boy was wicked?'[27]

Savage begins with a series of elegant witticisms about his illegitimate birth. He then turns briefly aside to thank his fellow-poets for their contributions, and especially Aaron Hill for his *Plain Dealer* articles which 'point out my Unhappy story to the World'. Finally he returns 'to the Lady, my Mother', assailing her with grotesque accusations of infanticide and sadistic cruelty.

The black humour of this third section, with references to cannibalism, castration and being buried alive, is psychologically revealing: both ingenious and pathological. It suggests an imagination not free and light-hearted, as Johnson suggests and as Savage may consciously have intended; but a mind trapped by its own fantasy, obsessive and self-lacerating. It indeed expresses the genuinely outcast and alienated personality to which Johnson was responding at a far deeper level.

The darkness and violence in Savage's wit increases as the Preface progresses. From genial flourishes of well-turned and extended irony – like the doffing of a hat – Savage descends to bitter sarcasm, painful fragments of autobiography and barely suppressed fury – like the jabs of a sword.

He opens with a deft apology for 'so constantly' referring to himself as the son of the late Earl Rivers, which readers might 'impute to a ridiculous Vanity'. But his 'hard Fortune' has forced this upon him. He is an outcast 'savage', just like any American Indian.

This contemporary joke is skilfully unravelled:

I am to be pardon'd for adhering a little tenaciously to my Father, because my Mother will allow me to be No-body; and has almost reduced me, among heavier Afflictions, to That uncommon kind of Want, which the Indians of America complain'd of at our first settling among them; when they came to beg *Names* of the English, *because* (said They) *we are Poor Men of ourselves, and have none we can lay Claim to.*[28]

This initial identification of himself with the nameless, ethnic tribes beyond white civilisation is a clever stroke to which he will return.

He continues with the history of Lady Macclesfield's adultery with Earl Rivers and her divorce from Lord Macclesfield, which deprived him of *two* fathers simultaneously. The argument here becomes both legal and philosophical, and is again turned with great deftness.

> Thus, while *legally* the Son of one Earl, and *naturally* of another, I am, *nominally*, No-body's Son at all: For the Lady, having given me *too much Father*, thought it but an equivalent Deduction, to leave me *no Mother*, by way of Balance. – So I came sported into the World, a kind of Shuttlecock, between Law and Nature.[29]

This bounce of paradox, with its mixture of playfulness and pathos, shows Savage's insidious charm. He presents himself as tossed between the absurdities of the legal system and the failures of his mother's natural instincts, and so suffering from a double injustice. It is an injustice of which he can accuse society as a whole. Johnson was particularly delighted by the sporting analogy, and much later used it to describe the fluctuations of literary reputation, which should be 'struck like a shuttlecock, at both ends' to keep it before the public.

Savage ends this section of his Preface with a reference to the disputes over Earl Rivers's will, and the good fortune of Rivers's other illegitimate children (including Bessy Rocheford). Through the 'unaccountable Severity of a Mother' who denied his very existence, he is the 'single unhappy Instance, among that Nobleman's natural children' of an illegitimate son 'thrown, friendless on the World' without means of support or authority to apply for it. (He makes no mention here of his 'convincing Original letters' proving his birthright.)

Deprived of the 'Privilege of a Man of Quality', he is forced to depend upon the free gifts of wit and intelligence to make his way in society. This is the subject he had debated in poems with John

Dyer, and about which Johnson himself felt so strongly. 'Thus, however ill-qualified I am to *live by my Wits*, I have the best Plea in the World for attempting it; since it is too apparent, that I was *Born to it*.'[30] Here Savage has touched skilfully on a subject that was to preoccupy eighteenth-century philosophers with increasing urgency: the conflict between inherited privilege and 'natural rights' and talents.

Thus far, the Preface is a clever, spirited and well-judged claim for redress. In the second part, Savage gracefully thanks his friends for furnishing the *Miscellany* with their verses, which give it 'Wit enough to deserve a Subscription'. He particularly acknowledges Aaron Hill, 'whose writings are a shining Ornament'. He refers to the *Plain Dealer* campaign and the two articles 'which I entreat his Pardon, for reprinting'. This could either mean that Savage had not consulted Hill about reprinting them beforehand, which seems unlikely from their correspondence; or it was a way of extricating the magazine if Lady Macclesfield should bring a case of libel.

Great stress is laid on the many distinguished people who, unlike Lady Macclesfield, had responded to his 'unhappy Story' with money 'in the most liberal, and handsome Manner' as Hill had hoped: 'many Persons of Quality, of all Ranks, and of both Sexes, distinguish'd themselves with the Promptness he had hinted to the Noble-minded.'[31]

The clear suggestion is that the 'Noble-minded' might provide more, with equal promptness. There is no further discussion of the literary content of the book (we are far from the delicate, critical exchanges with Thomson and Mallet), and the accent here is unblushingly commercial. Savage then returns, with a vengeance as one might say, to the subject of Lady Macclesfield.

The third part of the Preface is so extraordinary that one would have to look to the excoriations of Swift to find its equivalent. Savage turns abruptly to the philosophical writings of John Locke, and launches into a tirade against his mother. The angle of attack is devastating. Lady Macclesfield is an example of the most extreme form of maternal barbarity that exists on historical record. She belongs in Locke's casebook examples of inhumane practices, in Chapter Three of his *Essay Concerning Human Understanding* (1690). 'Had the celebrated Mr Locke been acquainted with her Example, it had certainly appeared in his Chapter against "Innate Practical Principles"; because it would have completed his Instances of Enormities.'

In this chapter, 'No Innate Practical Principles', Locke is attacking the idea that humane behaviour is generated (as Shaftesbury argued) by innate or instinctively benevolent impulses. To disprove this, Locke cites a series of anthropological examples – his 'Instances of Enormities' – in which parents refuse to nurture children. These cases of infanticide do not contradict the social norms of the tribal group and so produce no guilt or condemnation. They therefore disprove the idea that an 'innate principle' of parental love and nurturing exists.

'Have there not been whole Nations', Savage quotes gleefully from Locke, 'and those of the most Civilized People, amongst whom the exposing of Children, and leaving them in the Fields, to perish by Want or Wild Beasts, has been the Practise, as little condemned or scrupled as the begetting them?'

Savage applies this passage specifically to himself. 'Were I inclinable to grow serious, I cou'd easily prove that I have not been more gently dealt with by Mrs Brett.'[32] The shift away from the decorous previous references to 'the late Countess of Macclesfield (now widow of Colonel Henry Brett)' indicates the complete shift in tone. Referring to her abruptly as 'my Mamma', Savage goes on to pick three of Locke's tribal 'Enormities' and apply them directly to his Mother's behaviour. He claims to do this in a 'whimsical' manner.

The first is Locke's example of the Mengrelians, who it is said 'bury their Children alive without Scruple'. Savage comments that his 'Mamma's' industrious attempts to obscure his identity as a baby were exactly equivalent to being buried alive. 'And sure, like a Mengrelian, she must have committed the action without Scruple, for she is a Woman of Spirit, and can see the Consequence without Remorse.'[33]

The second example is that of the Caribees. 'The Caribees (continues my Author) were wont to castrate their Children, in order to fat and eat 'em.' Savage's choice of this form of persecution of course invites a Freudian interpretation; and this may well be appropriate. By refusing to love him, Lady Macclesfield has disabled his own ability to grow up and find love and companionship in a full, adult way. His social deprivation is in some sense an emotional and sexual one. His identification with the figure of the Hermit, in *The Wanderer*, perhaps unconsciously confirms this.

Yet in his own commentary on the Caribee example, Savage studiously avoids the castration image and concentrates sarcastically on the fattening and eating. He also now introduces one of his wildest and most melodramatic claims (one that Johnson entirely accepts), that Lady Macclesfield tried to smuggle him as a child to the slave colonies.

> Here indeed I can draw no Parallel; for to speak but Justice of the Lady, she never contributed ought to have me pamper'd, but always promoted my being starved: Nor did she, ev'n in my Infancy, betray Fondness enough to be suspected of a Design to devour me; but, on the contrary, not enduring me ever to approach Her, offer'd a Bribe to have had me ship'd off in an odd Manner, to one of the Plantations.[34]

Why Savage should make this sudden, novelettish charge (evidently adapted from Eliza Haywood's *Utopia*) is puzzling. Perhaps it linked curiously well with his opening image of barbarous anonymity, as if he were a poor benighted American Indian, without a land or name.

His final example touches on astrology and witchcraft. It is his funniest, but also his most sinister. 'Mr Locke mentions another Set of People, that despatch their children, if a pretended Astrologer declares 'em to have unhappy Stars.' This is his parting shot, and he handles it lightly. But the implication is that old Lady Macclesfield has gone mad.

'Perhaps my Mamma has procur'd some *cunning Man* to calculate my Nativity; or having had some ominous Dream, which preceded my Birth, the dire Event may have appear'd to her in the dark and dreary bottom of a China cup, where Coffee-stains are often consulted for Prophecies, and held as infallible as were the Leaves of the ancient Sybils.'[35] He prefers to believe she is 'tainted' with such crazy superstitions, rather than to suppose that she can be 'Mistress of a sear'd Conscience, and act on no Principle at all'. The Preface ends abruptly on this last bitter jest.

It is little wonder that Lady Macclesfield paid to have this document suppressed. But it is very strange that she did not also sue for libel, and this must give us pause for thought, as it evidently did Johnson. Meanwhile Richard Savage went on living in comparative comfort, between his two addresses in Richmond and Westminster, and making regular sorties to meet his less poetical friends in Grub Street. Unknown to anyone he was also preparing a new work, of less sublime aspect than *The Wanderer*. It was to be called *The*

Bastard, 'a poem inscribed with all due reverence to Mrs Brett, once Countess of Macclesfield'. The rejected bard was now in the ascendant: or so he thought.

CHAPTER 6

MURDER

On the night of 20 November 1727, at a coffee-house near Charing Cross, Savage was involved in a brawl during which a maidservant was wounded in the head and a man was stabbed to death.

It might be natural to suppose that this appalling incident was somehow arranged, or indirectly caused, by Lady Macclesfield in an attempt to silence Savage or frighten him off from further blackmail. Some fifty years previously Dryden had been attacked in Rose Alley, by henchmen of the Earl of Rochester, in revenge for his satires. But the fight in which Savage took part was of an entirely different kind.

Savage was not alone, but with two drinking companions. The affray took place at two o'clock in the morning, at Robinson's Coffee-house, which was generally known as a 'house of ill fame' or brothel. Evidence showed that Savage and his two friends were acting in a violent and drunken manner, and were the aggressors in the fight. Moreover, it was Savage who admitted under oath that he was responsible for both the killing of the man and the wounding of the maid. In consequence Savage was facing a murder charge at the Old Bailey.

The trial transcript, which has survived in shortened form, puts it as follows:

Thursday Dec 7, 1727. Richard Savage, James Gregory, and William Merchant were indicted for the Murder of James Sinclair: Savage by giving him with a drawn Sword, one mortal Wound in the lower part of the Belly of the length of half an Inch, and the Depth of nine Inches, on the 20 Nov last, of which mortal Wound he languished till the next Day, and then died: And Gregory and Merchant by being present, aiding, abetting, comforting, and maintaining the said Savage, in committing the said Murder.[1]

This charge, and its consequences, become the crisis and then the turning point of Savage's entire career. It is also a key episode in Johnson's biography, and provides the next crucial test in the romantic interpretation of his friend's misfortunes. If he could not defend Savage at this point, by at least retaining the sympathy of the reader, then his case was lost.

Johnson now had several new sources with which to work: besides the 'Newgate' pamphlet (written for this very occasion) there is the *Select Trials* transcript, Savage's own extensive reminiscences, and sections from the poetry which refer to the event. Johnson handles the evidence in masterly but adversarial manner, acting throughout as if he is counsel for the defence. He pleads mitigating circumstances, underplays or frankly omits hostile evidence, harries the prosecution witnesses, impugns the judge, and finally manages to introduce Lady Macclesfield in her customary role of pursuing demon – his trump card.

Johnson begins by raising doubt in the reader's mind as to whether Savage was not more a victim than a perpetrator of evil. Nothing in Savage's previous behaviour or impulsive character is allowed to bear on the affray at Robinson's. It may simply be one more stroke of his unhappy destiny: 'both his Fame and his Life were endangered by an Event, of which it is not yet determined, whether it ought to be mentioned as a Crime or a Calamity.'[2]

In fact the circumstances leading up to the killing give us a vivid picture of the Grub Street side of Savage's life (as opposed to his country-gentleman existence) at this period of comparative affluence. Savage had come into London that day from Richmond to pay off his Westminster lodgings. He had met two cronies, William Merchant and James Gregory, and embarked on a drinking expedition which continued the whole evening until the ordinary coffee-houses closed at about midnight. Unable, or perhaps unwilling, to obtain rooms for the night (they were not short of money) the three agreed 'to ramble about the Streets, and divert themselves with such Amusements as should offer themselves till Morning'. Johnson omits the possible inference that they were going whoring.

Neither William Merchant nor James Gregory were literary men; neither could give fixed addresses or employments to the court, and all three were said to 'possess no goods'. Both Savage and Gregory carried swords. Gregory was said to be tall and well-built. Merchant wore brightly 'coloured Clothes' by which he was later identified. Savage was dressed in black, wore hat and wig in a dandified manner, and was the smallest and quietest of the three.[3] His unusual silence, and impulsive actions, might suggest that he was very drunk, though he afterwards emphatically denied this to Johnson. He also denied that he knew that Robinson's was a brothel, or even suspected it; though since he had lived in this part of the city for thirty years, wandering all its streets, such ignorance might seem unlikely.

Johnson glosses over this particular late night-walk with an indulgent smile: Savage 'sat drinking till it was late, it being in no Time of Mr Savage's Life any Part of his Character to be the first of the Company that desired to separate. He would willingly have gone to Bed in the same House, but there was not Room for the whole Company . . .'[4] One recalls uneasily at this point his lines from *London*:

> Prepare for death, if here at Night you roam,
> And sign your Will before you sup from home . . .
> Some frolic drunkard, reeling from a feast,
> Provokes a broil, and stabs you for a jest.[5]

The real purpose of the night-walk remains unsolved. What were the three up to, between midnight and two o'clock, if not looking for whores and trouble? The 'Newgate' pamphlet, perhaps less subtle than Johnson in defence, tries to explain it away but only succeeds in raising further awkward questions. The three decided 'to waste Time as well they could till morning, when they purposed to go together to Richmond'. But was it not possible to find a ferry, boatman or coach at that hour? Or were there really no alternative lodgings?

'In their Walks, seeing a Light in Robinson's Coffee-house, they thought that a Place proper to entertain them, tho' Mr Savage protested he was entirely ignorant of the Character of the House, and had never been there in his Life before.'[6] But if Savage did not know it was a brothel, what of Gregory or Merchant? This part of the story is never properly clarified. Nor is any further light ever shed on the identity of the two raffish companions, or the nature of their connection with Savage.

The events at Robinson's Coffee-house were described by five prosecution witnesses, who were cross-examined separately in front of the jury. The witnesses were Mr Nuttal and Mr Lemery, friends of the dead man; Jane Leader, a prostitute; Mrs Enderby, the keeper of the coffee-house; and Mary Rock, the maidservant who was wounded by Savage. Important evidence was also given by Mr Taylor, a clergyman, who afterwards attended the dying man; and Mr Wilkey, a surgeon, who later examined his wound.

Very little was established about James Sinclair himself, the man whom Savage killed, except that he was young, unemployed – 'an idle Person' – and had no fixed address. One witness also testified that he had previously been involved in a fight.[7]

Everyone directly involved had been drinking, and towards the end of the brawl all the candles were knocked over, plunging the room into darkness. This added to the confusion, and incidentally allowed Savage and Merchant the chance to escape; though it meant abandoning Gregory, who was still fighting with Nuttal. The affray was finally brought to an end by three soldiers from a nearby night-cellar, who were called by Lemery. The soldiers 'secured' Gregory and disarmed him, and then found Savage and Merchant hiding in a 'back Court' outside the coffee-house. They gave themselves up without a struggle, Savage appearing pale and 'confused'. All three, together with Nuttal, were arrested and taken to the Watch House.

In the morning Nuttal was released, while Savage and his party were committed by three Justices to the Gatehouse Prison. When James Sinclair died from his wound later that day, they were transferred to Newgate Prison. The following morning, 22 November 1727, all three were charged with murder.

Normally they would have been chained among other serious criminals to await trial. But in deference to Savage's claim to be the son of the late Earl Rivers, they were all placed in the open Press-Yard, where they could receive friends. As Johnson put it, they were 'treated with some Distinction, exempted from the

Ignominy of Chains, and confined, not among the common Criminals, but in the Press-Yard'.[8]

The machinery of eighteenth-century justice worked rapidly by modern standards. On 23 November they went before a coroner's court, which decided that James Sinclair had been wilfully 'killed', and that the prisoners had to answer an indictment for murder. A fortnight later, on Thursday 7 December, 1727, the trial opened at the Old Bailey. It lasted eight hours. This was a protracted length for a common trial, which normally had to be concluded within a single day's sitting.

The case was the talk of literary London, and the public gallery was 'crowded in a very unusual manner'. No record was kept of those who attended from Savage's extensive circle of acquaintance, but it is indicative of the excitement that Alexander Pope came up from Twickenham and took notes.[9] Many celebrities from the world of theatre and journalism were evidently there, and this seems to have tempted Savage to play to the gallery in the latter part of the proceedings. Aaron Hill was present, and fearing the worst, was already preparing an appeal by having shorthand notes made of the leading speeches. These were to form the basis of the 'Newgate' pamphlet.

Johnson's first method of defence was to summarise the prosecution evidence, but not to quote directly from it. The prosecution witnesses are so vivid that however biased their testimony is, it tells sharply against the more abstract and grandiloquent style of Savage's later explanations. The prosecution speaks in the voice of the authentic London streets, colloquial, forceful and specific. Savage views the whole proceedings as he feels a nobleman should, insouciant and detached.

What emerges is a clash of social hierarchies and class assumptions. This points towards the heart of the trial, and the underlying cause of the affray. Savage and his friends had assumed social precedence, the privilege of moneyed gentlemen to command and bully, which the habitués of Robinson's Coffee-house were not prepared to grant them. In this sense, the events of that drunken night were not mere chance. They were a logical outcome of all Savage's obsessively pursued claims to social distinction and recognition.

Johnson summarises the initial action as follows:

In their Walk they happened unluckily to discover Light in Robinson's Coffee-house, near Charing-Cross, and therefore went in. Merchant with some Rudeness, demanded a Room, and was told that there was a good Fire in the next Parlour, which the Company were about to leave, being then paying their Reckoning. Merchant not satisfied with this Answer, rushed into the Room, and was followed by his Companions. He then petulantly placed himself between the Company and the Fire, and soon after kicked down the Table. This produced a Quarrel, Swords were drawn on both Sides, and one Mr James Sinclair was killed.[10]

Various points should be remarked in this initial summary. Savage's name is not mentioned at this stage, not even in reference to the actual killing. The choice of the brothel is simply the 'unlucky' discovery of a light in the dark streets. The blame of aggressive behaviour is placed exclusively on Merchant, while the other two simply 'follow'. Nor is it made clear – and Johnson only mentions it at the very end of his account of the whole trial – that Merchant was the only one of the three not carrying a sword.

The evidence from both Mrs Enderby and her maid is much more specific than Johnson makes out, and suggests rather more than 'some Rudeness' in the behaviour of Savage's party on arrival. In fact they were violent, drunken and menacing.

Mrs Enderby: 'I keep Robinson's Coffee-house. When I let the Prisoners in, I perceived they were in Drink. I shewed them a Room. They were very rude to me. I told them, if they wanted any Liquor, they should have it; but, if they did not, I desired their Absence. Upon which one of them took up a Chair, and offered to strike me with it. – They went into the next Room, which is a publick Coffee-Room in the Day-time. Merchant kicked down the Table. – Swords were drawn.'[11]

Mrs Enderby may not have been a reliable witness. But her testimony was corroborated by the maid, and when asked if Sinclair's party was actually occupying the table that was kicked down, she did not make the obvious response in their favour. 'Whether the other Company were sitting or standing at that Table, I cannot be positive.' Instead, she made a true landlady's observation that the table was a big one (perhaps one of her more valuable pieces of furniture) which required considerable violence to turn over, and that there was plenty of other space in her coffee-house. 'It is a folding Table with two leaves, and there were two other Tables in the same Room.'

This evidence is significant, and was later picked up by the judge, because it suggests the manner in which Savage's party burst into a private room hired for the night. They expected instantly to take it over for their own use, while everyone else deferred to them and got out of the way of the fireplace.

The maid's evidence, not unnaturally, supported her employer's. It did so convincingly; and, perhaps unwittingly, emphasised the whole party's insistence on having absolute and immediate deference paid to their wishes.

Mary Rock, the maid: 'My Mistress and I let the prisoners into the House. My Mistress shewed them a Room. Merchant pulled her about very rudely, and, she making Resistance, he took up a Chair, and offered to strike her with it. Then asking, who was in the next Room? I answered – "Some company that have paid their Reckoning, and are just going, and you may have the Room to yourselves if you'll have but a little patience." But they would not, and so they ran in. I went in not long after, and saw Gregory and Savage with their Swords drawn, and the Deceased with his Sword in his hand, and the Point from him.'[12]

It seems clear from this evidence that once inside Robinson's, Savage's party were prepared to offer violence to anyone who got in their way, including the landlady Mrs Enderby. The maid's phrase, 'pulled her about very rudely', even suggests sexual menaces. In both testimonies, Merchant appears to be leading the group at this stage, with a drunkard's enthusiasm for breaking the nearest piece of furniture. There is no suggestion that either Savage or Gregory were restraining him, and the precipitous rush into the coffee-room – 'and so they ran in' – is a general one.

All that can be said is that neither the maid nor the landlady saw who drew their swords first, once inside the coffee-room. But Mary Rock's statement, when she went into the room 'not long after', gives a clear picture of Savage and Gregory both simultaneously advancing on Sinclair with drawn swords, while Sinclair himself stands in a position of defence with his sword held downwards, 'the Point from him'; that is, turned aside towards the floor.

Again, biased witnesses might be expected to make claim – not easy to contradict – that they had seen Savage draw first. (Other witnesses actually involved in the fight would indeed say this.) But neither Mary Rock nor Mrs Enderby make this damaging claim against the defendants. Their testimony is therefore not only consistent, but carries a degree of conviction, as far as it goes. The impression they give of the generally aggressive behaviour of Savage's party, immediately prior to the killing of Sinclair, is sufficiently circumstantial for a murder charge to be sustained; and it evidently carried great weight with both judge and jury. Johnson prefers to omit it altogether.

Johnson summarises the testimony of Nuttal and Lemery, as to the next and fatal stage of the brawl, with a similar lack of specific detail. Once again, he appears anxious to avoid the evidence that is most damaging to Savage. He had evidently reflected a good deal on the varied and often conflicting accounts of the action, for his summary has a masterly brevity and logic about it, which gives the impression of great fairness. But matched against the transcripts, which suggest a confused and violent confrontation, Johnson's approach seems specious. He defends Savage, ultimately, by suggesting that it is impossible to know the precise truth about what occurred in the coffee-room. Yet in fact a great deal of the truth can be elicited; and it is damning to Savage, as Johnson must have realised.

Johnson puts the prosecution case as follows:

They swore in general, that Merchant gave the Provocation, which Savage and Gregory drew their Swords to justify; that Savage drew first, and that he stabbed Sinclair when he was not in a Posture of Defence, or while Gregory commanded his Sword; that after he had given the Thrust he turned pale, and would have retired, but that the Maid clung round him, and one of the Company endeavoured to detain him, from whom he broke, by cutting the Maid on the Head, but was afterwards taken in a Court.[13]

Initially Johnson appears to accept this testimony without comment. He leaves the impression that Savage was somehow involved against his will, even if guilty of the killing itself; and the strongest image is that of Savage 'turning pale' (presumably with remorse) and wishing to 'retire' (a delicate word) from the coffee-room.

Johnson has to admit that the prosecution witnesses are powerful, and if 'there was some Difference in their Depositions' these are 'very far from amounting to Inconsistency'. This all appears admirably fair. He adds that in the 'Hurry of the Quarrel' it is not easy to establish the exact sequence of events, and therefore 'some Deductions' are to be made from the credibility of the witnesses.[14]

He does not suggest at this point, however, what these deductions might be.

He has also subtly inserted the word – and notion of – a 'Quarrel': that is, a disagreement between the two parties, rather than a sudden assault by one party on the other. But it is precisely the idea of a sudden and unprovoked assault which is the whole burden of the prosecution case against Savage and his friends.

Johnson has thus begun, under the appearance of magisterial impartiality, a steady deflection of the charges. Savage *may* have acted against his will; he seems to have shown immediate remorse; the evidence against him is not *entirely* credible; there was a great deal of confusion in the coffee-room; and anyway the whole affair was simply a late-night quarrel that unfortunately got out of hand. At the worst, Johnson implies, Savage may have been guilty of manslaughter; an inadvertent killing, even a terrible mistake, one more of his tragic 'Misfortunes'.[15]

But Johnson's defence of his friend has only just begun. From impartiality he suddenly switches to an outright attack on the prosecution witnesses. Again he studiously avoids specific reference to or quotation from their evidence, but turns to the general question of character. In a single sentence, of gathering rhetorical force, he unleashes a scathing commentary on the hostile witnesses and follows through with a passionate plea for Savage's essential innocence. His underlying appeal is to that of class-distinction: the lay-abouts of a brothel are inherently less credible than a poet with distinguished friends. If this is a surprising tactic for Johnson to deploy, given his wide social sympathies as a young man, his adversarial role evidently forced him to make the best of it:

> The Witnesses which appeared against him were proved to be Persons of Characters which did not entitle them to much Credit; a common Strumpet, a Woman by whom Strumpets were entertained, and a Man by whom they were supported; and the Character of Savage was by several Persons of Distinction asserted, to be that of a modest inoffensive Man, not inclined to Broils, or to Insolence, and who had, to that Time, been only known for his Misfortunes and his Wit.[16]

Whether the judge, the jury or even Johnson himself were convinced of this assessment of the character evidence, remains to be seen. It is now necessary to examine in a little more detail what the prosecution witnesses actually said in court, and what Johnson so carefully omitted or veiled from his readers.

The trial transcript records long statements from three of them: Nuttal, who carried a sword and fought with Gregory; Lemery, who was unarmed but who wrestled with Savage in an attempt to prevent his escape; and Jane Leader, who claims to have seen much of the fighting, including the actual stabbing of Sinclair.

All three were friends, and Jane Leader was living with Nuttal and probably working as a prostitute. As witnesses they were clearly anxious to support each other's testimony, and Jane Leader particularly entangled herself in contradictions as to what exactly she saw. Nevertheless, the body of their evidence is surprisingly circumstantial, and gives a clear impression of how Savage's party behaved in the coffee-room that night.

After Merchant kicked down the table, all three testified that Gregory and Savage simultaneously set about Sinclair with swords; and that Savage made the fatal thrust while Sinclair was distracted by Gregory, or at least not in a full posture of defence. No evidence was offered that Nuttal joined the fight until after Sinclair was wounded.

The most doubtful point arising from their evidence was as to which of the three combatants – Gregory, Savage or Sinclair – drew his sword first. Both Nuttal and Jane Leader insisted it was Savage, but in this they may have been perjured. Significantly, Lemery remains mute on this important issue. At the request of the defendants, the witnesses gave their evidence 'apart', so they could not hear what the others had said. Nuttal appeared first.

Mr Nuttal: 'On Monday 20th November about eleven at night, the Deceased, and Mr Lemery, and his Brother, and I, went to Robinson's Coffee-house, near Charing Cross, where we staid till one or two in the morning. We had drank two Three-Shilling Bowls of punch, and were just concluding to go, when the Prisoners came into the Room. Merchant entered first, and turning his Back to the Fire, he kicked down our Table without any provocation. "What do you mean?" says I. "And what do *you* mean?" says Gregory. Presently Savage drew his Sword, and we retreated to the farther End of the Room. Gregory drawing too, I desired them to put up their Swords, but they refused. I did not see the Deceased draw, but Gregory, turning to him, said, "Villain, deliver your Sword"; and soon after, he took the Sword from the Deceased.'[17]

At this point Sinclair was wounded, and the rest of Nuttal's evidence concerns his own fight with Gregory. He states that Gregory's sword was broken in the preliminary scuffle with Sinclair, *before* the wounding. This gives some indication of the violence of Gregory's attack. He also states that all the candles were put out by one of Savage's party (presumably Merchant) shortly after Sinclair was wounded. On one other point he is surprisingly frank. Even though convinced that Savage had killed Sinclair, he did not claim to have seen the actual stab delivered. 'I did not see Savage push at the Deceased, but I heard the Deceased say, "I am a dead Man!" And soon after the Candles were put out.'[18]

Lemery's evidence is similar to Nuttal's, except that he does not claim that Savage drew his sword first. Nevertheless he maintains, like Nuttal, that Savage and Gregory set upon Sinclair while the rest of the party drew back across the coffee-room. Like Nuttal, he describes Gregory shouting at Sinclair. Like Nuttal, he states that Savage delivered the fatal sword-thrust to Sinclair. But he is also able to describe the wounding in some detail, having seen it with his own eyes, and also observed Savage's reactions.

Mr Lemery: 'I was with the Deceased, and Mr Nuttal, and my Brother, at Robinson's Coffee-house, and we were ready to go Home, when somebody knocked at the Street Door. The landlady opened it, and let in the Prisoners, and lighted them into another Room. They would not stay there, but rudely came into ours. Merchant kicked down the Table. Our company all retreated. Gregory came up to the Deceased, and said: "God damn ye, you Rascal, deliver your Sword!' Swords were drawn. Savage made a thrust at the Deceased, who stooped, and cried "Oh!" At which Savage turned pale, stood for some Time astonished, and then endeavoured to get away; but I held him. The lights were then put out.'[19]

Before going on to Jane Leader's evidence, which attempts to corroborate both Nuttal and Lemery, two discrepancies should be noted between the witnesses. The first concerns the order in which swords were drawn. Nuttal says that Gregory began shouting at Sinclair to 'deliver up his Sword' *after* Gregory and Savage had drawn their own swords to attack Sinclair. But Lemery says that Gregory began shouting at Sinclair *before* he had drawn his own weapon.

Why this difference? Who really drew first? Is it possible that it was in fact Sinclair, after all? Did Gregory shout and draw his sword in response to Sinclair? And did Savage do likewise? This must be a possibility. Nevertheless, even if this were so, it seems clear that Sinclair was defending himself against an assault, simultaneously, from Gregory and Savage. The evidence for the violent and threatening behaviour of the whole party is overwhelming, from the moment they entered Robinson's.

The second discrepancy is this. Why did Lemery claim to see Savage actually stab Sinclair, while Nuttal did not? Savage never disputed that it was his thrust that killed Sinclair. So if Nuttal was not already fighting Gregory, why didn't he see this stab delivered?

In such a flurry of action, it is in fact a commonplace that witnesses miss or misinterpret crucial events. Yet all the other evidence suggests that Nuttal did not begin fighting Gregory until Sinclair was already wounded. Gregory had broken his own sword in the preliminary attack on Sinclair, and he used Sinclair's sword when he turned to fight Nuttal. He could not have taken this sword until Sinclair was already stabbed by Savage. So why was Nuttal not in a position to observe it? Whatever the explanation, it does seem that both Gregory and Savage were *simultaneously* attacking Sinclair, and that Savage wounded him, before Nuttal intervened. The prosecution would later produce further evidence to sustain this crucial point of a combined assault on Sinclair alone.

Yet the discrepancies remain an issue, and one is surprised that Johnson did not raise them. Alexander Pope, in his notes taken from the public gallery, concluded that Nuttal was perjured on both counts. He does not think that Savage drew first: 'Upon throwing down the table four swords were drawn. It appeared their all four swords were drawn before any wound was given.' Nor does he think that Gregory and Savage were fighting Sinclair simultaneously. 'One Lembury [sic], who was of their company, swore that he saw Savage give the wound, and did not see Gregory at the same time, his back being toward Gregory and his face to Savage and Sinclair.'[20]

In fact, according to the trial transcript, Lemery did not say this about Gregory. He merely says he saw Savage give the wound. There is an obvious area of dispute here, and Johnson does not exploit it for the defence. He chose not to do so because it would have involved a detailed reconstruction of the fight which could only have damaged Savage since it showed him in such a deadly light among a party of drunken assailants.

Jane Leader, the prostitute and friend of Nuttal, gave the most succinct and hostile evidence against Savage.

Jane Leader: 'I was in the Room, and saw Savage draw first. Then Gregory went up to the Deceased, and Savage stabbed him; and turning back, he looked pale.' She was cross-questioned about the actual moment of the stabbing, and stuck to her story that Gregory 'passed, or struck his Sword, while Savage stabbed him'.[21]

This does not quite square with what Lemery said, also under cross-examination: 'When Savage gave the Wound, the Deceased had his Sword drawn, but held it with the Point down towards the Ground, on the Left side.'[22] But in both cases the implication is that Sinclair was not prepared for the thrust, and not turned in a posture of defence towards Savage. In eighteenth-century law this would not be regarded as a 'fair engagement' between two armed men but as a 'malicious' assault with intent to kill by the aggressor. It would tell very heavily against Savage and any plea of self-defence or 'inadvertent' wounding that he might make.

Johnson, as we have seen, dismissed this evidence without examining it in any detail, preferring to regard a 'Strumpet's' testimony as inherently unreliable. Pope, in his notes, saw by contrast that it was extremely important. But he concluded that Nuttal and Jane Leader had concocted this account together, and that they were both perjured, since they had given false testimony about their own relationship.

> It was sworn by Nuttal and his whore, that Mr Gregory passed Mr Sinclair's sword when Savage gave him the wound. But it appeared from the evidence of the defendant, that both these were perjured, for the whore swore she never had been but *once before in her life* at the said Robinson's Coffee-house, and that she never saw Nuttal *but once before*, which *he* also swore. But the woman of the coffee-house attested that she had lived with her *above nine months*. And another evidence swore that Sinclair, Nuttal, and Jane Leader all cohabited together for *three months* in one house in Southwark.[23]

The argument here is that a witness who gives false evidence on a minor or subsidiary issue cannot be trusted to tell the truth on a major one. It is effective in a courtroom cross-examination, and is a classic method of discrediting evidence. Yet in fact it may not be decisive, and Jane Leader may have had several reasons for trying to hide her intimacy with Nuttal; not least, that it might have opened her to a charge of living on immoral earnings.

So was Jane Leader telling the truth about Savage's attack on Sinclair? This is the question that Johnson crucially avoids.

One may ask if Jane Leader was corroborated in any way, except by Nuttal? Her statement was partly supported by Lemery; but here too it could be argued that the story was concocted between friends. The maid, Mary Rock, whose testimony is always careful and circumstantial, specifically denies that she saw the moment of Sinclair's wounding. But she does say that she saw Gregory and Savage facing Sinclair *alone* at the beginning of the fight; and that the fight between Gregory and Nuttal took place *after* the wounding. 'I did not see the Wound given to the Deceased, but I afterwards saw the Encounter between Mr Nuttal and Mr Gregory.'[24] This appears to support Jane Leader.

So one may summarise the prosecution case up to this point in rather sharper terms than Johnson. Five witnesses had testified, with a fair degree of consistency, that Savage had taken part in the drunken and aggressive entry into a privately hired coffee-room; that he had drawn his sword first; that he had joined in a combined and simultaneous assault against Sinclair, who stood at that moment alone; and that he had fatally stabbed Sinclair when he was not in a posture of defence.

But the prosecution case did not rest here. Johnson does not quote the evidence that Sinclair himself gave while he was dying, and after the fight had been broken up by the soldiers from the Watch Station. Two of these Watch soldiers reported his words, and they had no obvious motive for lying. Characteristically, their evidence is not quite the same. One Watchman, Rowland Holderness, reports Sinclair as saying, 'I was stabbed barbarously before my Sword was drawn.' The other Watchman, John Wilcox, remembered Sinclair's words as: 'I am a dead man, and was stabbed cowardly.'[25] Yet the evidence of both amounts to Sinclair saying it was not a fair fight.

The following morning, just before Sinclair died in hospital, he was attended by a clergyman, Mr Taylor, who heard his confession. Afterwards, Sinclair talked about the fight, and he repeated that it was not a fair encounter. 'The tallest [Gregory] commanded my Sword, and the other [Savage] stabbed me.'[26] Again, this is not decisive evidence; dying men may have many reasons for not telling the truth. However, it is clear that Sinclair was not disposed to think that his assailant had acted honourably, or was in any way moved to forgive him. This evidence – for what it is worth – also supports Jane Leader's account.

Finally, there is one other piece of testimony that Johnson astonishingly omits. It is of a different kind from all the previous statements, as it is based on simple forensic fact, which cannot be disputed. It concerns the nature of the wound that Sinclair received, and was given by the surgeon called to attend the dying man. This is perhaps the most damning evidence in the whole transcript, and it emerges in a piece of straightforward cross-examination, which Johnson cannot have failed to read.

Mr Wilkey, the surgeon: 'I searched the Wound, it was on the Left side of the Belly, as High as the Navel. The Sword had grazed on the kidney, and I believe that Wound was the Cause of his Death.'

Court: 'Do you think the Deceased could receive that Wound in a posture of Defence?'

Mr Wilkey: 'I believe he could not, except he was Left-handed.'[27]

The significance of this medical evidence is clear. Sinclair's wound was received on the left, or undefended, side of his body. Had he been facing Savage at the moment he was attacked, the sword must have entered through his right side. Either Sinclair was turned away to face Gregory, or his sword was 'passed' by Gregory's, or he was standing with lowered guard between the two men. Once again, Jane Leader's testimony is upheld.

As to the events immediately following the wounding, there seems little dispute. Savage stood still in the middle of the coffee-room, turned pale, and seemed stunned by what he had just done. He did not join in the fight between Gregory and Nuttal. Lemery, and the maid Mary Rock, both unarmed, were able to approach him and seize hold of him. Only when the candles were put out (probably by Merchant), did Savage begin to struggle, and then his one idea was to get away.

Lemery's account seems accurate enough, and was not challenged.

Mr Lemery: 'We struggled together. The Maid came to my Assistance, pulled off his Hat and Wig, and clung about him. He, in striving to force himself from her, struck her, cut her in the Head with his Sword, and at last got away. I went to a Night-cellar, and called two or three soldiers, who took him and Merchant in a back Court.'[28]

Mary Rock, despite her head-wound, meanwhile went over to nurse Sinclair where he lay. Instructed by the landlady, she opened

Sinclair's coat, bent down and sucked the wound, a treatment that was thought to encourage bleeding and thereby clean away any impurities and promote healing. Gregory and Nuttal continued to fight until parted and arrested by the soldiers.

Savage's actions may have been those of panic. But they do not seem compatible with the behaviour of an innocent man, who had just beaten off an unprovoked attack. He did not help Gregory, or attempt to stop further fighting, or go himself for the Night Watch. Instead he simply fled and tried to hide.

Johnson attempts to put this in the best possible light:

> Savage having wounded likewise a Maid that held him, forced his way with Merchant out of the House; but being intimidated and confused, without Resolution either to fly or stay, they were taken in a back Court by one of the Company and some Soldiers, whom he had called to his Assistance ... With regard to the Violence with which he endeavoured his Escape, he declared, that it was not his Design to fly from Justice, or decline a Trial, but to avoid the Expences and Severities of a Prison, and that he intended to have appeared at the Bar without Compulsion.[29]

The speciousness of Savage's explanation is passed over in silence.

The process of a trial, with its conflict of evidence and various possible interpretations of the truth, is to some extent a paradigm of the whole biographic enterprise. I have been severe with Johnson's approach thus far because he so clearly throws himself into the role of Savage's defence counsel, suppressing or slanting evidence without regard to obtaining an overall picture of what probably occurred at Robinson's on that fatal night. At the least, one can say that Savage was far more guilty of the crime than Johnson is prepared to allow. While claiming narrative impartiality, he consistently adopts an adversarial rather than a judicial stance; and this profoundly affects the nature of the literary genre he is developing.

As a biographer, however, Johnson laboured under a disadvantage which was characteristic of much of Savage's career. He did not have the full evidence of the story from Savage's own point of view. Astonishingly, neither the trial transcript, nor the 'Newgate' pamphlet, carried any record of Savage's own statement of defence in court. All that is known is that Savage elected to conduct the defence himself, and that his main speech to the jury lasted for over an hour.

Johnson desperately attempted to secure a copy of this statement, both from Edward Cave at the *Gentleman's Magazine* and from friends who knew Savage in his latter days at Bristol. But he never succeeded in tracking it down. All he could discover was that Savage brought his own witnesses to impugn the characters of each of the hostile witnesses (except the maid); that he insisted that he himself was not drunk; that he argued that Merchant's behaviour – not his own – initiated the affray; that he himself had drawn his sword purely in self-defence; and that the fatal wound occurred in the flurry of combat and without premeditation.

Rather than examine the court evidence in further detail, Johnson had recourse to the technique that he had learned in his parliamentary reporting for Cave. He reconstructed Savage's defence speech from these points, and also from the judge's summary of the case which was heavily weighed against the defendants.

Such reconstruction of course violates the discipline of modern biography, for it creates a 'text' where none exists as a matter of historical record. But Johnson could claim the classical precedent of Thucydides, in his great literary reconstruction of the speeches made during the Peloponnesian Wars; and it was still a method accepted in much contemporary eighteenth-century journalism. Although Johnson had claimed that he would use no fiction, and no romance, in Savage's biography, he felt that the trial was in its own way a special, semi-dramatic interlude in the course of his narrative, which could be conducted according to the special conventions of historical writing. He could best defend Savage by speaking for him, in his own dramatised persona, and by bending his own rules of biographic realism, at this most perilous point.

Johnson slides into Savage's voice gradually, and with great skill, so that the exact line between the reportorial or factual voice and the dramatic or projected one is effectively blurred. So as a biographer he slips almost undetected from the defending counsel's table to the prisoner's position at the bar:

Sinclair had declared several Times before his Death, that he received his Wound from Savage, nor did Savage at his Trial deny the Fact, but endeavoured partly to extenuate it by urging the Suddenness of the whole Action, and the Impossibility of any ill Design, or premeditated Malice, and partly to justify it by the Necessity of Self-Defence, and the Hazard of his own Life, if he had lost that Opportunity of giving the Thrust: He

observed, that neither Reason nor Law obliged a Man to wait
for the Blow which was threatened, and which, if he should suffer
it, he might never be able to return; that it was always allowable
to prevent an Assault, and to preserve Life by taking away that
of the Adversary, by whom he was endangered.[30]

The cool elegance of this plea sounds very much like Savage in
his most suave and high-principled mode. His way of transforming
the impulsive actions of a drunken, late-night brawl into the oper-
ation of 'Reason and Law' gives his explanation a remarkably auth-
entic ring. He smoothly reverses all the evidence raised against
him, and presents himself – not Sinclair – as the object of a murder-
ous assault. He stands confidently on the age-old right of a gentle-
man dispassionately using his sword to preserve his honour and
his life.

Johnson adds that Savage was heard by 'the Multitude that
thronged the Court with the most attentive and respectful Silence'.
Even those who thought that he ought not to be acquitted neverthe-
less 'owned that Applause could not be refused him; and those who
before pitied his Misfortunes, now reverenced his Abilities'. Had
his audience been his judges – rather than the jury – he would have
'undoubtedly' been found innocent.[31]

In all this Johnson is presenting the courtroom drama purely from
Savage's point of view and gaining sympathy for his predicament as
best he can. There is no real or independent record of what the
public thought, or of how the hour-long defence was received,
except that it irritated the judge to the point of fury. Pope, for
instance, makes no comment at all on Savage's speech. The 'New-
gate' pamphlet also gives no particulars, except to enter an openly
emotional plea on his behalf, which again emphasises Savage's
gentlemanly demeanour in the face of his beastly accusers.

Let the Reader now behold a Man of his unspotted Character,
and inoffensive Behaviour, until this fatal Action, involved all on
a sudden in all the wretched Circumstances and Sufferings of the
most inhuman Criminals and abandoned Profligates, and admire
at the decent Fortitude and Serenity of Mind, with which, accord-
ing to the report of all who saw him, he supported so shocking
and unexpected a Misfortune as well before as at the Time of his
trial . . .[32]

Johnson now turns his dramatic skills on the attitude of the judge; and here he found a valuable target. Judge Francis Page was a political appointee, and renowned for his severity and sarcasm. Pope lampooned him, and Henry Fielding later caricatured him in *Tom Jones* (1749) where he appears in Book Eight as a comic monster of cruelty and injustice, joking sarcastically that he will give a hangman's 'halter' to the trembling prisoner who has stolen a horse. On the West Country circuit, where London 'hanging judges' frequently indulged in their worst excesses, he was the subject of a popular song among the labourers of Dorchester: 'God in his rage made old Judge Page'. He was notorious for making caustic jokes at the expense of men he was about to condemn, and juries were said to be terrified of his wit, laughing sycophantically at his appalling puns like schoolchildren before a sadistic master.

Savage, with his gentlemanly airs, his 'distinguished Friends' in the gallery and his assumptions of superiority and nonchalance, provided Judge Page with a perfect butt for his gallows humour. Johnson makes great play with Page's reputation, saying that he treated Savage 'with his usual Insolence and Severity' and endeavoured to 'exasperate' them against him by mockery. This mockery amounted to misdirection of the jury because it undermined Savage's credibility.

Johnson again invents a 'text' for part of Page's summary, for there is no record in the transcript. Johnson says he gives a version 'as Mr Savage used to relate it'. The suggestion is that this became a favourite performance of Savage's in later years: how Judge Page condemned him to the gallows. So we are again being given Savage's voice, as reproduced by Johnson. But this time we have Savage *pretending* to be Judge Page for the benefit of admiring listeners. Biographically speaking, it is a double ventriloquism on Johnson's part. He mimics Savage mimicking Page; and he does it to tremendous effect, for this becomes the single most memorable speech in the whole trial.

Johnson wants to show Savage rising above his calamity. The mockery turns back against Judge Page's 'eloquent Harangue' and leaves Savage heroically at bay in the face of a hostile court and a cowed jury, hopelessly misrepresented but still coolly demanding justice. That at any rate is Johnson's intended effect. But for the modern reader Johnson's advocacy has a curious double edge. Despite all the stage directions we end up wondering if Judge Page did not have a point after all about Savage's behaviour:

Gentlemen of the Jury, you are to consider, that Mr Savage is a very great Man, a much greater Man than you or I, Gentlemen of the Jury; that he wears very fine Clothes, much finer Clothes than you or I, Gentlemen of the Jury; that he has an abundance of Money in his Pocket, much more money than you or I, Gentlemen of the Jury; but, Gentlemen of the Jury, it is not a very hard Case, Gentlemen of the Jury, that Mr Savage should therefore *kill* you or me, Gentlemen of the Jury.[33]

In fact this speech, shorn of its sly repetitions, goes to the heart of the question of social privilege. Savage evidently did not appear as a penniless, romantic outcast to the Old Bailey court. He appeared as a vain and extravagant man, well-dressed, well-heeled and well-connected, making claims to special rank and treatment. If there had been no truth in this impression, Page's sarcasms would have been harmless to damage the defendant.

Yet they enraged Savage, for according to Johnson he took the perilous step of interrupting the judge in mid-flow, to assert 'that his Cause was not candidly explained'. He began to 'recapitulate what he had before said with regard to his Condition' and why he had tried to escape from the coffee-house. Judge Page ordered him to be silent, but Savage persisted. The judge again commanded him to be quiet. But again Savage launched into further explanation. Finally, amid uproar, the judge 'commanded that he should be taken from the Bar by Force'.[34]

Johnson, in recording this climactic incident, states that it demonstrated Savage's 'resolution'. No one who knows the temper of an English jury can doubt that such an uncontrolled outburst, especially in a case that turned on the probability of a defendant's aggression, would have told against Savage far more than any judicial irony. For Savage to be dragged shouting from a courtroom simply reminded the jury that the defendant could be a violent man.

Judge Page's actual directions to the jury, on the points of law arising in the case, do not in fact appear unreasonable. He concentrated on the character evidence; the credibility of the various witnesses; the distinction between manslaughter and murder; and the question of shared responsibility for the killing. It is clear that he believed the inmates of the coffee-house were, broadly speaking, telling the truth, despite their dubious social backgrounds. He also believed that Savage's party had demonstrated persistent aggression from the moment they entered Robinson's, and that they had been offered no real provocation for their attack on Sinclair. Johnson summarised this direction:

> The Jury then heard the Opinion of the Judge, that good Characters were of no Weight against positive Evidence, though they might turn the Scale, where it was doubtful; and that though when two Men attack each other, the Death of either is only Manslaughter; but where one is the Aggressor, as in the Case before them, and in Pursuance of his first Attack, kills the other, the Law supposes the Action, however sudden, to be malicious.[35]

Pope's notes add two interesting clarifications. One concerns the privacy of the coffee-room. The other suggests that Page actually left a loophole for Savage, by pointing out that Merchant alone may have initiated the assault:

> The Court was of opinion that a coffee-room, although a public room *by day*, was not so in the *night* when a set of company was drinking in it . . . The Court also was of opinion that when an unlawful act is done and murder ensues, all the company are equally guilty; that these men had no right to go into the coffee-room, and that the original of this quarrel proceeded from Merchant's throwing down the table.

This final remark must have set the jury thinking that perhaps there were degrees of guilt, even if it was shared. Nevertheless, Pope adds that Judge Page directed them to find 'all three guilty of murder'.[36]

Such positive direction would never be countenanced in a modern courtroom; yet it was not unusual in an eighteenth-century one. Nor did the jury entirely follow it. After a brief retirement, Savage and Gregory were found guilty of 'wilful murder' but Merchant only of manslaughter. Merchant was branded in the hand with a hot iron, according to law, and released. Savage and Gregory were taken to the condemned cells at Newgate and loaded with 50-lb iron fetters round their legs. This was a notable severity which made all physical movement painful and exhausting, and prolonged sleep almost impossible.

Savage's prospects were now bleak. Conditions in the prison were bad, and time was short. He had four days in which to prepare a plea for mercy, which would be read in open court when the sentence of death was confirmed by the Bench of Judges. But this was a mere formality. Normally the execution would be carried out within a month: at the latest, allowing for the Christmas recess, by mid-January. Friends gathered round, though they were evidently shocked by the whole affair. Pope sent money, but did not visit; Edward Young prayed for him and sent a letter 'passionately kind'; Theophilus Cibber helped with correspondence; and Mrs Oldfield made a private approach to the Prime Minister.[37] But Savage's one real hope lay in the possibility of a royal pardon, which required some groundswell of popular feeling in his favour coupled with a discreet approach through Court circles.

It was Aaron Hill who skilfully set this rescue operation in motion. He immediately commissioned the 'Newgate' pamphlet to put Savage's case and misfortunes in the best possible light, employing a young Grub Street poet, Thomas Cooke, who had previously praised Savage's work in an amusing satire, *The Battle of the Poets* (1725). He also had the brilliant idea of concluding the pamphlet with an open letter, not to Lady Macclesfield but to Lord Tyrconnel who, Hill had heard, was critical of his aunt's behaviour.

This subtle change of tactic would prove decisive. The 'Letter to a Noble Lord in the behalf of Mr Savage and Mr Gregory', which Hill wrote himself, was addressed anonymously (so as not to embarrass Tyrconnel) and phrased with great care. In it Hill described Savage as an old friend, and tactfully held out the promise of reformed behaviour:

> I have discovered in him a Mind uncapable of Evil; I have beheld him sigh for the distressed, when more distressed himself; I have seen him give that Relief to others, which not long before he has in some degree wanted. He is so far from a litigious Man, that he was always more ready to stifle the Rememberance of an Injury than to resent it.[38]

That Grub Street held a more cynical view of Savage's merits, and his chances of a pardon, appears in a note that Thomas Cooke received, while slaving to complete the text of the pamphlet in the upstairs room of a tavern, on 3 December. Recalling that they were all drunk on their last meeting ('the wine drowned a great deal'), Cooke's correspondent cheerfully implied that the whole exercise was a waste of good drinking-time in a bad cause: 'Sir – I had the happiness to be under the same roof with you last Tuesday evening, but you had a *brother poet*, how unworthy soever of the appellation, to save from the gallows, and the Coroners Inquest took up all your time and thoughts above stairs, while your Friends below could have cursed the Inquest and cause of it, for depriving them of your company . . ."[39] Here the feeling seemed to be that Savage was about to receive his just deserts.

How far did Savage really deserve a conviction for 'wilful murder'? The evidence that has come down to us – through the incomplete transcript, the 'Newgate' pamphlet, Page's summary, Pope's notes and Johnson's extremely partial advocacy – is surely conflicting. The modern biographer is also forced to put Savage on trial, with the knowledge that much evidence has been lost, obscured or deliberately slanted.

The drunken and aggressive behaviour of Savage's party seems unavoidably established. So too does the fact that Savage and Gregory fought Sinclair simultaneously, and that Savage delivered the fatal sword-thrust when Sinclair was not facing him with his sword at readiness. Savage's violent efforts to escape the scene of the fight, wounding the maid and abandoning his friend at a moment of peril, also tell heavily against him.

Yet even on this hostile evidence a defence of manslaughter can still be made. The essence of such a defence must turn on the question of 'equally' shared guilt, in the progress of the whole affray. Even though Savage delivered the actual blow that killed Sinclair, was he as guilty of unprovoked aggression in the coffee-house as his friends? Did he initiate the quarrel as Merchant did, or pursue it as Gregory did? Could a case be made that he was drawn, against his will and intention, into acting impulsively in *their* defence?

Judge Page himself stated that for a murder charge to be sustained the accused must be proved to be, first, 'the one who is the Aggressor' in a quarrel; and, second, the one who kills 'in Pursuance of his first Attack'. Was this, beyond reasonable doubt, Savage's role and situation at Robinson's that night?

A modern advocate for Savage, following in Johnson's footsteps, might put the case as follows. First, let us try to fit the details into an overall picture of Savage's character and psychology; and his social position as a writer in 1727. Taking all the evidence and not just friendly evidence, let us see not merely what can be proved but what on balance is most *likely* to have occurred.

Everything about Savage's behaviour at the trial indicates that he felt himself to be the real protagonist of the case. He was the cleverest, the best known, the richest of the defendants. He claimed to be the son of the late Earl Rivers, and had to deport himself as such. On the day of the killing he was drinking with friends who were his social inferiors. He had gone along willingly on the night-adventure through the back streets, and claimed that he intended to take his two companions to his lodgings in Richmond the following day. As a gentleman, he felt responsible for their behaviour, however outrageous.

He was often outrageous himself, had a quick temper, was vain and waspish (as James Thomson had noticed) and could be violent – as the court saw. But as Johnson elsewhere insists, he was also capable of moments of great loyalty and generosity. He was probably deeply ashamed of having abandoned Gregory during the latter part of the fight. So he was determined not to abandon his friends again, during the trial.

From a legal point of view this put him at a great disadvantage. He threw in his whole case with theirs, and took on the burden of the defence himself, another characteristic example of both his courage and his vanity. The entire affair at Robinson's was not one more meaningless misfortune but a logical outcome of Savage's overriding notion of himself as 'son of the late Earl Rivers'.

His behaviour that night can, in fact, be sharply distinguished from that of Merchant and Gregory, even on the evidence of the hostile witnesses. There is, to start with, the outstanding fact that no one reported him saying, shouting or doing anything aggressive up to the moment that swords were drawn. Savage's silence throughout is one of the notable features of the case. He may have been more drunk than anyone else, but no witness accused him of this. His mere presence may have encouraged his friends to act in a high-handed way (and he himself may have thought this); but again there were no accusations levelled on this ground. The very identification of him as 'the least man, in Black', somehow suggests that his presence only emerged as decisive during the fight. Up till then Savage remained in the background.

Next, there is the fact that Savage was not the initiator of the affray. All the evidence shows that it was Merchant who precipitated events. Merchant offered violence to the landlady, threatening to strike her with the chair; Merchant led the rush into the coffee-room; Merchant kicked down the large table where Sinclair's party had been drinking in front of the fire. No one accused Savage of directly abetting these actions. Even Judge Page pointed out in his directions to the jury that Merchant alone carried out these 'unlawful' provocations, though he added that the guilt for them should be shared. But this question of shared guilt is precisely the point that must be disputed in Savage's defence, though Savage himself would not do so.

Then there is the vexed question of who drew the first sword. Savage claimed he only drew in self-defence; that is, after other swords had been drawn by Sinclair's party. The evidence against this claim is not, as it emerges, very strong. Mrs Enderby, the landlady, did not give it. The maid, Mary Rock, perhaps the most reliable prosecution witness, did not give it. Even Lemery, who later struggled with Savage to prevent his escape, did not give it. The only two witnesses who gave it were Jane Leader and Nuttal. How reliable is their testimony at this point?

A good deal of Jane Leader's evidence, as to the development of the fight, has been shown to be corroborated by several other witnesses. But on this point she was only corroborated by Nuttal, who was her lover (according to Pope's notes), and since she was also a prostitute, very probably her pimp. Her evidence is therefore not necessarily reliable, and she could reasonably be suspected of simply supporting Nuttal's version, under duress.

Moreover, in cross-examination she appeared to contradict her first forthright statement that she had seen *everything* at the beginning of the fight: 'I was in the Room, and saw Savage draw first.' On being pressed as to when Sinclair drew his sword in response, she answered: 'I did not see the Deceased's Sword at all.'[40] This is a crucial admission. For if Jane Leader never saw Sinclair's sword, how could she tell if it was not *already drawn* before Savage's? Indeed, how could she tell if Sinclair himself was not the first to draw a sword in the coffee-room?

On inspection, Nuttal's evidence contains exactly the same admission. 'Presently Savage drew his Sword, and we retreated to the farther End of the Room . . . I did not see the Deceased draw, but Gregory, turning to him, said "Villain, deliver your Sword." '[41] The same objection applies: how could Nuttal know that Sinclair had not drawn first, before Savage? Neither witness is wholly reliable on this crucial point. It is therefore quite possible that Savage was telling the truth when he said that he drew in defence against Sinclair. And in this case a rather different picture begins to emerge of the progress of the actual fight.

The defence explanation would run as follows. It was William Merchant who was out of control that evening, despite the best endeavours of Savage and Gregory. Pursued by them, Merchant burst into the coffee-room and drunkenly kicked down the table. Sinclair's party leapt away from it ('we retreated to the farther End of the Room'), and Sinclair – who was acknowledged to be a tough character, involved in a previous brawl[42] – angrily drew his sword in response. As Merchant was unarmed, and so suddenly in peril, Savage drew his own sword to protect his friend, as a gentleman should. He stood on guard, but made no gesture of attack.

Gregory then drew his sword and shouted to Sinclair to 'deliver' his weapon, in a vain attempt to bring the situation to order. Both Nuttal and Lemery gave versions of this shouting at Sinclair, and it evidently took place. But Sinclair stood his ground. This was the suspended scene that Mary Rock witnessed as she entered the room. Nuttal now also drew his sword. As Pope noted: 'all four swords were drawn before any wound was given.'

Gregory then advanced on Sinclair, with the aim of securing his sword, but a fight immediately broke out. Savage came up to protect Gregory against any possible attack from Nuttal. But still Savage did not engage. Once again, the defence would argue that Savage was drawn into events initiated by his friends, but his role was essentially protective. He never attacked Nuttal, as an aggressive man would have done. Nor is there any evidence, though he stood by supporting Gregory, that he made any attack on Sinclair until the moment of the fatal thrust.

We come now to the final stage of the action, as far as Savage is concerned. The hostile evidence, and the surgeon's testimony, show that when Savage did attack Sinclair the latter was turned away from him and 'not in a posture of Defence'. *But no one tried to establish why this was so.* Lemery said Sinclair's point was turned away defensively; Jane Leader said it was 'passed' by Gregory. But it is Nuttal himself, a hostile witness, who provides the most convincing explanation. Nuttal said that 'Gregory's sword was broke in the Scuffle' with Sinclair.[43] So Sinclair was turned *away* from Savage, at that moment, because he was turned *towards* Gregory – and had him at his mercy.

This breaking of Gregory's sword undoubtedly occurred *before* Sinclair was wounded, for on Nuttal's own admission Gregory subsequently attacked him using Sinclair's own sword after it dropped from his hand. So the defence would argue that Gregory was in imminent danger of death himself, facing Sinclair with only a broken sword. It was not until this critical moment that Savage intervened to save his friend. An instant action was required. With a single, powerful and impulsive thrust, the 'son of the late Earl Rivers' ran Sinclair through the belly. It was his only decisive action of the entire evening.

Immediately afterwards Savage was obviously in a state of shock. He went pale, and he stood irresolute. Far from joining in Gregory's attack on Nuttal, as an aggressive man would have done, he allowed himself to be seized by Lemery and the maid, neither of whom was armed. Only when the candles were put out, plunging them all into the dark, did he suddenly panic. His only thought was to get away from the coffee-house. He could not know, in the dark, if he was about to be attacked himself; or that Sinclair was mortally wounded. Striking out blindly, he tore himself from his invisible captors, and rushed into the street with Merchant. They did not run further, but hid near by in a back street, hoping Gregory would join them. When the soldiers came up, they offered no resistance.

Such would be the case for the defence; and such, a biographer might argue, is the most likely version of events that night.

Whatever else can be suggested, it does not seem a case of deliberate or premeditated murder. Savage was drawn in by his friends; he acted impulsively to defend Gregory; he represented himself badly in court. He had no friendly witnesses to rely on, and he was committed to maintaining his superior role as the responsible member of the party.

Four days later, on 11 December 1727, Savage submitted his plea for mercy. He reflects ruefully on the nature of the crime, and now states his desire to be alone in the dock. Johnson gives the whole text of this speech, which is also recorded in the 'Newgate' pamphlet and is evidently authentic. Savage speaks of the fight as 'a casual absence of Reason, and sudden impulse of Passion'. He begs for 'an Extension of that Mercy, which the Gentlemen of the Jury have been pleased to shew Mr Merchant, who (allowing Facts as sworn against us by the Evidence) has led us into this our calamity'. He concludes with a revealing gesture of splendid isolation. 'For my Part, I declare nothing could more soften my Grief, than to be without any Companion in so great a Misfortune.'[44]

The panel of judges confirmed his sentence of death. To which Johnson added dramatically: 'Mr Savage had now no Hopes of Life, but from the Mercy of the Crown, which was very earnestly solicited by his Friends, and which, with whatever Difficulty the Story may obtain Belief, was obstructed only by his Mother.[45]

Johnson's story of how Lady Macclesfield allegedly intervened to prevent the process of a royal pardon is his final and indeed sensational manoeuvre for the defence. He says himself that this is difficult to believe, and can give no source for its authenticity. There is no hint of it in the 'Newgate' pamphlet, or in the letters that Aaron Hill subsequently wrote to her nephew, Lord Tyrconnel, about his own part in the appeal. It is not mentioned by Pope, although he was sympathetic enough to send Savage £10 to defray his prison expenses. Nor is it mentioned by Theophilus Cibber, to whom Savage wrote from the condemned cells. All that is known from these sources is that Savage did write to Lady Macclesfield at this time, and apparently received no reply.

The letter itself has not survived, but a covering note to Cibber has. In it Savage reveals something of his feelings. He also shows that, like much of his previous writing about his mother, the letter was intended to be circulated among his friends and supporters. Even at this eleventh hour Savage was continuing his relentless campaign to win sympathy and recognition.

Dear Theo, – My love to good Mr Wilks, in answer to his kind message by Mr Ray, and desire him to get delivered the enclosed to my Mamma ... which I wrote, as you will find, in an inexpressible conflict of passions ... I hope you are mended in your health, as for death I am easy, and dare meet it like a man
All that touches me is the concern of my friends, and a reconcilement with my Mother. – I cannot express the agony I felt when I wrote the letter to her ... If you can find any decent excuse for shewing it to Mrs Oldfield, do ... for I would have all my friends (and that admirable lady in particular) be satisfied I have done my duty towards her.[46]

This note does seem to show genuine and conflicting emotions, and it is one of our rare glimpses into Savage's innermost world. Horror at his own position combines with the gentlemanly pose of calm detachment: 'as for death I am easy, and dare meet it like a man.' Intensely personal feelings about Lady Macclesfield – 'I cannot express the agony I felt when I wrote the letter to her' – are inextricably mixed with the need publicly to justify his behaviour towards her with all his friends. The one element lacking in this turmoil is an expression of remorse for the killing itself.

For Johnson, who evidently did not see this letter, it is Lady Macclesfield's implacable vengeance against Savage which now is the decisive fact. It is the final proof that Savage was a victim of circumstances. The 'story' of her intervention with Queen Caroline, to block the appeal which was being mounted by Aaron Hill and his friends, can only of course have come from Savage's subsequent accounts. Johnson accepts it without demur, and brilliantly turns it to Savage's advantage.

'To prejudice the Queen against him, she made use of an Incident, which was omitted in the order of Time, that it might be mentioned together with the Purpose which it was made to serve.' This was the incident of Savage's breaking into Lady Macclesfield's house at night, as we have already seen, and reducing her to terrified screams for help. When Queen Caroline heard of it, Johnson explains, 'she could not think that Man a proper Object of the King's Mercy, who had been capable of entering his Mother's House in the Night, with an Intent to murder her'. As a result, the Queen 'for a long Time refused to hear any of those who petitioned for his Life'.[47] So Johnson is able to make his biting summary: 'Thus had Savage perished by the Evidence of a Bawd, a Strumpet, and his Mother . . .'[48] It is his last appeal for the defence.

How far did Johnson really believe this sensational claim of Savage's? It fitted with his increasingly melodramatic portrait of Lady Macclesfield, as seen through Savage's eyes; and that the story was in circulation in Court circles must seem very probable, since Savage's hounding of Lady Macclesfield was already a public scandal. But that Lady Macclesfield herself should have urged his execution on these grounds still seems extraordinary. Yet perhaps it partly explains the known fact, which Aaron Hill records, that her nephew Lord Tyrconnel at this very moment responded to the pamphlet appeal, began to interest himself on Savage's behalf, and would shortly become his official patron.

None the less Johnson must have had doubts, and indeed a close reading of his biography subtly reveals them. In an aside, he asks what motives she could have had to persecute him 'in a Manner so outragious and implacable'. He claims there are none, but falls back on his notion of some terrible, meaningless malignity: '. . . only this can be said to make it probable, that it may be observed from her Conduct, that the most execrable Crimes are sometimes committed without apparent Temptation.[49] In this admission, Johnson again seems to expose something of his own terrors and fantasies of evil.

In considering Johnson's refusal to engage more openly with the whole question of feminine motive and psychology, perhaps we should also invoke the Judgement of Solomon. If Lady Macclesfield *knew* Savage to be someone else's child and an impostor, then she had every reason to block the pardon. She had been harassed, persecuted and blackmailed by Savage for some nine years. *Pace* Johnson, she had every 'apparent Temptation' to urge the execution, and rid herself of a pursuing demon. But if, on the other hand, she knew that Savage was really her offspring, then how would such an impulsive and generous woman be expected to respond? Surely she would have pleaded 'on her knees' before the King, just as she had done years before for her cruel and detested first husband, Lord Brandon? Considered in this light, the story of her intervention to secure the execution – if true – reverses the biblical parable with exemplary force. One could argue that it demonstrated that Savage was not her child, precisely because at the moment of crisis Lady Macclesfield abandoned him. Perhaps some reflections such as these made Johnson particularly uneasy at this point.

In another aside, he hesitates significantly over the question – central to Savage's accusation – of whether Lady Macclesfield actually intervened in her own person with the Queen: 'By whom this atrocious Calumny had been transmitted to the Queen, whether she that invented it, had the Front to relate it; whether she found any one weak enough to credit it, or corrupt enough to concur with her in her hateful Design, I know not . . .'[50]

Here the biographer appears to waive responsibility; he simply cannot know the objective truth. It is Savage's version, and he passionately wants to believe it, that is all. Yet in making these admissions Johnson acutely draws the reader into his own dilemma, divided between the duties of the historian and the friend. As a result, I think, we too want to believe him; and this is the most subtle defence of all.

Savage's fate hung in the balance for nearly five weeks. Though physically much weakened, it is remarkable that mentally he showed no signs of breaking under the stress of deprivation, filth and imminent death. There were no confessions, conversions, or cries for mercy. Johnson was tremendously impressed by this stoicism, as well he might be, and later argued that 'resolution' and 'compassion' in suffering were Savage's strongest traits.

A letter written to Theophilus Cibber, one 'Saturday Night' in late December, displays Savage's peculiar grace under pressure in a marked light. Subject to the 'insipid visits' of the Newgate padré (who incidentally, by a curiosity of prison regulations, had the publishing rights to any written confession he could extract from his charges), Savage showed himself fully equal to the occasion: 'I have this afternoon had a visit from the poor illiterate Ordinary, Mr Guthrey, and received him with a decent respect for my own sake; but had no way of getting rid of him, except one; which was by talking on points of religion, and learning, a little above his capacity . . .'

Nor was Savage beyond a little heroic irony on his own behalf. Knowing full well that the 'Newgate' pamphlet had made his life-story the talk of London, he dismissed all such interest with a pained but nonchalant sigh. 'The weight of my fetters has so weakened me (being obliged to lie in them) that I can scarce drag myself across a room. – I could not help smiling this afternoon – a kind of Bookseller visited me, in order to solicit me for an Account of myself, to be printed at my decease. – What indecencies will not wretches commit thro' hopes of money?'[51]

The royal pardon for Savage and Gregory finally arrived on 6 January 1728, and they were released on bail a fortnight later. No record exists of the last, delicate manoeuvres at Court; but by 28 February Savage was formally freed by the King as a 'pauper Convict in Newgate'. Following Savage, Johnson says that the decisive intervention came through the Countess of Hertford – well-known patroness of poets – with Queen Caroline. But from Aaron Hill, who had organised the whole appeal, we know that the key figure was really Lord Tyrconnel. For obvious reasons, Savage preferred to boast of the distinguished and literary Lady Hertford.[52]

Another story which Savage told Johnson was that the prostitute, Jane Leader, subsequently retracted her evidence against him.[53] Some time afterwards, Savage said he met her in the street, destitute, and freely forgave her, dividing 'the only Guinea that he had' with her. Johnson accepts this story, and says it could be regarded as the action of a 'Saint or a Hero'. We might well be sceptical, but Johnson emphasises 'compassion' as Savage's distinguishing quality, and evidently believes it. However, he adds that Savage never forgave Judge Page, and lampooned him bitterly.

Johnson wonders, with some anxiety, how Savage himself looked back at his part in the affray, after he was free from the danger of execution and 'under no Necessity of using any Art to set his Conduct in the fairest Light'.[54] It is interesting that he goes directly to the poetry for this evidence, saying that Savage was not otherwise 'willing to dwell upon it' in conversation. Quoting from a section of *The Bastard*, he decides that Savage's reactions were mixed, but essentially philosophical: he regretted the killing of young Sinclair but did not feel guilty of murder and put the whole thing down to unhappy 'chance'.[55]

In fact the passage also suggests that Savage was always haunted by the affair: 'Still the pale *Dead* revives and lives to me, / To me, through Pity's Eye, condemn'd to see.'[56] Moreover when Savage returned to his interrupted work on *The Wanderer*, he inserted several nightmare visions in which images of guilt and horror, clearly drawn from his experience in the Newgate cells, erupt with peculiar violence. One of these suggests not merely suppressed guilt, but a terrible cycle of compulsive recall, especially at night.

> Now *Sleep* to *Fancy* parts with half his Pow'r,
> And broken Slumbers drag the restless Hour.
> The Murder'd seems alive, and ghastly glares,
> And in dire Dreams the conscious Murd'rer scares,
> Shews the yet-spouting Wound, th' ensanguin'd Floor,
> The Walls yet-smoking with the spatter'd Gore . . .[57]

Savage never admitted in his waking hours that he felt himself to be a 'conscious Murderer'; but in dreams begin responsibilities. Certainly *The Wanderer* became a far more self-dramatising and disturbing poem after the events of winter 1727.

Johnson ends his account of the whole affair at Robinson's by suggesting that all the mitigating circumstances largely absolve his friend: 'perhaps the Memory of Savage may not be much sullied by his Trial.' One concludes that Johnson could not accept the idea of Savage as genuinely guilty of murder.[58] It is essential to him to believe that Savage was a victim of circumstances: Merchant's impetuosity, Judge Page's severity, Lady Macclesfield's malice. By contrast, Savage shows great resolution during his trial and imprisonment, and exceptional compassion afterwards.

What finally emerges is not merely Johnson's adversarial skill in defending his friend but his enormous loyalty and moral generosity. At one level we may not be convinced by Johnson's pleas and explanations; but at another we are deeply moved by his stubborn refusal to abandon faith in Savage. Even if we think it is blind faith, we are left with a crucial question: what *kind* of man could inspire this sort of loyalty in his biographer; especially in a biographer like young Johnson, with his supreme commitment to moral truth?

CHAPTER 7

FAME

It is perhaps the greatest irony of Richard Savage's career that the conviction for murder, followed by the royal pardon, brought him exactly the fame and fortune he had so long and so deviously sought. Thousands of copies of the 'Newgate' pamphlet had been circulated in London, and 'were in a few Weeks dispersed over the Nation'.[1] Booksellers were anxious for his work, and Society hostesses for his company. Smart gossip in the salon and coffee-house speculated on the truth of his identity, and on the behaviour of Lady Macclesfield.

His confessional poem, unblushingly titled *The Bastard*, was issued in April 1728, and ran to five editions. It made specific mention of Lady Macclesfield, his trial for murder and his pardon by Queen Caroline. It was Savage's first, and as it turned out his only popular success. The mask of the 'poor poet' was thrown aside for a triumphant celebration of his own energy and genius:

> Blest be the *Bastard*'s birth! through wondr'ous ways,
> He shines eccentric like a Comet's blaze.
> No sickly fruit of faint compliance he;
> He! stampt in nature's mint of extasy!
> He lives to build, not boast, a gen'rous race:
> No tenth transmitter of a foolish face.[2]

It is this swaggering passage which now enshrines him, two centuries later, in *The Oxford Dictionary of Quotations*.

The Bastard also contained his most open and sardonic attack on Lady Macclesfield which the general public had then seen:

> O Mother, yet *no* Mother – 'tis to you,
> My thanks for such distinguish'd claims are due.
> You, unenslav'd to nature's narrow laws,
> Warm championess for *freedom*'s sacred cause,
> From all the dry devoirs of blood and line,
> From ties maternal, moral and divine,
> Discharg'd my grasping soul; push'd me from shore,
> And launch'd me into life without an oar.[3]

It might seem extraordinary that Savage, fresh from the condemned cells at Newgate, should become instantly so fashionable and so confident. But London Society was in a mood for rakish figures, and bored and disillusioned with the respectable Whiggish establishment that had solidified round Sir Robert Walpole and the new king. Nothing demonstrates this more clearly than the overwhelming success of John Gay's *Beggar's Opera*, which took Drury Lane by storm in this same spring of 1728, running for an unprecedented sixty-two nights to packed houses.

This 'Newgate pastoral', centred on the highwayman MacHeath and his simultaneous love-affairs with Lucy Lockit (the jailer's daughter) and Polly (daughter of his friend and fence in the underworld, the rascally Peachum), caught the imagination of the city. Using popular folk-songs and street ballads, it championed a sentimental world of outcasts and criminals, the despised and rejected of society who now seemed authentic and glamorous, in a reversal of values closely parallel to Savage's own fortune in escaping Tyburn.

Henry Fielding (1707–54), as both Justice and novelist, was an acute observer of these shifts in literary fashion, and noted how the booksellers quickly seized on the new market in notorieties. Writing later in *The Covent Garden Journal*, he wryly remarked on the speed with which publishers and journalists took up the Newgate vogue:

Of this probably they received the first hint from the case of one Mr Richard Savage; an author whose *manufactures* had long lain uncalled for in the Warehouse, till he happened very fortunately for his Bookseller to be found guilty of a capital crime at the Old Bailey. The merchant instantly took the hint, and the very next day advertised the 'Works of Mr Savage, now under sentence of death for Murder'. This device succeeded and immediately (to use their phrase) carried off the whole Impression.[4]

Fielding added that thenceforth the gallows was found to be a great friend of the press, and booksellers made it their chief care 'to provide themselves with such writers as were most likely to call in this assistance; in other words, were in the fairest way of being hanged'.

But it was not just Newgate that carried cachet; it was also the whole world of Grub Street, with its hack-writers, its penniless poets and unproclaimed geniuses. For the other notable publication of the spring was Pope's first version of *The Dunciad*. With brilliant, scatological satire, Pope mocked and celebrated this underworld of writers in the Kingdom of Dullness, centred on the East End of London:

> ... where Fleetditch with disemboguing streams
> Rolls the large tribute of dead dogs to Thames.[5]

Savage was known to be one of Pope's chief sources for the literary libels and scandals which gemmed the darkness of this epic of Grub Street. A denizen of Grub Street himself, he also was a chorus and commentator on its follies. He was in the know, and could give the liveliest account of both the poem's inception and triumphant publication. Indeed he soon after published and edited a pamphlet in its praise, vividly describing the riotous success of its first appearance:

> On the Day the Book was first vended, a Crowd of Authors besieged the Shop; Entreaties, Advices, Threats of Law, and Battery, nay Cries of Treason were all employed to hinder the coming out of the *Dunciad*: On the other Side, the Booksellers and Hawkers made as great Efforts to procure it.[6]

Johnson records this sudden, unexpected meridian of Savage's popularity with grave detachment. He observes it with sombre irony, but with none of Fielding's cynicism: 'This was the Golden Part of Mr Savage's Life; and for some Time he had no Reason to complain of Fortune; his Appearance was splendid, his Expences large, and his Acquaintance extensive ... To admire Mr Savage was a Proof of Discernment, and to be acquainted with him was a Title to poetical Reputation. His Presence was sufficient to make any Place of Publick Entertainment popular; and his Approbation and Example constituted the Fashion.'[7]

The dizzy up-swing in Savage's fortunes was not merely the result of the murder case. It was also the consequence of his renewed campaign against Lady Macclesfield, which finally quadrupled the money he had extorted from her to a fixed pension of £200 per annum. For a bachelor living in London, this by itself was an income that provided ease bordering on opulence (an equivalent today might be £25,000, tax free). But with the money, Savage also obtained an apartment in Arlington Street, near St James's, and various luxuries including those most notable appendages to the poetical life – free supplies of wine and books, of which he took the fullest advantage. All these benefits – the money, the rooms, the poetical supplements – came from Lord Tyrconnel.

How exactly Savage obtained this support, and how soon after his release from Newgate it began, remains something of a mystery. Johnson begins to be vague about dates at this juncture. He suggests there was a period of some months in 1728 and 1729 when Savage was wildly indulged by his friends and fashionable supporters, fluctuating between 'Beggary and Extravagance'. At length he determined to 'extort from his Mother' a settled income, using what Johnson calls evenly, 'rougher Methods'.[8] His account of this renewed campaign of menaces is succinct, and apparently approving.

Savage 'threatened to harass her with Lampoons, and to publish a copious Narrative of her Conduct, unless she consented to purchase an Exemption from Infamy, by allowing him a Pension. This Expedient proved successful. Whether Shame still survived, though Virtue was extinct, or whether her Relations had more Delicacy than herself ... Lord Tyrconnel, whatever were his Motives, upon [Savage's] promise to lay aside his Design of exposing the Cruelty of his Mother, received him into his Family, treated him as his Equal, and engaged to allow him a Pension of two hundred Pounds a Year.'[9]

Savage's campaign had been much 'rougher' than Johnson allows, and was not merely confined to threats. Here the question of dates becomes crucial. Johnson implies that the publication of *The Bastard* was held over until at least 1735, *after* Tyrconnel had withdrawn the Pension, not before it was conferred.[10] Yet all five editions appeared in 1728, the first in April of that year. Savage had also republished the *Miscellaneous Poems* in June 1728, reinstating the satyric Preface attacking Lady Macclesfield. Tyrconnel's motives were obviously an attempt to stem this tide of libel and mockery against his aunt.

How Johnson misplaced the publication of Savage's most famous poem by seven years is an interesting question. Was his research (as in much else) simply faulty? Or was he deliberately misled by Savage, who later boasted at length about its effect on Lady Macclesfield? Or was he trying to cover up the most outrageous of his friend's blackmailing attempts? It is possible that Johnson did not read the poem until it was reprinted in the *Gentleman's Magazine* in 1737, the year he arrived in London and became aware of Savage's existence. But even in this reprint, his editor Cave noted that *The Bastard* had first been published 'some years ago', and over the lapse of time had since 'become scarce'.[11] This alone should have alerted Johnson to a much earlier date than 1735.

Moreover Johnson gave a very full description of Savage's delight at the acute public shame and discomfort he at last succeeded in causing Lady Macclesfield. By placing this in 1735, at the end of Savage's brief 'Golden' period, the suggestion is one of a last, and partially justified, act of revenge, from a man again reduced to poverty by callous aristocrats. It is passed off as a kind of poetic justice, and this is made to sustain Johnson's ironic and indulgent view of Savage's temporary fame. But biographically, this gives a quite false impression of the real sequence of events, and of Savage's relentless pursuit of justice of a much more practical and financial kind. It also obscures the extraordinary generosity and patience of young Tyrconnel towards the wayward poet.

If we move Johnson's account of Savage's revenge back to its proper place, in the summer of 1728, then the full effect of *The Bastard*'s appearance is instantly revealed. 'One Circumstance attended the Publication,' wrote Johnson, 'which Savage used to relate with great Satisfaction. His Mother, to whom the Poem was *with due Reverence* inscribed, happened then to be at Bath, where she could not conveniently retire from Censure, or conceal herself from Observation; and no sooner did the Reputation of the Poem begin to spread, than she heard it repeated in all Places of Concourse, nor could she enter the Assembly Rooms, or Cross the Walks, without being saluted with some Lines from *The Bastard*.'[12]

It is clear that Johnson identifies and rejoices here, with Savage, in Lady Macclesfield's public humiliation. He notes that she fled immediately from Bath – then the most fashionable of all summer resorts – to 'shelter herself' in the comparative anonymity of London. It was an occasion when 'the Power of Wit' was triumphantly and conspicuously vindicated against money and privilege. 'Thus Savage had the Satisfaction of finding, that though he could not reform his Mother he could punish her, and that he did not always suffer alone.'[13]

There is something unbearably bleak in that last phrase of Johnson's justification of Savage. It suggests a degree of self-identification with Savage that has blinded him to the small, stubborn fact of the poem's actual date. In 1735 it could be a lonely act of poetic revenge; but in 1728 it was a calculated, repeated demand for money and position. Far from suffering alone, Savage at that moment was capable of mobilising all the forces of fashionable society. He was even building on an anonymous broadside, *Nature in Perfection*, which also attacked her, and had appeared three weeks before *The Bastard*.[14] But Johnson could not face this revelation of his friend's opportunism and malice. So once again, consciously or not, he obscured the record.

Indeed, in discussing *The Bastard* Johnson returns to his most powerful plea, that we consider Savage as an outcast and orphan who was never given the chance of moral maturity. At the moment of Savage's greatest and most vindictive triumph (at the age of thirty) Johnson asks us to reflect that he is still really a helpless, defenceless victim.

He may be considered as a Child *exposed* to all the Temptations of Indigence, at an Age when Resolution was not yet strengthened by Conviction, nor Virtue confirmed by Habit; a Circumstance which in his *Bastard* he laments in a very affecting Manner –

– No Mother's Care
Shielded my Infant Innocence with Prayer;
No Father's guardian Hand my Youth maintain'd,
Called forth my Virtues, and from Vice restrain'd.[15]

One may even feel here that Savage had succeeded in the emotional blackmail of his own biographer.

There are no letters that reveal the exact negotiations between Savage and Lord Tyrconnel. But these must have been completed by January 1729, when Savage fulsomely dedicated *The Wanderer* to him:

> I am persuaded . . . that to forgive Injuries, and confer Benefits, is your Delight; and that to deserve your Friendship is to deserve the Countenance of the best of Men: To be admitted into the Honour of your Lordship's Conversation (permit me to speak but Justice) is to be elegantly introduced into the most instructive, as well as entertaining, Parts of Literature; it is to be furnish'd with the finest Observations upon human Nature, and to receive from the most unassuming, sweet, and winning Candour, the worthiest and most polite Maxims – Such as are always enforc'd by the Actions of your own Life.[16]

Such grandiloquence in dedications was the currency of the day. Yet there is not a phrase here that cannot be read as ironic hyperbole, at Tyrconnel's expense.

Savage was fully aware of the nature of the contract he was making with his new patron: pension and lodgings in return for silence on the subject of Lady Macclesfield, adherence to Tyrconnel's Whig associations in Parliament, and no more scandalous dining-out on street-tales of the Bastard's tragic lot. In short, Savage was to become a respectable member of society, and forget his Grub Street past.

One of the unforeseen consequences of this deal was that, with the exception of a peculiar arrangement that became his 'Volunteer Laureateship' to Queen Caroline (an acceptable and loyal eccentricity), Savage fell almost silent as a poet for the next five years of his life, until his dramatic return to scandalous publication in 1735. The paradox was that fame and fortune actually gagged him and cut off the publicity he craved. Eventually he had to decide which was more necessary to him, and whether the elegant friendships at my lord's table at Arlington Street could substitute for those of the old iniquities of Grub Street.

Although there are no letters, there survives one poem which shows Savage meditating on the choice to be made in 1728. Entitled

'Fulvia', it reconstructs a fashionable dinner-party with a Society hostess in 1728, when *The Bastard* was all the rage and Savage the darling of the literary salons. The poem has the additional interest that Savage withheld it until 1737, when he published it in the *Gentleman's Magazine* – so Johnson cannot have missed it, though he never refers to it.

The scene is sketched in by Savage with rapid strokes. Fulvia is one of the London smart set, 'her darling passions, scandal and Quadrille', known for her delicious dinners and her wicked tongue. She is piqued with Lady Macclesfield, and therefore quite capriciously decides to take up Savage. She lionises him, flirts with him and shows him off to her rich, aristocratic friends:

> The banquet serv'd, with peeresses I sit:
> She tells my story, and repeats my wit.[17]

With her drawling voice and pouting 'distorted' mouth, Fulvia urges him to continue his attacks upon Lady Macclesfield, hoping for more piquant scandals and more suggestive revelations:

> 'How fine your BASTARD! why so soft a strain?
> 'What *such* a *Mother?* satirize again!'

Reluctantly (according to Savage) he is persuaded, 'the verse now flows', and manuscript copies of a new poem begin to circulate among the over-excited Society beauties of Fulvia's circle. His fame is a kind of sexual excitement for them: 'The fame, each curious fair enflames.' The poems spread scandal like a house fire, until finally Lady Macclesfield and her daughter by Colonel Brett are forced to negotiate with him (significantly, there is no mention of Lord Tyrconnel):

> The wildfire runs; from copy, copy grows:
> The Bretts alarm'd, a sep'rate Peace propose.

Then comes the twist. The moment that Fulvia hears of peace being 'ratified' between Savage and his mother, her attitude changes. Instead of congratulating her poet, she spurns him:

> 'Tis ratified – How alter'd Fulvia's look?
> My wit's degraded, and my cause forsook.

Her excitement at the whole story rapidly cools – 'This tale is old'. Savage is treated as a tiresome bore – 'what's poetry but to amuse?' His only hope of recapturing Fulvia's favours is to break the peace with Lady Macclesfield and publish new attacks – 'All love the satire, none the satirist.' Savage realises his dilemma – either the safe pension or the smart friends. This moment of ironic enlightenment is cleverly caught:

> I start, I stare, stand fix'd, then pause awhile;
> Then hesitate, then ponder well, then smile.
> 'Madam – a pension lost – and where's amends?'
> 'Sir (she replies) indeed you'll lose your friends.'

The speed of the social reversal is effectively dramatised, and soon turned against Fulvia herself:

> Let Fulvia's friendship whirl with ev'ry whim!
> A reed, a weathercock, a shade, a dream.

Savage departs with a mocking bow, 'despising and discerning' all. So the poem abruptly ends, a mocking allegory of his fame told in just twenty-six couplets.

The lightness and venom of the style is very like *The Bastard* itself, and so far from the solemn, decorous musings of *The Wanderer* that it is difficult to believe they come from the same pen. Together they seem like the revelation of a second personality: one creates Fulvia, the other creates the Hermit. This sudden shift in voices, or masks, will eventually emerge as a crucial aspect of Savage's talents.

But there is something stranger still. In the lethal swiftness of the social encounter there is the subliminal imagery of a duel. The Bastard fighting the Lady is now an armed conflict, even if their weapons appear to be only words tipped with wit. In the exchange of thrust and counter-thrust, the one instant of pause – that moment of Savage's enlightenment – 'I start, I stare, stand fix'd, then pause awhile' – one cannot help recalling Jane Leader's account of Savage at the moment of killing Sinclair.

Johnson never refers to 'Fulvia' directly, or the hard, calculating side of Savage's personality that it reveals. But he does seem to have understood the way in which Savage's fame led him to declare war on everything that Lady Macclesfield stood for. From now on, he writes, 'she was to be considered as an Enemy implacably malicious, whom nothing but his Blood could satisfy'.[18] From this point of view Savage's arrangement with Lord Tyrconnel in 1729 was no more than an armed truce. It is perhaps surprising that it lasted so long.

None the less, Tyrconnel was astonishingly generous and long-suffering. Everything suggests that he had genuine affection for the wayward poet and that initially that affection was returned. Johnson, who is our main source about Savage's patron, concentrates on the quarrels that arose between them; but this merely reflects Savage's retrospective view in 1737. By that date, in a typical gesture, Savage would heavily ink out the dedication to Tyrconnel in any copy of *The Wanderer* which happened to come into his hands.[19]

However, it was less easy to delete the praise that was incorporated in the poem itself, in which Tyrconnel is described as 'a generous Soul, approaching to Divine', and his house in Arlington Street as a sacred retreat for the Muse:

> When bless'd beneath such Patronage I write,
> Great my Attempt, though hazardous my Flight.[20]

It is possible to piece together something of the actual relations between poet and patron. John Brownlow, Viscount Tyrconnel, was the son of Lady Macclesfield's sister, Lady Brownlow, and must have known his aunt well during the twelve-year period she stayed at Beaufort House, immediately before her affair with Earl Rivers. Whatever he thought of her behaviour he clearly differed from her view of how to handle Savage and his claims. Tyrconnel was a sociable, easy-going man, confident of his position: a Member of Parliament, a Knight of the Bath, an estate owner in Ireland. He was married, kept a large town house in Arlington Street, dabbled in the Arts, gave private concerts and poetry-readings. (One such reading, in November 1731, was of Aaron Hill's appalling epic *Athelwold*, which possibly reflects a certain naïvety in milord's critical faculties.[21]) He kept a large library and a good wine cellar, and liked literary chat. After 1730, when his beloved wife Eleanor suddenly died, he may also have been a lonely man. Like so many of Savage's supporters, he conforms to a certain type: kindly, literary, long-suffering, and easily imposed upon.

As we have seen, he enters Savage's story in December 1727, in response to Aaron Hill's desperate appeal to save Savage's life. Using his Whig connections, and access to the new king and queen, he was able to put forward a case for mercy. In 1728 he intercedes again, this time to protect his aged aunt from further scandalous publications, by providing the lavish pension. But he does more than this: he urges Savage to concentrate on the imaginative, confessional poetry of *The Wanderer*, and to complete a serious work that is intended to rival Thomson's *Seasons*.

We know this from Savage's own remarks in the dedication (however vehemently he later tried to suppress them). Savage wrote in 1729: 'Part of this Poem had the Honour of your Lordship's Perusal when in Manuscript, and it was no small Pride to me, when it met with Approbation from so distinguishing a Judge: Should the rest find the like Indulgence, I shall have no Occasion (whatever its Success may be in the World) to repent the Labour it has cost me.'[22]

It is significant that Tyrconnel took Savage's poetry seriously, and may throw some light on his forgiving, but somewhat ambiguous attitude to Savage's claim to be Lady Macclesfield's son. Did Tyrconnel recognise his claim, or regard it as a poetical eccentricity, an unfortunate obsession? We simply do not know. What is certain, and perhaps far more surprising, is that on the strength of *The Wanderer*, Tyrconnel recommended Savage in 1730 for the official post of Poet Laureate. He wrote to Mrs Clayton, the Queen's Mistress of the Robes, urging his merits and adding that Pope himself supported the application. The post had fallen vacant in September 1730, on the death of Laurence Euden; and was eventually filled – to universal hilarity, as so often on these occasions – by Colley Gibber in December of that year.[23]

Savage was so incensed by this failure that he did something unique in the annals of official patronage. In March 1731 he published a 60-line ode 'Most humbly Addressed to her Majesty on Her Birthday', announcing that he had appointed himself Queen Caroline's 'Volunteer Laureate', and would thenceforth celebrate her virtues annually. Cibber's reaction was to remark that Savage might 'with equal propriety style himself a Volunteer Lord, or Volunteer Baronet'.[24]

Savage continued to publish these 'Volunteer Laureates' for seven years. Curiously, Lord Tyrconnel was not discountenanced by the astonishing cheek of these proceedings, but himself presented the second Laureate Ode to the Queen in March 1732. Most remarkably of all, Queen Caroline responded with an annual £50 grant, which appears in the royal account books from 1732 and continued until her death in 1737.[25] This brought Savage's regular income up to the modern equivalent of some £30,000 per annum.

The content of the odes, typified by 'Volunteer Laureate No. 1', is much what we would expect of Savage in his campaign style of piteous grievance alternating with extravagant praise:

> *Two* Fathers join'd to rob my Claim of *One*!
> My *Mother* too thought fit to have *no Son* . . .
> The pitying MUSES saw me Wit pursue,
> A BASTARD-Son, alas! on that Side too . . .
> Great Princess! 'Tis decreed – once ev'ry Year
> I march uncall'd, Your LAUREATE VOLUNTEER;
> Thus shall Your Poet his low Genius raise,
> And charm the World with Truths too vast for Praise.[26]

Savage never afterwards acknowledged Tyrconnel's help in this laureate campaign, either at the official or the 'voluntary' stage. Indeed he later emphasised to Thomas Birch that 'the author had not at that time a friend either to get him introduced, or his poem presented at Court'.[27] Johnson believed him, and also omitted Tyrconnel from his account. He did not rate either the odes themselves, or the Queen's patronage, very highly. Of the £50 grant, he observed drily: 'though by no Means unkind, [it] was yet not in the highest Degree generous: To chain down the Genius of a Writer to an annual Panegyric, shewed in the Queen too much Desire of hearing her own Praises . . .'[28] In the circumstances this seems an odd reflection, as Savage's 'chains' were entirely self-imposed. But then Johnson hated the very idea of patrons and panegyrics.

One may guess that Savage and Tyrconnel grew closer on Lady Tyrconnel's death in September 1730. During her prolonged illness, with convalescent periods at Bath, Savage dedicated verses to her recovery, jauntily entitled 'The Triumph of Health and Mirth'. These evidently pleased Tyrconnel at the time; although when Savage republished them after their quarrel in 1737 he deleted her name from the title, as if she had never existed.

It was probably at this point, in the winter of 1730, that Savage took up residence at Arlington Street, and received a handsome gift of books, each bound for him and adorned with Tyrconnel's crest. We know about these books for the simple reason that Tyrconnel later complained that he spent so much time and money retrieving them.

Johnson supplies the anecdote with grim satisfaction: 'Having given him a Collection of valuable Books, stamped with his own Arms, [Lord Tyrconnel] had the Mortification to see them in a short Time exposed to Sale upon the Stalls, it being usual with Mr Savage, when he wanted a small Sum, to take his Books to the Pawn-broker.'[29]

Tyrconnel's faith in Savage was not easily shaken. He was delighted with 'An Epistle to Sir Robert Walpole', which Savage published in 1732, praising the Whig contribution to commercial enterprise and religious values. The fact that this was entirely the opposite of Savage's own beliefs did not apparently alarm Tyrconnel. By contrast, Johnson was for once genuinely shocked by this duplicity, considering that Savage 'was very far from approving the Conduct of Sir Robert Walpole, and in Conversation mentioned him sometimes with Acrimony, and generally with Contempt...'[30]

Johnson later asked Savage 'what could induce him to employ his Poetry in Praise of that Man who was, in his Opinion, an Enemy to Liberty, and an Oppressor of his Country?' Savage replied that he was dependent on Lord Tyrconnel and had been 'enjoined' by him to write in praise of the Whig leader, 'not without Menaces'. This seems highly unlikely, given Tyrconnel's easy and kindly disposition. Moreover, Savage earned £20 for the poem and went on trying to get a government pension from Walpole until 1737. Johnson concluded that during the period of his fame Savage would always sacrifice 'the Pleasure of Affluence to that of Integrity'.[31] But he did not believe that Savage's real political principles, 'zealous' for the Opposition and 'jealous of the Rights of the People', were really undermined. No doubt they had re-emerged by the time of their long night-conversations.

A letter of Aaron Hill's to Lord Tyrconnel in March 1731 also underlines the kindness of Savage's patron. He speaks of Lord Tyrconnel's exceptional generosity and 'all the charge you have been at, in comforting the life, you have saved him'. He also implies that some tacit admission of Savage's claims may have been made by Tyrconnel, since he refers to 'this unhappy kinsman' and how Tyrconnel has 'avowed his blood, and asserted his good qualities'. Hill dared not be more explicit on this point, and there is some suggestion that even at this date Savage is proving an awkward guest: 'Whatever *good* he does; whatever *love* he merits, must be yours; and nothing left him, which the world will call his own, except he should have follies, which, I hope, he has not...'[32]

At all events, it seems that Savage continued at Arlington Street until 1735, and Tyrconnel continued to grant him not only the pension but a great deal of latitude in his bohemian way of life. Indeed there is something almost pathetic in Tyrconnel's resolute indulgence of his troublesome poet's behaviour. When he spent 'all his Nights in Taverns', says Johnson, Tyrconnel would mildly exhort him to 'regulate his Method of Life' and tell him how much he missed his company in the evenings, appearing 'very desirous, that he would pass those Hours with him, which he so freely bestowed upon others'.[33]

For us to understand Lord Tyrconnel's sympathy and forbearance during these years, various factors have to be considered. It is clear that he thought Lady Macclesfield had behaved unwisely, if not unjustly, towards Savage. His response to the trial of 1727 also suggests that he was caught up in the pathos of Savage's case. The fashionable image of the Newgate poet, of the literary outcast and orphan, must have touched him deeply. As he got to know Savage personally, like so many others, he was evidently charmed and even infatuated.

Above all he was impressed by Savage's gift as a poet, and like many other literary patrons of the period – Pope's Lord Burlington or Thomson's Lady Hertford – sought to cultivate and encourage him. The dedication of *The Wanderer* was taken seriously, and Savage's fame as a poet – however temporary – was a matter of pride. For Tyrconnel to promote him as candidate for the laureateship (a candidacy which did not, incidentally, appear ludicrous to Johnson ten years later) vividly demonstrates this. Even James Thomson had considered this a possibility in 1726, when *The Wanderer* was still in manuscript.

So what was it about the poem which so impressed Savage's contemporaries? Today it is entirely forgotten, not least because it appeared so close in time to the two master-poems of the epoch: the florid pastoral of Thomson's *Seasons* (1730) and the stinging scatological satire of Pope's *Dunciad* (1729). *The Wanderer* is written in a different key, formal and yet weirdly fragmented, with a chilling undercurrent of nightmare confessional that makes it unique to the period.

Johnson, who seems to have been puzzled and haunted by the poem for most of his life, used to recite passages of it by heart fifty years later, to Mrs Thrale. To him it conjured up the image of one of those gothic follies which were shortly to become so fashionable in the gardens of the rich aristocracy. This is curiously apposite, since Savage himself might be said to occupy a similar ornamental position in the lives of Lady Macclesfield and Lord Tyrconnel, and by extension the world of Augustan literary fashion. Johnson wrote: 'the whole Performance is not so much a regular Fabric as a Heap of shining Materials thrown together by Accident, which strikes rather with the solemn Magnificence of a stupendous Ruin, than the elegant Grandeur of a finished Pile.'[34]

Savage considered *The Wanderer* to be his masterpiece. He had been 'labouring' on the poem for many years, and it had gone through several metamorphoses. As early as 1721 he mentioned to Aaron Hill that he was working on an extended piece to be called 'The Enthusiast'. Its primary imagery was to be that of the Garden of Eden, and it seems to have involved some kind of Fall. Hill suggested that its title might be 'The Inspired', and this seems to imply that Savage already had in mind some version of his Poet-Hermit figure.[35]

By 1726 at Richmond, the poem had become 'The Misfortunes of Life', as Savage told Mallet. The Garden of Eden had been abandoned for a winter landscape, initially much influenced by Thomson. At this time parts of Cantos I and II had been drafted, which include the famous 'Tooth-Ache' and 'Suicide' passages. By 1729 the poem had expanded to five cantos and just under two thousand lines. Savage told Johnson that having impetuously sold it for ten guineas, he gave back two guineas to have it reset when he discovered a few small errors overlooked by a careless proof-reader in the last two sheets. His profits for his most important work were thus derisory. For once it was the poem alone that mattered.

Johnson himself, early hardened to the vicissitudes of journalistic publication and creeping misprints, noted this Quixotic desire for perfect typesetting with shrewd amusement. To him it revealed an obsession wholly characteristic of Savage's lack of realism in daily affairs.

A superstitious Regard to the Correction of his Sheets was one of Mr Savage's Peculiarities; he often altered, revised, recurred to his first Reading or Punctuation, and again adopted the Alteration; he was dubious and irresolute without End, as on a Question of the last Importance, and at last was seldom satisfied; the Intrusion or Omission of a Comma was sufficient to discompose him, and he would lament an Error of a single Letter as a heavy Calamity.[36]

For all the minute care lavished on *The Wanderer*, its general structure remains vague. 'The Design is obscure, and the Plan perplexed,' observed Johnson. Savage thought the opposite, and that 'his Drift could only be missed by Negligence or Stupidity'.[37] It seems to have been composed as a series of separate episodes around the central figure of a Hermit-Poet, living in rural retreat outside a great city, which is evidently London. The Hermit is obviously some idealised projection of Savage's vision of himself, working at Richmond and away from the snares and worldly struggles of Grub Street. It is also Savage's first extended treatment of the 'pastoral retirement' theme, a wish-fulfilment which would eventually take him as far as Wales.

Each episode moves into realms of allegory, dream or persecution fantasy, whose private meanings are increasingly difficult to interpret. Savage subtitled the poem 'A Vision', and this suggests the strong confessional and introverted current that gradually dominates its development. Indeed the lack of control, the absence of a logical Augustan design and the intrusion of unconscious autobiographical elements, is what finally gives *The Wanderer* its peculiar fascination.

Canto I presents a bitter winter landscape, in which the Hermit has established a surprisingly comfortable cave, equipped with well-stocked parlour and handsome library. The favoured books are those of Savage's friends: Thomson, Mallet, Hill, Young and Pope.

Canto II further explores the cave, in which the Hermit has furnished an elaborate allegorical grotto – complete with statues, pictures, waterfalls and reflecting mirrors – all remarkably similar to the grotto which Pope was steadily excavating under the riverside gardens of his own house at Twickenham. The grotto is dedicated to Love and Friendship, and in particular to the Hermit's dead wife – a voluptuous Muse-figure – who is called Olympia. The grotto also seems to be an image of the Hermit's own mind, which is haunted by another and repulsive woman, the figure of Suicide. It is significant that Johnson was particularly struck by the fifty lines describing her – a 'terrific Portrait' – knew them by heart and quoted them in the *Life* in full.[38]

In Canto III, night falls, with vivid evocations of moon and frosty stars, nocturnal animals, funeral bells and ghosts, and dreamlike skating on a frozen lake. The Hermit begins a long night-walk which takes him into the shrouded, sinister city, where he speaks of his sufferings and loneliness, the cruelty of wealth, the terrors of poverty, the evils of sexual entanglements. Visions of murder, and resurrected ghosts, obsess him. Finally, at dawn and the ringing of the Matin Bell, he is granted a vision of Olympia who leads him safely back to his cave.

Canto IV appears to form an interlude, in which the Sun revolves through the signs of the Zodiac, and visits various natural marvels over the surface of the globe. Polar icecaps crash into the sea; birds migrate; rainbows form and melt; wild animals hunt and couple; and primitive tribes worship ancient gods. This section may perhaps be a fragment of the original Garden of Eden poem. The kaleidoscope of disconnected images succeed each other, as Johnson noted, strange and beautiful in themselves but alarmingly 'without Order'.

The shifting of what Savage calls the 'strange, visionary Land' is almost terrifying in its mobility, tilting and slipping from precise botanical observations – 'Snakes, that lurk to snap the headless fly' – to dreamlike evocations of ruins and colonnades paced by huge, misty allegorical figures like Ignorance, Superstition, Sleep, and Scorn. A feeling of drunkenness, hallucination, even madness, seems to permeate the whole canto; and despite Nature's fertility and richness it is the images of destruction, hunting, killing, terror and loss which seem to predominate. Even the landscape can be pitiless:

> A waste, pale-glimm'ring, like a Moon, that wanes,
> A wild Expanse of frozen Sea contains.
> It cracks! vast, floating Mountains beat the Shore!
> Far off he hears those icy Ruins roar,
> And from the hideous Crash distracted flies,
> Like One, who feels his dying Infant's Cries.[39]

The 'he' who hears and observes in this passage, and climatologically causes this bleak destruction is, formally speaking, the Sun. But in the narrative of the canto it is also Savage himself, who witnesses some geological catastrophe in his own spiritual nature. Again and again this uncontrolled transformation from outer to inner world occurs. The canto ends with the return of the 'Hermit-Friend', who warns of the danger of such visions which the mind cannot 'endure'.[40]

Canto V is the longest and most circuitous in structure, again based on a walk with the Hermit, and a series of philosophical discussions about the powers of Good and Evil in Nature and society. There is a symbolic encounter with a beggar at a field-gate, 'whose russet Rags hang flutt'ring in the Wind', which leads to an extended debate on Poverty and Genius.[41] The Beggar is then revealed as a Seraph, wandering the land in search of the spirit of friendship and charity among mankind, like the disguised angel in the Old Testament. He is of course one more projection of an idealised Savage:

> Though now a Seraph, oft he deigns to wear
> The Face of human Friendship, oft of Care;
> To walk disguis'd an Object of Relief,
> A learn'd, good Man, long exercis'd in Grief;
> Forlorn, a friendless Orphan oft to roam,
> Craving some kind, some hospitable Home;
> Or, like Ulysses, a low Lazar stand,
> Beseeching Pity's Eye, and Bounty's Hand;
> Or, like Ulysses, Royal Aid request,
> Wand'ring from Court to Court, a King distrest.[42]

One is tempted to believe that this passage reveals one of Savage's deepest fantasies – one often associated with orphaned adolescence – that he was really 'a Ulysses', a secretly disguised king on his wanderings, searching for his royal home.

The mood of this final canto changes abruptly with the fall of night, and the experiences of three political rebels in a prison death-cell. There is no attempt to fit these scenes of imprisonment and violent death into the previous, consoling pattern of the Hermit's talk; and the effect is like the uncontrolled eruption of a nightmare. They are evidently based on Savage's own experiences in Newgate.

They end with equal abruptness, and the bleak but companionable night-pacing resumes, without comment. It is as if everything in Savage's life eventually came back, with a kind of fatality, to this grim nocturnal patrol, and the whole poem is encircled and contained in this movement, going relentlessly on and on. For once the steady, mechanical beat of the heroic couplet perfectly expresses the purgatorial, ceaseless pacing through the dark and gives it a bitter beauty of its own:

> Distinction now gives way; yet on we talk,
> Full Darkness deep'ning o'er the formless Walk.
> *Night* treads not with light Step the dewy Gale,
> Nor bright-distends her Star-embroider'd Veil;

Her leaden Feet inclement Damps distill,
Clouds shut her Face, black Winds her Vesture fill;
An Earth-born Meteor lights the sable Skies,
Eastward it shoots, and, sunk, forgotten dies.
So Pride, that rose from Dust to guilty Pow'r,
Glares out in vain, so Dust shall Pride devour.[43]

Savage insists on one final, visionary transformation which brings the poem back within the norm of Augustan decorum. In a sudden blaze of celestial light the Hermit, the Seraph Beggar and the Bard are revealed as one, happily reunited with his Olympia. The Hermit's last words are a promise of eternal friendship and poetic inspiration:

Of that no more! my deathless Friendship see!
I come an Angel to the *Muse* and *Thee*.[44]

The two friends, Hermit and narrator, part in tears: 'Farewell – Nay stop the parting Tear! – I go! / But leave the *Muse* thy Comforter below.'[45] The Hermit ascends into heaven like a baroque angel.

From every point of view, *The Wanderer* is an extraordinary work. Ornate but chaotic in form, it uses the solemn diction of Augustan ceremony to describe those intensely introverted states of elation, despair and wish-fulfilment which we have come to associate with Romanticism. Its fragmentation and abrupt shifts of mood and place are enough to startle even a reader schooled in Post-Modernism. The impact it must have had on readers like Tyrconnel and Johnson can only be imagined. Johnson recognised in it 'a Genius truly poetical', and knew that at best Savage's work contained something unique and unprecedented: 'an original Air, which has no Resemblance of any foregoing Work; that the Versification and Sentiments have a Cast peculiar to themselves, which no Man can imitate with Success, because what was Nature in Savage would in another be Affectation.'[46]

All the main figures – the narrator, the Hermit, the Seraph-Beggar and the Bard – are clearly autobiographical projections, whose identities slide into each other in moments of apocalyptic self-revelation. Yet Lady Macclesfield, the obsessive mother-figure, is notably absent, weirdly subsumed into the figure of Olympia, part erotic fantasy and part classical Muse. The one moment that she appears, in the night-walk of Canto III – 'Ye *cruel Mothers*! – Soft! those

Words command! / So near, shall *Cruelty*, and *Mother* stand?' – the
Hermit immediately stops the conversation: 'Then with a Sigh his
issuing Words oppos'd! / Straight with a falling Tear the Speech
he clos'd.'[47]

All of Savage's concerns with greatness and friendship, with
poverty and persecution, with political power and unrecognised
genius are relentlessly rehearsed and debated. Sometimes Savage
finds highly original images for these, as in the passage that Johnson
recalled for his *Dictionary*, where Savage compares the effects of
Fame and Money with oxygen introduced into an experimental
bell-jar which contains an animal dying in an airless vacuum:

> Now rising Fortune elevates his Mind,
> He shines unclouded, and adorns Mankind.
> So in some Engine, that denies a Vent,
> If unrespiring is some Creature pent,
> It sickens, droops, and pants, and gasps for Breath,
> Sad o'er the Sight swim shad'wy Mists of Death;
> If then kind Air pours pow'rful in again,
> New Heats, new Pulses quicken ev'ry Vein,
> From the clear'd, lifted, life-rekindled Eye,
> Dispers'd, the dark and dampy Vapours fly.[48]

Many other poets, especially James Thomson, were fascinated
by the new science of the day – optics, physics, astronomy – but
none of them used it quite like this.

Savage also demonstrated a special sensitivity to the colour,
movement and pain of hunted animals – birds, fish, snakes, rabbits,
wolves, bears. Here also one can surely trace an element of self-
identification, as if his life in the London streets were an endless
series of battles and escapes from the human predator. (One recalls
Thomson's image of him as a vengeful hornet, guarding his space
in the coffee-house with stinging wit.) Some of these Nature pass-
ages are like miniature epics of war and persecution, such as the
rabbit-hunt in Canto IV:

> The Tenants of the Warren, vainly chased,
> Now lur'd to ambient Fields for green Repast,
> Seek their small, vaulted Labyrinths in vain;
> Entangling Nets betray the skipping Train;
> Red Massacres through their Republic fly,
> And Heaps on Heaps by ruthless Spaniels dye.[49]

Others are single, horrifying images of capture and wounding, which almost burst the decorous bounds of Augustan diction, with what Thomson called their 'writh'd' lines, and knotting syllables. Thus the night-fishing in Canto V:

> Fishers, who yonder Brink by Torches gain,
> With teethful Tridents strike the scaly Train.
> Like Snakes in Eagles' claws, in vain they strive,
> When heav'd aloft, and quiv'ring yet-alive.[50]

There are moments when Savage's whole universe seems to be convulsed in pain like this, as if agony were the condition or proof of existence, 'quiv'ring yet-alive'. Even the lives of flowers and fruit mutely bear their burden of sacrificial carnage: 'For human Taste the rich-stain'd Fruitage bleeds'.[51]

From the stab of 'Tooth-Ache' to the desolation of the polar Sun, Savage's *Wanderer* witnesses not merely the Virgilian 'lacrimae rerum', the tears in ordinary things, but an active cruelty pulsing through the material of being. In its darkest moments – and so much of the poem takes place in the dark – Mother Nature seems to be persecuting an orphaned Earth. This is the central vision of *The Wanderer*.

Johnson, so deeply wounded in his own personal life, responded overwhelmingly to this conception of the world as witnessed by his friend. His answers, long struggled for, were to be founded on human compassion and religious faith. From now on, the word 'compassion' itself becomes an increasingly important emblem in his biography, as a final court of appeal. As he views the paradox of Savage's fame, he begins to remind the reader that if Savage's 'Miseries were sometimes the Consequence of his Faults, he ought not yet to be wholly excluded from Compassion, because his Faults were very often the Effects of his Misfortunes'.[52]

Johnson also believed that *The Wanderer* showed the possibility of spiritual triumph over suffering and cruelty. He claimed that it was fundamentally a 'moral Poem', whose 'Design' – however obscure – was comprised in these words of the Hermit:

> ... the Sons of Men may owe
> The Fruits of Bliss to bursting Clouds of Woe;
> That even Calamity by Thought refin'd
> Inspirits and adorns the thinking Mind.[53]

The great, positive value celebrated throughout the poem is that of companionship in suffering, the intimacy of talk, the consolation of friendship. Though the Hermit is a solitary, dedicated to retirement, his wisdom and experiences are released in conversation and confession during the long walks and visionary wanderings which the poem recounts. In this we can see an early model for the peregrinations of *Rasselas, Prince of Abyssinia* and for the circuitous explorations of the *Rambler* essays. As the Hermit asks at the end of Canto V,

> Did not the Soul abroad for Objects roam,
> Whence cou'd she learn to call Ideas home?[54]

The Hermit is Savage's best self, drawn out through dialogue into an idealisation of friendship and trust which the poet himself was notoriously incapable of sustaining in real life. Again and again throughout the poem the words 'Friend' and 'Friendship' recur at points of crisis and disenchantment. The very books in the Hermit's cavernous library are described as such: 'These Friends (said he) though I desert Mankind, / Good Angels never wou'd permit behind.'[55]

When the Hermit views the ultimate fears of the Bard's loneliness and isolation, he appeals to Friendship both immediate and in the future (as if Savage were already envisioning his compassionate biographer):

> But, O my Friend! mysterious is our Fate!
> How mean his Fortune, though his Mind elate!
> *Æneas-like* he passes through the Croud,
> Unsought, unseen beneath Misfortune's Cloud;
> Or seen with slight Regard: Unprais'd his Name:
> His after-Honour, and our after-Shame . . .
> Yet, *suff'ring Worth*! thy Fortitude will shine!
> Thy Foes are *Virtue*'s, and her Friends are thine![56]

Even at that most dangerous, confessional moment, when Savage turns obsessionally to the subject of his own mother – and the whole philosophic structure of the poem trembles, as if it may collapse into another bitter, railing version of *The Bastard* – it is the impulse of Friendship which saves Savage and his poem. This is expressed in the Hermit's sympathetic tears and resolute turning to other subjects, 'to general Views'. The dramatic simplicity of the exchange drawn as it were from life, from a conversation in the dark city street, inevitably conjures and prefigures the image of Johnson and Savage together:

> Yes, there *are* Mothers – There I fear'd his Aim,
> And, conscious, trembled at the coming Name;
> Then with a Sigh his issuing Words oppos'd!
> Straight with a falling Tear the Speech he clos'd.
> That Tenderness, which Ties of Blood deny,
> Nature repaid me from a Stranger's Eye.
> Pale grew my Cheeks! – But now to gen'ral Views
> Our Converse turns, which thus my Friend renews.[57]

By contrast, the ultimate false friend is Suicide, the 'Fiend in evil Moments ever nigh' when the 'lone Hour, a Blank of Life, displays'.[58] Here too we know that Savage's experience resounded in the depths of Johnson's mind.

The Wanderer reveals Savage, both as a man and as a poet, in a new light. His self-contradictions are greater and more extreme; but his sensibility is also more original, more tender, more tortured, than one might have supposed. Our whole assessment of him begins a subtle alteration, exactly as Johnson had intended by placing the poem at the centre of his career and at the moment of his most ludicrous vainglory. However reprehensible Savage appears, we now have to remember he is still 'the Author of *The Wanderer*'.

For a patron like Lord Tyrconnel the poem must have seemed like a profound appeal for patience and sympathy. He was convinced that he was dealing with a man of genius, whatever the reality of his birthright, and that he alone was in a position to offer Savage comfort and security. The house at Arlington Street could become the equivalent of the Hermit's cave, even down to the well-stocked library. He could soothe the man, nourish the poet and befriend the outcast spirit. Like Richard Steele and Aaron Hill before him, Tyrconnel buckled down to the thankless task of mentor.

What first puzzled him, then irritated him, and finally maddened him, was that Savage revelled in his fame and new-found wealth but produced no more poetry. Apart from the occasional verses to Lady Tyrconnel, and to Walpole, there was virtually nothing. Savage did use his time, however, to mock his erstwhile acquaintances in Grub Street in an anonymous pamphlet of singular venom and ungenerosity, *An Author to be Let*, which began to circulate in 1730.

This was a kind of miniature, prose version of Pope's *Dunciad*, satirising and libelling the private lives of most of the struggling writers he had known in his days of poverty. It was signed with bitter mockery 'Iscariot Hackney', as if he consciously revelled in the role of betrayal.

The pamphlet opens with a graphic London street scene, describing a compromising manuscript dropped in a muddy lane behind Charing Cross, and a leering satire on his old friend Eliza Haywood – 'the divine Eliza! ... and her Apron-String' – hinting at her freedom with sexual favours. Iscariot Hackney's style throughout the piece is sharp-eyed, knowing and sarcastic about the journalistic world. The pamphlet attacks numerous other friends, including his old adviser John Dennis, and even his recent defender, Thomas Cooke. Johnson noted that it contained 'many secret Histories of the petty Writers of that Time, but sometimes mixed with ungenerous Reflections on their Birth, their Circumstances, or those of their Relations.'[59] Much of it was the kind of material that Savage was now freely passing on to Pope for his *Variorum* edition of *The Dunciad*, to appear in the mini-biographies and scandals of the footnotes. Theophilus Cibber later recalled that 'Savage was of great use to Mr Pope, in helping him to little stories, and idle tales, of many persons whose names, lives, and writings, had been long since forgot, had not Pope mentioned them in his Dunciad.'[60]

Johnson was not much perturbed by this, for he admired Savage's 'exact Observations on human Life', though he admitted that Savage was 'making use of the Confidence which he gained by a seeming Kindness, to discover Failings and expose them'.[61] But soon it would open Savage to a series of widespread attacks and retaliations, from friends who felt he had abandoned them in his new prosperity. Savage was not abashed, and republished the pamphlet in a signed collection dedicated to Pope in 1731.

Johnson saw something deeper. In the new mask or persona of Iscariot Hackney, 'a prostitute Scribler', Savage now appeared to be satirising – almost exorcising or punishing – his own, opportunistic self in the desperate days before his glory. He jeers most bitterly at himself, grubbing for a living. 'Some passages,' observed Johnson quietly, 'are such as Iscariot Hackney might himself have produced.'[62] Between the high-flown, tender sensibility of *The Wanderer* and the railing, cynical adventurer of *The Bastard* was a third personality, a pathetic hack. At some level, the invention of Iscariot Hackney was an attempt to accuse himself of this, to mock his own clever performances. There is an element of self-laceration, which Johnson immediately recognised.

Ironically it produced some of the best writing in the pamphlet. Once again it was confessional. What else is one to make of the following self-caricature, which so deftly includes not only his sponging tavern-life but stories about the Robinson's affair and even his pretensions as Tyrconnel's visionary house-poet? It is surely a deliberate act of self-exposure, in the hard, unforgiving vernacular of Grub Street:

> The Time has been when, after an Evening's hard boozing, my Brother Bards (who have been what we call Seedy or Cropsick) have bilked the Publick House, and barbarously left me in pawn for the Reckoning. On this Emergency, I have written an 'Account of a Sharp and Bloody Fight', a 'Vision in the Air', of a 'Wonderful Prophesy' to be hawked about the Street. And (would you believe it?) even these Productions of mine have passed for design'd Wit . . .[63]

Johnson took a philosophic view of Savage's fame, knowing that it would soon end because Savage's unstable personality could never sustain it. He saw it above all as a time when Savage educated himself in the nature of greatness and power in eighteenth-century society. 'The Distinction which was for some Time paid him by Lord Tyrconnel, intitled him to Familiarity with Persons of Higher Rank . . . and to examine, whether their Merit was magnified or diminished by the Medium through which it was contemplated.'[64] Mixing with lords and politicians, he could see 'whether the Splendour with which they dazzled their Admirers, was inherent in themselves . . .'

Savage's conclusion, deeply satisfactory to the subversive streak in Johnson, was profoundly negative. Power was a mirage. His 'discoveries' indeed were so penetrating that they were not 'entirely safe to relate', since the 'Persons whose Characters he criticised' were still in a position to exercise their 'Resentment'. Johnson did however risk giving Savage's verdict on the Prime Minister, Walpole: 'the whole Range of his Mind was from Obscenity to Politics, and from Politics to Obscenity.'[65] This was good Opposition talk, and Johnson loved it in those days. For the rest, Savage 'did not appear to have formed very elevated Ideas' about statesmen or party leaders.[66]

Johnson knew that Savage's formal education (at the St Albans school) had been slight, but he was fascinated by Savage's natural 'Inquisitiveness' and human penetration: 'He took all Opportunities of conversing familiarly with those who were most conspicuous at that Time, for their Power, or their Influence; he watched their looser Moments, and examined their domestic Behaviour, with that Acuteness which Nature had given him . . .'[67]

He concluded that such concentration, the ability to find significance in small, mundane details, was a mark of genius and one clue to Savage's capacity to engage with those around him and find out so unerringly their strengths and weaknesses. 'His Discernment was quick, and therefore he soon found in every Person, and in every Affair, something that deserved Attention.'

Savage registered human life with greater intensity than most people, and this too was a product of a desire to break in, to gain access, to a society that had denied him recognition. He would indeed be 'a volunteer Lord' if he could. But with that discernment also came disenchantment; the disenchantment of the outsider who finds 'merit' to be inherited, not earned. So Savage scorned what he also coveted. His fame made him restless, uneasy, destructive. He mocked those above him, and those below. A weak man in a powerful position, observed Johnson balefully, could not 'admit an Acquaintance more dangerous than that of Savage'.[68]

Indeed it soon became clear that Savage had lost all respect for Lord Tyrconnel, and from 1734 the stories of his outrageous behaviour at Arlington Street begin to accumulate. The incident of the pawned library books was just one among many. There was 'Coldness, Peevishness, or Neglect' on both sides, developing into open quarrels and insults. Savage complained that the £200 pension was not enough, and could not support his taste in 'the most expensive Wines'. He brought back rowdy friends from the taverns and took over Tyrconnel's house after midnight as if it were his own.

Johnson gives a Hogarthian account of these proceedings, in which it is difficult not to detect a certain relish. Savage would 'assume the Government of the House, and order the Butler in an imperious Manner to set the best Wine in the Cellar before his Company, who often drank till they forgot the Respect due to the House in which they were entertained, indulged themselves in the utmost Extravagance of Merriment, practised the most licentious Frolics, and committed all the Outrages of Drunkenness.'[69] There is a hint here that Savage's 'Company' also included whores.

At some point, perhaps in 1735, Tyrconnel appears to have for-
bidden Savage to continue living at Arlington Street, though he did
not immediately terminate the pension. Insults, threats and unpaid
bills now became frequent. Savage particularly revelled in one inci-
dent where he claimed that, like Dryden, he was threatened with
an aristocratic beating-up. Johnson is happy to tell this story, which
confirmed his low view of patrons in general. Lord Tyrconnel was
'so much provoked by the Wit and Virulence of Savage, that he
came with a Number of Attendants, that did no Honour to his
Courage, to beat him at a Coffee-house. But it happened that he
had left the Place a few Minutes, and his Lordship had without
Danger the Pleasure of boasting, how he would have treated him.'

Savage boasted in turn that he had gone alone to Arlington Street
the next day, 'to repay his Visit', but that he was prevailed upon
by the domestic staff to leave without seeing Tyrconnel. Whatever
credit we give to this story, it has an uneasy echo of Savage's much
earlier, unheralded night-visit to Lady Macclesfield.[70]

Johnson evidently believed such accounts, and partially explained
them by various 'Provocations' which had induced Tyrconnel to
'seize' whatever property Savage had left in his rooms at Arlington
Street. It does not seem to have occurred to him that most of this
'property' must have been Tyrconnel's in the first place.

Nor does Johnson quite give the flavour of what a 'provocation'
from Savage might feel like to a peer of the realm. Boswell was
particularly intrigued by this point, which eloquently confirmed his
low opinion of Savage, and managed to ferret out one undated but
undoubtedly genuine scrap of correspondence between the poet
and his patron at this time. The subject appears to be a bill of
Savage's which Lord Tyrconnel has evidently refused to honour.
The poet's response perhaps lacks a certain diplomacy:

Right Honourable Brute, and Booby,
   I find you want (as Mr— is pleased to hint) to swear away
my life, that is, the life of your creditor, because he asks for a
debt. – The publick shall soon be acquainted with this, to judge
whether you are not fitter to be an Irish Evidence, than to be an
Irish Peer. – I defy and despise you. I am, your determined
adversary, R.S.[71]

Johnson attempts to arbitrate between poet and patron, sug-
gesting there were faults on both sides. He also sees that Savage

always expected to be forgiven by Tyrconnel in the end, and that when the final break came in 1735, Savage was utterly unprepared for his fall from grace. In this Johnson again shrewdly emphasises the childlike element in Savage's psychology, which assumed that fame was his right and that nothing he did would have the painful consequences that any adult could reasonably have foreseen: 'Though it was undoubtedly the Consequence of accumulated Provocations on both Sides, yet everyone that knew Savage will readily believe, that to him it was sudden as a Stroke of Thunder; that though he might have transiently suspected it, he had never suffered any Thought so unpleasing to sink into his Mind, but that he had driven it away by Amusements, or Dreams of future Felicity and Affluence . . .'[72]

Yet there is some evidence that Savage was also shrewdly calculating. From 1734 onwards he began surreptitiously to rebuild his reputation in Grub Street with various journalistic jobs and publication schemes. He seems to have begun working for *The Grub Street Journal*, as a collector of literary gossip and scandal; and, on a higher level of respectability, to work as an assistant for Thomas Birch's *General Biographical Dictionary* which was to be based on a translation of Pierre Bayle's famous reference book, the *Dictionnaire Historique* (1702). Both publications fascinated Savage as a lifelong raconteur.

From 1734 he also began contributing reworked poems to Cave's newly-launched *Gentleman's Magazine*, a deliberate attempt to replace an aristocratic patron with a journalistic one. Typically Savage adopted a unique approach to magazine publication. The same poems were simultaneously offered to rival publications, so that the *London Magazine* often found itself printing the same work as the *Gentleman's Magazine* in the same month.[73] That the respective editors allowed this situation to endure for several years can only suggest that his name was still considered a special attraction for Society readers. Savage also planned and advertised a new collected edition of his works, pulling in subscriptions but failing to supply the actual copy to his bookseller.[74]

Johnson saw the final break with Tyrconnel in something close to heroic terms. It was a vindication of Savage's spirit of independence and his determination to continue on his own way as a writer: 'The Spirit of Mr Savage indeed never suffered him to solicit a Reconciliation; he returned Reproach for Reproach, and Insult for Insult; his Superiority of Wit supplied the Disadvantages of his

Fortune, and inabled him to form a Party, and Prejudice great Numbers in his favour.'[75]

In fact Savage was manoeuvring for new supporters, and despite his patron's commitment to the Whigs he now decided to return to Opposition politics. It was this that must have caused the ultimate breach with Tyrconnel. In 1735 he published a poem to the Prince of Wales, the official leader of the anti-Walpole faction at Court; and in May of the same year the *Daily Courant* reported him as somehow involved on the Tory side in 'a *Riot* at a late Election in Flintshire'.[76] Ironically, this appears to have been a genuine confusion of identities with another 'Mr Savage'. At all events, the 'real' Savage denied the charge and later told Johnson he had brought a libel action against the paper, though no legal records of such a case have ever been found. It emerges too that Savage was by now deeply involved with a branch of the Freemasons committed to the Opposition, a characteristic interest in secret machinations.

One would like to know more of this Masonic connection (of which Johnson was unaware). It seems to date back to Pope's membership in 1730, also on Opposition grounds. The name of John Savage appears alongside that of Pope's on the membership list of the Haymarket branch in 1730, and this may suggest a possible link.[77] Certainly by 1737 Savage was a leading member of the Charing Cross branch, and the *Daily Gazetteer* of September 1737 notes that 'Richard Savage, Esq., son of the late Earl Rivers, officiated as Master' at a meeting which enrolled James Thomson.[78]

But Savage's full re-emergence into the world of popular scandal was marked by his publication of 'The Progress of a Divine' in July 1735. This poem of 400 lines was a lively and obscene attack on contemporary corruption among Society clergymen. It was inspired by a dispute over preferments between the Bishop of London and the Lord Chancellor, a subject of no conceivable interest in itself to Savage but one which guaranteed a maximum of publicity.

Savage used it to paint a sort of Rake's Progress of a profligate priest, from a country curacy to a smart London parish, deliberately allowing all kinds of personal references to the most successful career-clergymen of the day. It joyfully enumerates the full range of canonical temptations, from spiritual cynicism to fleshy exploitations:

He feeds, and feeds, swills Soop, and sucks up Marrow;
Swills, sucks, and feeds, 'till leach'rous as a Sparrow.
Thy pleasure, Onan, now no more delights;
The lone Amusement of his chaster Nights.
He boasts – (let Ladies put him to the Test!)
Strong Back, broad Shoulders, and a well-built Chest.
With stiff'ning Nerves, now steals he sly away;
Alert, warm, chuckling, ripe for am'rous Play;
Ripe, to caress the Lass; he once thought meet,
At Church to chide, when pennanc'd in a Sheet.
He pants, the titillating Joy to prove;
The fierce, short Sallies of luxurious Love.[79]

The success of the poem was indicated by an immediate summons to the Court of King's Bench on a charge of obscenity. Johnson says that Savage extricated himself by the plea that he had 'only introduced Obscene Ideas with the View of exposing them to Detestation, and of amending the Age by shewing the Deformity of Wickedness'.[80] He was released, Johnson tells us, on the grounds of the 'Purity and Excellence' of his previous writings.

This seems so unlikely that it is no surprise to find a complete absence of any such case in the record of King's Bench for 1735. Savage was again boasting to Johnson of his feats as a writer in the lists of Virtue. What probably occurred was simply a threat of prosecution, and Savage fantasised the rest. This is borne out by the *Gentleman's Magazine* which noted a temporary suspension of publication but no actual court case, an occurrence which would otherwise have merited a lively editorial. Yet one is surprised that Cave did not bother to correct Johnson on this fact; perhaps he too was curiously entranced by Savage's gifts for myth-making.

Why Savage should suddenly in 1735 seize upon the question of clerical corruption might appear puzzling. Had he buried his old cause and turned to the nobler task of reforming the world? Or was this part of his courageous breakaway from the patronage of Tyrconnel and the compromises of his lavish, aristocratic style of life, to renew his self-dedication as the outcast, satirising poet? One might expect Johnson to believe this, or at least hope for it; yet here he is remarkably clear-eyed about Savage's motivation.

Though he was an 'indefatigable Opposer of all the Claims of Ecclesiastical Power' (as he was – once again – of the Whig Government) Savage's real interests were quite 'remote' from the Bishop of London's dispute. Johnson admits that Savage had friends who were involved, but the real attraction was the acrimony and the fierce topicality which the subject offered. Savage desperately needed to feel back at the centre of things; he needed to feel embattled and talked about. He hungered for the publicity, the notoriety. So Savage 'in Pursuance of his Character, endeavoured to become conspicuous among the Controvertists with which every Coffee-House was filled on that Occasion'.[81] Johnson drew from this an unflinching perception of Savage's unappeasable desire for self-glorification. To exist at all, Savage had to shine in the public gaze, wherever it was directed.

'It was always Mr Savage's Desire to be distinguished, and when any Controversy became popular, he never wanted some Reason for engaging in it with Ardour, and appearing at the Head of the Party which he had chosen.' In daring to plunge into the ecclesiastical fray, Savage had no other 'visible Design than that of drawing upon himself the Attention of Mankind'.[82]

The attention that Savage drew was no longer friendly. Without Tyrconnel's money or protection the world of fashion finally deserted him, and from 1735 he himself became the butt of a growing number of satires and attacks. 'The Progress of a Divine' drew 'more Infamy upon him than any incident of his Life'. Grub Street began to take its revenge. Old allies ridiculed his pretensions. John Dennis called him a 'Fool', and Thomas Cooke referred to him as 'a Spy'. A leading scandal sheet, *The Hyp-Doctor*, dedicated an entire issue to heaping scorn on his literary career, describing him as a 'Mad Animal' and a poetical impostor, 'an impotent *Creature mad* with the Imagination of being a Satyrical Poet'.[83] Not only his claims but his literary connections were subject to furious mockery, especially that with Alexander Pope and *The Dunciad*. He was 'the *Jack-all* of *that Ass* in *Lion's Skin*, he was his *Provider*: Like *Montmaur*, the *Parasite of Paris*, he rambled about to gather up *Scraps* of *Scandal*, as a Price for his *Twickenham Ordinary*; no Purchase no Pay; No Tittle-tattle, no Dinner . . .'[84] From now on Pope, whose own star (like his income) was in the ascendant, began to regard Savage as less of a poetical ally and more of a personal liability – for which he would eventually have to pay.

A whole series of poems, attacking and (with rather less conviction) defending Savage, appeared in *The Weekly Miscellany* and the *Gentleman's Magazine*. The subject of the murder trial came back to haunt him, with the accusation that he had capitalised shamelessly on its publicity. He was the horrible opportunist who 'by Free

Thinking to free Action fir'd, / In midnight Brawls a deathless Name acquir'd'.[85] His cynical impiety and ingratitude were pilloried:

> For cruel Murder doom'd to Hempen Death,
> Savage, by royal Grace, prolong'd his Breath.
> Well might you think, he spent his *future* Years
> In Prayer, and Fasting and repentant Tears.
> But, O vain Hope! – the truly *Savage* cries,
> 'Priests, and their slavish Doctrines, I despise.'[86]

Edward Cave, at the *Gentleman's Magazine*, attempted to answer these attacks, but the best he could do was to publish an unsigned poem from 'a Wiltshire Correspondent' which exhorted Savage to 'Exert thy Pen to mend a vicious Age'. Even though the killing of Sinclair was referred to as an 'equal Brawl' and the criticism of clerical corruption as a 'Patriot' duty, the defender from Wiltshire could only end on an uncertain note, which did not show much enthusiasm for Savage's fast-plummeting reputation:

> – But grant –
> – Maliciously that Savage plung'd the *Steel*,
> And made the Youth its shining Vengeance feel;
> My Soul abhors the Act, the Man detests,
> But more the Bigotry in priestly Breasts.[87]

It seemed that the pathos of his situation, upon which Savage had so long depended, was now almost exhausted; as were his friends and his finances.

It also appears that Savage's late-night dissipations had undermined his health, and in the winter of 1735 he was seriously ill. His desultory letters to Thomas Birch suggest that he holed up in a top-floor room at the Cross Keys Inn in St John Street, very close to Cave's offices in St John's Gate, Clerkenwell.[88] The cause of the illness is unknown, but it lasted on and off for several months, and was probably connected with his drinking. It may also have involved a venereal infection, judging by later remarks of James Thomson about his fondness for 'Girls'. It is possibly significant that one of the new members Savage introduced to the Freemasons in 1737 was Dr John Armstrong, a specialist in venereal diseases.

From this time Savage began to make short convalescent trips down the river to Greenwich, renowned for its good air and royal parklands; and the idea for his 'rural retirement' from London took on new urgency. He was now in his late thirties, with a constitution and physical appearance much weakened since the early days of his Grub Street glory. It was this gaunt and 'mournful' figure that young Johnson would encounter, not the glamorous, expensive dandy who in 1727 had so antagonised Judge Page.

Savage's illness and depression appear for the first time in his 'Volunteer Laureate' poem to Queen Caroline of 1735. The old story, virtually his signature-tune, is rehearsed as before; but there is a new softness, a plangent self-pity. We hear the voice of the Wanderer again, but from an older, genuinely suffering man:

> In Youth no Parent nurs'd my infant Songs,
> 'Twas mine to be inspir'd alone by Wrongs;
> Wrongs, that with Life their fierce Attack began,
> Drank Infant Tears, and still pursue the Man.
> Life scarce is Life – Dejection all is mine;
> The Power, that loves in lonely Shades to pine;
> Of faded Cheek, of unelated Views;
> Whose weaken'd Eyes and Rays of Hope refuse ...
> Thus sunk in Sickness, thus with Woes opprest,
> How shall the Fire awake within my Breast?
> How shall the Muse her flagging Pinions raise?
> How tune her Voice to Carolina's Praise?[89]

Dreams of the countryside, of warm sun and healing breezes, also begin to haunt the verse. Savage thinks back to his days at Richmond, before the disaster of the trial, and imagines remaking his life there amid the cheerful groves of songbirds (who are also his happier fellow-bards like Thomson and Pope). There is a tactful reference to Queen Caroline's new hunting-lodge being built at Richmond, known as Merlin's Cave, which was to have gardens, grottoes and a library, much on the lines already established by Pope and long-occupied by the imaginary Hermit.

> 'Come then (so whisper'd the indulgent *Muse*)
> 'Come then, in Richmond Groves thy Sorrows lose!
> 'Come then, and hymn this Day! – The pleasing Scene
> 'Shews, in each View, the Genius of thy *Queen*.
> 'Hear Nature whispering in the Breeze her Song!
> 'Hear her Sweet-Warbling through the feather'd Throng!
> 'Come! with the warbling World thy Notes unite,
> 'And with the vegitative Smile delight!

'Sure such a Scene and Song will soon restore
'Lost Quiet, and give Bliss unknown before . . .'[90]

As so often with Savage, this pastoral vision also had its strictly practical aspect. It was known that Queen Caroline was looking for a literary man to be her official librarian at Merlin's Cave, and Savage's 'Volunteer Laureate' was also a form of job application for the royal post. It is likely that he was considered, but the scandal over 'The Progress of a Divine' must have wrecked his chances.

In August the Queen appointed Stephen Duck (1705–56), the famous 'Thresher-poet' from Wiltshire whose career had some parallels with Savage's meteoric rise to temporary fame, as the well-salaried custodian. His official title was 'Cave and Library Keeper', a position which would certainly have suited the Hermit. But Duck had led a comparatively respectable life, and he also had a wife who could very properly be appointed the 'Necessary Woman' or housekeeper there, so the Queen got poet and charlady into the bargain. It must have seemed doubly ironic that Stephen Duck was first recommended to the Queen by Lord Macclesfield. However, even Stephen Duck's fortunes did not hold: he soon burnt out as a poet, took holy orders and drowned himself in a fit of despondency.

By 1736 Savage was fast returning to his original state of obscurity and indigence. Repeated applications to Walpole for a government sinecure were rejected. Nothing except the Queen's £50 pension, and occasional payments from Edward Cave, sustained him. His behaviour became steadily more eccentric and mysterious, as Johnson observed:

His Conduct with regard to his Pension was very particular. No sooner had he changed the Bill, than he vanished from the Sight of all his Acquaintances, and lay for some time out of the Reach of all the Enquiries that Friendship or Curiosity could make after him; at length he appeared again pennyless as before, but never informed even those he seemed to regard most, where he had been, nor was his Retreat ever discovered.[91]

Savage would tell people that he 'retired to study . . . in Solitude' and therefore gave no address; but he used to reappear in so short a time that it was generally concluded that he must have dissipated the money in a few weeks' riotous living in taverns and brothels, somewhere deep in the East End or across the river at Southwark.

Johnson did not pursue these darker possibilities and obtained no further information on Savage's life in 1736, perhaps fearful of what he might discover.

There are however a few hints to be uncovered. They suggest not so much a secret life of riot and extravagance as something approaching a breakdown in Savage's spirits which led him to creep away from company whenever he could. Johnson says stoutly that 'To despair was not, however, the Character of Savage, when one Patronage failed, he had recourse to another'.[92]

It is true that in January 1736 Savage published his 'Birthday Poem to the Prince of Wales'; but he was not able to find anyone to present it for him at Clarence House. In March 1736 his 'Volunteer Laureate No. 5' ran to a mere 46 lines and suggests a state of illness and dejection both chronic and crushing. For once there is not even a reference to his mother. Instead he observes the spring (perhaps from the window of some lost lodging at Greenwich) once more filling the parklands with sunlight and birdsong, but feels remote and disenchanted, cut off from Nature and above all from friendship.

> Yet mildest Suns, to *Me*, are Pain severe,
> And Music's self is Discord to *my* Ear.
> I, jocund Spring, unsympathizing, see,
> And Health, that comes to All, comes not to Me.
> Dear Health once fled, what Spirits can I find?
> What Solace meet, when fled my Peace of Mind?
> From absent Books, what studious Hint devise?
> From absent Friends, what Aid to Thought can rise?[93]

There is something haunting about this passage, as if we were hearing for the first time the intimations of a new and historic mood, like a horn echoing through a distant woodland. It is with a slight shock that one registers the adjective 'jocund', that has since become so exclusively associated with Wordsworth, 'in vacant or in pensive mood', contemplating the friendly host of spring daffodils beside the Lakes long after.

In May, Savage seems to have written – without disclosing an address – to James Thomson, recently returned from a comfortable Italian tour. Thomson mentions this letter in passing to another old friend and supporter, Aaron Hill. His tone is solicitous, but puzzled. 'Poor Mr Savage would be happy to pass an Evening with you,' Thomson tells Hill, 'his Heart burns towards you with the eternal Fire of Gratitude: But how to find him, requires more Intelligence than is allotted to Mortals. Life is too short to lose Years without the Conversation of those one most loves, and esteems . . .'[94]

Thomson, perhaps unaware of the full extent of the rows and scandals now surrounding Savage (or perhaps for the very reason that he had recently become aware of them), genially suggests arranging a supper-party at Richmond with Hill, Pope and the elusive Savage.

Aaron Hill's reply, dated 20 May 1736, is a cat's-cradle of compliments, vague allusions and careful evasions. It becomes clear that, like many others, he is now anxious to maintain a prudent distance from the disaster area of Savage's fall from grace and fashion. Thomson's own letter is pleasingly described as coming 'charged, like the winds of Arabia, with the fragrant exhalations of the climate, they belong to'; and this is followed by a long panegyric on Thomson's new poem, 'Liberty'. But the subject of Savage is treated like an unexploded petard:

> Your good nature was justly and generously employed, in the mention you make of poor Mr Savage: – It is a long time, since I saw him: I have been told, some of his friends make complaints of certain little effects of a *spleen* in his temper, which he is no more able to help, and should, therefore, no more be accountable for, than the *misfortunes*, to which, in all likelihood, his constitution may have owed it, originally.[95]

Hill goes on to observe that it is a great pity that there remains nobody who has 'weight enough, and will enough' to recommend him once again to the King. That Hill himself once enthusiastically undertook such recommendations for patronage on Savage's behalf is prudently glossed over. Instead he remarks innocently that a crown pension would lift Savage 'above those mortifications in life, which, no doubt, must have soured his disposition, and given the unreflecting part of his Acquaintance, occasion to complain, now and then, of his behaviour'. The feline irony of 'now and then' shows the Hillarian touch.[96]

Characteristically, Savage could not believe that Hill would really abandon him, and throughout 1736 made determined efforts to re-establish himself with his old Svengali of the *Plain Dealer* days. In June he wrote a long letter to Hill describing his illness and depression (it has not survived); and later in the year republished in the *Gentleman's Magazine* a greatly enlarged version of his 1726

poem to Hill, 'The Friend'. He removed much of the hyperbole
and the self-vaunting gestures and admitted the many follies of
which Hill had tried to cure him. He appealed directly to their old
friendship in terms which were, for Savage, remarkably modest.
Here is part of the rewritten poem, an open verse-letter to his old
patron:

> Oft when you saw my youth, wild error, know,
> Reproof, *soft-hinted*, taught the blush to glow.
> Young and unform'd, you first my genius rais'd,
> Just smil'd when faulty, and when mod'rate prais'd.
> Me shun'd, me ruin'd (such a *mother's* rage!)
> You sung, 'till pity wept o'er ev'ry page . . .
> Welcome the wound, when blest with such relief!
> For *deep* is felt the *friend*, when felt in *grief*.[97]

Johnson makes no comment on this poem but he read it in Cave's
file of contributions to the magazine. He may even have seen it
before he came to London the following year. One can only imagine
what chords it must have touched: 'For deep is felt the *Friend*, when
felt in grief.'

As for Aaron Hill, only one of his letters to Savage from 1736 sur-
vives, and it is not altogether reassuring. Though superficially benev-
olent, there are uncomfortable traces of dismissive mockery. What is
one to make of this elegant show of extravagant sympathy, in which
every subordinate phrase and emphasis seems to contain a jibe?

> After having heard nothing, for a long time, concerning you, but
> what you, so sparingly, bestow'd on the public, I felt much delight
> in the news my Brother brought me, that you had recovered
> from a dangerous illness. The name of your distemper should
> have been *Legion*, from its dreadful description in your letter:
> Any *one* of the branches, had been *too much* for the *easy* in mind,
> and the *strong* in constitution: How then, have you struggled with
> so malignant a *confederacy*, oppress'd, as you are, by ill health,
> and ill fortune![98]

Hill goes on to commiserate with the failure of Savage's 'Birthday
Poem to the Prince of Wales', adding lightly that possibly it might
do better 'under a different title'. He supplies some guarded infor-
mation about the playwright Gay, on whom Savage was gathering
material for Birch's *General Biographical Dictionary*; but refuses to

send a copy of his own new poem 'Zara' – 'it is a *virtue*, to be cold and indifferent, to what we have *written*'.

Hill then turns to the explosive subject of Lord Tyrconnel, about which, strangely, he professes to be ignorant: 'What you say of Lord Tyrconnel, reminds me of something, I have heard (tho' very obscurely) concerning a breach in that friendship, which was once, so *useful*, and so *ornamental*, to you: – I am heartily sorry for the *cause*, whatever it may have been.' He urges a reconciliation, suggesting that the 'hand of some friend' (but not, of course, his) might 'methinks, interpose, and soon blot out all unpleasing impressions, on both sides'.

Hill reserves his most candid, and disinterested, thrust of friendship for his final paragraph. What he says is astute and possibly well-meant; but it hardly has the warmth for which Savage must have hoped. In fact, with its sudden reference to the Rivers birthright – perilously close to open sarcasm – it was cold comfort indeed for the poet back in his anonymous lodgings:

> Shall I add, so near the end of my paper, that tho' I own and *distinguish* the proofs, you have given of your genius, and spirit, for satire, yet I see you with *pain*, in persuits that must multiply *enemies*. – Were you Lord Rivers (as well as his *son*) I should have been of a different opinion. – But the merits of the *Unhappy*, will (in a world so maliciously active) be most shown to their benefit, in its softest and most *inoffensive* exertions.[99]

To remind Savage that he was now again one of 'the Unhappy' and that his future writings should be soft and 'inoffensive', suggests something very like a dismissal from the old Plain Dealer. It is certainly different from the language Hill used to the spectacularly successful Thomson. No prospect of future aid, or work, or even a meeting is held out to Savage. The signature appears to be an ironic valediction: 'Forgive me, my dear Sir, this mark of that Friendship, with which I have ever been sincerely, and still am, your most affectionate, and obedient humble Servant, A. Hill.'

As Johnson surveys the wreckage of Savage's fortunes at the end of 1736 his hand begins to tighten its grip almost imperceptibly on the narrative. He is now fast approaching his own arrival on the scene of Savage's desolation (though it will be unmarked and anonymous), and he wishes the reader to be prepared for Savage as he first encountered him. There will be little further confusion in dates and chronology. The essential drama begins to turn on moral questions. What are we to make of Savage's behaviour; how are we to judge the absurd contradictions of his character; and how confident can we be in condemning him, like the rest of the world?

The revolution of Savage's fortunes between 1727 and 1737 struck Johnson with the force of moral allegory. However much Savage himself was to blame for his own catastrophe, a wider pattern of human life was revealed. Fate was fickle in its operations, society was ravenous for success and cruel to failure. The wheel of fortune turned relentlessly. It tested men's dreams and hounded down their weaknesses. For a man as gifted, as unstable, as self-deluding as Savage it was a lethal process that might bring total destruction. What remained was the poetry, the stubbornness of the individual spirit and the moral wisdom – the exemplum – that might be drawn, especially by a friend. It was on this aspect that Johnson began to concentrate all his powers.

Johnson carefully gathered up the strands of the story so far, to show Savage as a man at bay before the whole world and therefore as still worthy of attention and even sympathy. He touches on the central chord of friendship with skill and irony, obliquely asking the reader not yet, not yet at least, to join in the chorus of condemnation:

It does not appear, that after this Return of his Wants, he found Mankind equally favourable to him, as at his first Appearance in the World. His Story, though in Reality not less melancholy, was less affecting, because it was no longer new; it therefore procured him no new Friends, and those that had formerly relieved him thought they might now consign him to others. He was now likewise considered by many rather as criminal, than as unhappy; for the Friends of Lord Tyrconnel and of his Mother were sufficiently industrious to publish his Weaknesses, which were indeed very numerous, and nothing was forgotten, that might make him either hateful or ridiculous.[100]

At the same time Johnson reiterates something crucial to his own estimate of the man he is about to meet. Out of disaster, Savage had achieved a certain stoicism:

... he never considered himself as levelled by any Calamities; and though it was not without some Uneasiness, that he saw some, whose Friendship he valued, change their Behaviour; he yet observed their Coldness without much Emotion, considered them as the Slaves of Fortune and the Worshippers of Prosperity; and was more inclined to despise them, than to lament himself.[101]

In this mood of renewed determination Savage emerged from hiding in the spring of 1737 and took the ferry up-river to stay with one of his few remaining allies, James Thomson, at his new house in Kew Foot Lane, Richmond. He set to work on his poem 'Of Public Spirit'. There, wrote Johnson, 'he might prosecute his Design in full Tranquillity, without the Temptations of Pleasure, or the Solicitations of Creditors, by which his Meditations were in equal Danger of being disconcerted . . .'[102] And as the ragged Hermit retired to his cave, his misshapen champion arrived in the dark city.

CHAPTER 8

FRIENDSHIP

Johnson the biographer now returns to our story as Johnson the friend: the gloomy, desperate, tender-hearted young teacher just up from the country, brilliant but grotesque, seeking his own fortune at the doors of the *Gentleman's Magazine* in Clerkenwell. But our perception of him can no longer be the same. For in recounting Savage's career thus far he has already revealed much of himself that is new: his stubborn loyalty, his strange credulity, his hunger for justice, his youthful political anger, his naïve romanticism and his extraordinary commitment to the fate of an outcast writer on the fringes of eighteenth-century society. This seems very different from the confident, wise, sententious, Tory Clubman of Boswell's great portrait.

Through the vivid but fragmented mirror of Savage's life we have glimpsed the reflections of a personality as anguished and unstable as Savage's own. The biographer has unconsciously written something of his own autobiography: and therein lies the peculiar mystery – or alchemy – of the form that Johnson is creating, for Boswell and so many others to develop after their own fashion.

As Johnson meets Savage he meets a version of his own literary future: a poet trapped in the toils of London, driven by unfulfilled ambitions, washed up by the tides of fortune and already dreaming of escape. He sees a whole curve of possible destiny. He identifies instantly with much that he hears from Savage, and about him: the poverty, the persecution, the hack-work, the incorrigible refusal to be beaten or humiliated. He is entranced by the stories, fascinated by the poetry, and weirdly beguiled by the battered elegance. According to Hawkins, Savage's first deep flourishes of salutation with his hat displayed 'as much grace as those actions were capable of'.[1]

But because of young Johnson's moral strength and intellectual power, he is also cautious of this faintly sinister, dandified Mephisto-pheles. He holds back, wanting a different future and a far greater one. He loves Savage – every grave excuse for him in the *Life*, every smiling complicity has made this clear – but he will also finally try to judge him. When they meet as friends they are also poised – the biographer and his subject – as if for a duel.

Johnson's first physical impression of Savage, which seems to have been in the street, is something of a shock. Neither the voluble, aggressive, quick-moving wit darting between the coffee-house tables whom Thomson encountered; nor the vain, extravagant, self-dramatising defendant at the Old Bailey whom Judge Page ordered from his court: neither is quite recognisable in this gaunt, slow, slyly amusing apparition.

> He was of a middle Stature, of a thin Habit of Body, a long Visage, coarse Features, and melancholy Aspect; of a grave and manly Deportment, a solemn Dignity of Mien, but which upon a nearer Acquaintance softened into an engaging Easiness of Manners. His Walk was slow, and his Voice tremulous and mournful. He was easily excited to Smiles, but very seldom pro-voked to Laughter.[2]

No doubt part of this unexpected *gravitas* was due to the ravages which Savage's health had suffered since 1735. But we may also feel that the subtle, observant changeling of Mrs Haywood's fiction may have been carefully adjusting his demeanour for a new and valuable young ally.

When and where did this meeting finally take place? Like so much else in Savage's life, this simple fact remains obscure and puzzlingly disputed. Johnson himself is silent on the point; Hawkins is anxious to establish it in 1737; Boswell is equally anxious to put off the evil moment as late as possible in 1738. No one really knows. But the crucial point of contact must surely have been the *Gentleman's Magazine* in the archway of St John's Gate. There is a curious satisfaction in the fact that this is the one physical monument to their friendship that has survived to this day, its decorated stonework painted with heraldic gold and red, amid the glassy business offices of modern London. Cave's editorial office above the actual arch can still be seen; and the big Jacobean staircase with its heavy mahogany balustrade up which both Johnson and Savage must have climbed, still gleams in the gothic half-light of mullioned windows.

The truth is that it would be difficult to avoid Savage at any time he was in Grub Street, either here or frequenting Button's and the other literary coffee-houses off the Strand. James Thomson met him within two months of his arrival in London. When Johnson first reached London in March 1737 he took an upstairs room with a staymaker, Mr Norris (who had Lichfield connections), in Exeter Street off the Strand, just three minutes away from Button's. Had Savage not been staying with Thomson at Richmond that spring their paths must have crossed almost immediately.

Johnson's intense loneliness is caught in a tiny memorandum he made of these early days, which touchingly records two points of treasured emotional contact: his beautiful landlady and her little cat. Cats, like women, always entranced Johnson; and, unlike women, lavished their attentions on him. The broken, almost indecipherable note also mentions children, rent payment in advance and what seems to be some sort of fortune-telling game about his future:

Norris the staymaker – fair Esther – w[ith] the cat – children – inspection of the hand – stays returned – lodging – guinea at the stairs – Esther died . . .[3]

How closely can we now pin down the circumstances of their meeting? Savage at this time was working on his poem 'Of Public Spirit', to be published in June 1737, which Johnson read immediately and with much attention, judging by the space he eventually gave to it in the *Life*. While at work, Savage wrote from Richmond at the end of May to Solomon Mendez, a rich Jewish merchant from Hackney whose family were later to provide him with one of his last-known lodgings in London. 'I think it an age since I have had the pleasure of seeing you and good Mrs Mendez. – I chose rather to trouble you with this, than you should think I have forgot you.

I have been here ever since Tuesday was fortnight, very much bemused, but not so much as to forget my best friends.'

He adds that he is in friendly touch with Pope, and that Thomson is also working hard at a new poem, so much so that he is still 'a-bed', and is thus too busy to write. 'The serious truth is, that this poem has quite absorbed every other thought of his for some time.' But Savage is almost ready to return to London, and he jauntily warns Mendez that he proposes to call on him 'very suddenly'.[4]

By July Savage had certainly returned from Richmond to the city, though not to the Mendez household; for Thomson was lamenting his absence, and Mendez was asking for news, and neither knew where to find him. July 1737 thus becomes the first time that Johnson and Savage could have met in London.

There is some reason to believe that the friendship began in a series of riverside discussions at Greenwich that summer. At this time Thomson writes to Mendez, with an appreciative glance at Savage's taunting wit: 'But (as Savage would say) to *passover* this, I propose to myself the pleasure of waiting on you soon, nor will I then leave you for two three days. The first time I see our brother bard, we will make an appointment; though where the Muses, or some sweeter girls, have hid him, I know not. He has lately published a fine poem on Public Works; a very impudent subject for one to write upon at this time o' day. When his annual fifty is turned into a thousand pounds, then will he see certain grounds like the sylvan scenes he describes . . .'[5] The letter continues with an affectionate satire on Savage's fantasies, including his desire to bridge the Thames, and to ride out of London into the country in a splendid 'coach and six'.

We know from Savage's 'Laureate' poems and from his brief notes to Birch about the *Dictionary* that since 1735 he was inclined to disappear to Greenwich in search of health during the hot summer months, his alternative rural retreat and 'sylvan scene'. And we know from Johnson's first London letter to Cave, dated 12 July 1737, that Johnson was already there in Greenwich, 'next door to the Golden Heart, Church Street'.[6] This proximity alone makes an encounter very likely.

Added to this is the fact that Johnson now proposed a meeting with Cave at Clerkenwell, to discuss a possible translation of Paolo Sarpi's *History of the Council of Trent*, his first serious attempt to obtain professional work. When this meeting took place it is highly likely that the talk turned to Savage, since the *Gentleman's Magazine* had been republishing much of his work and Johnson had long expressed interest in the 'Poetical Article' of the paper, which he thought could be improved.[7]

Cave was now campaigning for Savage, and for an increase in the famous £50 royal pension, much as Aaron Hill had done in *The Plain Dealer* in the early days. Savage made good controversial publicity for the magazine. In 1736 Cave had republished the retitled poem to the Duchess of Rutland; 'Volunteer Laureate No. 5'; 'An Epistle to Damon and Delia'; the revised 'The Friend' to Aaron Hill; and a long satire against Walpole's tardy patronage, 'A Poet's Dependence on a Statesman'. In 1737 he continued with 'Fulvia', an extract from 'Of Public Spirit' and the daring reprint of *The Bastard*, which Johnson can hardly have overlooked. For Johnson, Savage's name would have appeared that summer as a sudden star in the firmament, twinkling dangerously in his smoky glamorous reputation above St John's Gate. Here was the rejected poet of the city, brilliant, garrulous, sick and lonely; but still hungering for justice.

When, the following spring, Johnson sent in his first poems to the *Gentleman's Magazine*, they were dedicated to Cave as the best editor in London; and to Savage as its most idealistic poet, shamefully unrecognised by 'Mankind'. The poem to Savage, cast in the fashionable form of a Latin epigram, whose skilful word play was designed as a motto to be remembered and quoted, provides startling evidence of Johnson's initial feelings about Savage's persecuted genius. Though not published until April 1738, it suggests almost a kind of hero-worship. A literal translation runs as follows:

To Richard Savage, Bearer of Arms, Lover of Mankind.

Devotion to your Fellow Man burns brightly in your Breast;
O! that Fellow Man may cherish and protect Thee in return.

The embarrassed comment, by one modern Johnson scholar, that his Latin epigrams were naturally fulsome and 'jejune' shows just how emotionally Johnson had expressed himself.[8]

The strongest evidence that Johnson and Savage had heard of each other through Cave in 1737, and actually met while roaming the riverside at Greenwich that summer, comes in Johnson's *London*. If the 'injur'd Thales', dreaming of his escape to the rural fastness of Wales, really is Savage, then that is where the friendship was first, and so passionately, consecrated. This is how Johnson describes it, in that strange and memorable ceremony of kissing the earth, the two men dedicating themselves to poetic justice and the recovery of a lost Golden Age:

> On Thames's Banks, in silent Thought we stood,
> Where Greenwich smiles upon the silver Flood:
> Struck with the Seat that gave Eliza birth,
> We kneel, and kiss the consecrated Earth;
> In pleasing Dreams the blissful Age renew,
> And call Britannia's Glories back to view...[9]

There is a particular significance in establishing this early meeting at Greenwich, and hence the identification of Savage with Thales. It throws new light on *London* and the peculiar inspiration which Savage's friendship brought to Johnson's earliest months in the city. *London* is not merely the brilliant literary imitation of Juvenal's *Third Satire* it has always been taken to be. It also becomes an intensely personal poem about Savage's life and attitudes, as Johnson first learned about them. *London* becomes, in effect, a preliminary essay in biography, when Johnson's naïve admiration was at its height. It is the poetic investigation of a personality; and a monument to the heady, dazzling first days of an historic friendship.

The identification seems to be deliberately made in the opening lines of the poem, in which Johnson links Thales with Savage's figure of 'the Hermit' and his well-known fantasy of rural retirement from the city:

> Tho' Grief and Fondness in my Breast rebel,
> When injur'd Thales bids the Town farewell,
> Yet still my calmer Thoughts his Choice commend,
> I praise the Hermit, but regret the Friend,
> Resolv'd at length, from Vice and London far,
> To breathe in distant Fields a purer Air...[10]

Thales is Johnson's version of Juvenal's 'Umbricius', a man who was leaving Rome in disgust to seek virtue in the countryside. But Johnson also makes Thales a poet and satirist, like Savage, and echoes many of the lines describing country retirement from his recent 'Volunteer Laureate' poems. So this opening passage, besides its specific reference to Savage's 'Hermit', carefully picks up Savage's praise of the rural Muse in the 'Laureate' poem of 1735, with such lines as:

> Hark! she invites from city Smoke and Noise,
> Vapours impure, and from impurer Joys...[11]

Thales's place of retirement, like Savage's, will be Wales: 'on Cambria's solitary shore'. And like Savage, Thales uses the moment of departure to reflect on the evils and injustices of the London he has experienced, in a sparkling, mordant adaptation of Juvenal's satire on Rome. The body of the 260-line poem is thus given in Thales's voice, and allowing for the Juvenalian original (which Johnson would print in a series of Latin footnotes, to show both the parallels and the contemporary additions) this voice seems to be in many places a recognisable version of Savage talking to Johnson about his life in the city.

So, in one notable passage, we catch Thales making oblique reference to a typical catalogue of Savage's obsessions: the perjured witnesses at his trial; the plucking of his title 'Volunteer Laureate' from Cibber; the mockery of Sir Robert Walpole's policies; the farce of the royal pension; and even perhaps the social agonies of dining obsequiously with friends of Lord Tyrconnel:

> But what, my Friend, what Hope remains for me,
> Who start at Theft, and blush at Perjury?
> Who scarce forbear, tho' Britain's Court he sing,
> To pluck a titled Poet's borrow'd Wing;
> A Statesman's Logic, unconvinc'd can hear,
> And dare to slumber o'er the *Gazetteer*;
> Despise a Fool in half his Pension drest,
> And strive in vain to laugh at Clodio's Jest.[12]

There are at least half-a-dozen other passages where Thales appears to speak as Savage (some of which we have already met in the night-walks) and where he touches on specific aspects of his character as the Outcast Poet, a subject to which Johnson would return – though much more warily – five years later in the *Life*.

But above all it is Thales's presentation of himself as the persecuted writer, like the nomadic poet of *The Wanderer*, which seems to reflect Johnson's first and profoundly compassionate response to the extraordinary man he met at Greenwich:

Then thro' the World a wretched Vagrant roam,
For where can starving Merit find a Home?
In vain your mournful Narrative disclose,
Whilst all neglect, and most insult your Woes.[13]

This clearly echoes Savage's own image of the roaming, unrecognised 'Ulysses' from Canto V of *The Wanderer*.[14]

Moreover it was on exactly this note, and even with the same phrase, that Johnson would begin his *Life*. '... Volumes have been written only to enumerate the Miseries of the Learned, and relate their unhappy Lives, and untimely Deaths. To these mournful Narratives, I am about to add the Life of Richard Savage ...'[15]

Yet here a curious problem arises. Despite the internal evidence of the poem, and all the circumstances linking Johnson and Savage with its Greenwich setting, Boswell was adamantly opposed to this identification of Thales as in any way a portrait of Savage. This refusal to recognise Savage as the inspiration for Johnson's first great poem is resolutely maintained by most modern scholars, who seem equally anxious to deny such a controversial source of influence. *London* is simply a literary imitation of Juvenal, 'adorned with opposition catchphrases', and fuelled by a naïve political anger that Johnson rapidly outgrew.[16]

Boswell, indeed, is too sensitive not to catch something intensely personal about the poem. As it is political in inspiration, he argues that Thales's satire must therefore arise from a form of displaced autobiography. If Thales is anyone, he is young Johnson himself, prowling the streets with a gleeful, disenchanted eye. 'The nation was then in that ferment against the court and the ministry, which some years after ended in the downfall of Sir Robert Walpole ... Accordingly, we find in Johnson's *London* the most spirited invectives against tyranny and oppression, the warmest predilection for his own country, and the purest love of virtue; interspersed with traits of his own particular character and situation, not omitting his prejudices as a "true-born Englishman" ...'[17]

Yet Thales's situation is not Johnson's; and the 'spirited invective' – with its strong Jacobite caste against Walpole's Ministry – clearly reflects the voice of Savage's most recent poems, 'Of Public Spirit' and 'A Poet's Dependence on a Statesman', which had galvanised Johnson into political consciousness.

In contrast to Boswell, Hawkins immediately made this identification and stated that *London* 'anticipated the departure of his friend

Thales, i.e. Savage', for Wales. He added that Savage had long planned a retirement to some country place 'far distant from the metropolis', so although the event was 'antedated' in the poem, 'in every particular ... what is there said of the departure of Thales must be understood of Savage, and looked upon as true history'.[18] Yet Boswell continued to insist that such an identification was 'entirely groundless'.[19] He argued that since Savage did not actually leave the city until July 1739, and *London* was already published by May 1738, Thales could not be linked convincingly to Savage; and he accuses Hawkins of crediting Johnson with 'second-sight' as to Savage's plans in 1738.

Yet Savage's dream of a country retirement is evident in his work as early as 1729, with *The Wanderer*; and the theme is developed with increasing urgency in the 'Volunteer Laureate' poems of 1735–7. A friend like Thomson refers to it laughingly as one of Savage's well-known *folies de grandeur* (the 'coach and six') by the summer of 1737. Johnson would not have needed second-sight to incorporate this into his picture of Thales at Greenwich; and indeed one may rather suspect that it was Boswell, on the contrary, who had disdained to give Savage's poetry more than a first and cursory reading.

It is true that we do not know when the specifically Welsh or 'Cambrian' scheme emerged in Savage's mind, but there is some suggestion that he had been talking about it throughout the 1730s to any friend who would listen. The seed of the idea had been sown as early as 1724 by Sir Richard Steele's departure to Carmarthen; and Savage's old friend from the *Plain Dealer* days, John Dyer, had returned there permanently by 1735. Savage even seems to have reconnoitred as far as Bath and Bristol in the company of Lord Tyrconnel when Lady Tyrconnel was ill at Bath and taking the spa waters in 1730.[20] (This would explain, incidentally, how Savage got to hear of the pleasing story of Lady Macclesfield's humiliation at Bath on the publication of *The Bastard*.) Another country tour westwards, through Oxfordshire and Gloucestershire via 'Burford's hills', is also mentioned by Savage in a poem 'To Miss M.H. sent with Mr Pope's Works', published in 1736.[21] So the evidence that Savage's eyes had been turned towards Wales and the west for some years, like Thales's, is not insubstantial and certainly far from 'groundless'.

Boswell's final attempt to disassociate Savage from the poem (an attempt that becomes revealingly over-insistent) is an apparently authoritative statement that Savage and Johnson had not even met by May 1738. 'I have been assured, that Johnson said he was not so much as acquainted with Savage when he wrote his *London*.'[22] In fact, Boswell never had this assurance first-hand from Johnson but only as reported many years afterwards by an earnest young clergyman, the Rev. John Hussey, whom Johnson had been exhorting to spend his youth wisely and fulfil a missionary vocation in 1779. It seems more than possible that Johnson was simply trying to avoid scandalising Hussey. He reportedly asserted that 'when he imitated the third Satire of Juvenal, he did not intend to characterise anyone under the name of Thales'.[23]

However, this is not what he told Cave at the time, in April 1738. On the contrary, he asserted that much of the point of imitating Juvenal lay precisely in the parallels that could be drawn with contemporary events in London, and with contemporary *people* in the public eye: '. . . Part of the beauty of the performance (if any beauty be allow'd it) consisting in adapting Juvenal's Sentiments to modern facts and Persons.'[24] In other words, Johnson positively *wanted* his readers to look for clues to Thales's identity. One can only conclude that Boswell was in some sense covering up for Johnson, and trying to minimise the significance of these early links. The thought of someone like Savage inspiring Johnson, both politically and poetically, simply did not fit with Boswell's image of his sage.

Long after, when the *Gentleman's Magazine* published a memoir of Edmund Cave's career at St John's Gate, 'The Autobiography of Sylvanus Urban', it was given as an established tradition among the contributors that despite Boswell's assertions, Johnson and Savage were 'already intimate associates' by the end of 1737; that they met at Greenwich; and that Savage was 'certainly' the friend described in *London*, 'whatever doubts may have arisen on the point'.[25]

It is significant that Hester Thrale, who had so often talked with Johnson about Savage, came to the same conclusion. When in old age she acquired the 1816 edition of Boswell's *Life*, to add to her collection, she observed that the editor Chalmers had now respectfully footnoted Boswell's view as 'doubtful'. Impatiently she scrawled in the margin alongside: 'I thought we were all convinced that Thales was Savage.'[26]

Yet we still have to bear in mind how much of Savage the initial portrait of Thales omits. Nothing of his opportunism, his instability, his obsession with his mother clouds Johnson's first – and clearly idealised – picture of his friend. Perhaps this is partly what made Boswell, and others, so keen to deny the identification. Thales's anger against society is purely disinterested, in Johnson's view: he is the Accuser, the spokesman of the poor and the oppressed, and the voice of eternal opposition.

Imagining Savage's imminent departure for Wales in 1738, as Johnson supposed, he invokes his spirit as the guide for his own youthful writing. Savage, as the honoured Hermit retired to the mountains, will always be ready to return to the city to inspire his own work should he flag or lose heart. He is the hero who will one day come back from the hills. As Thales says in his stirring valediction at Greenwich:

> Much could I add, – but see the Boat at hand,
> The Tide retiring, calls me from the Land:
> Farewell! – When Youth, and Health, and Fortune spent,
> Thou fly'st for Refuge to the Wilds of Kent;
> And tir'd like me with Follies and with Crimes,
> In angry Numbers warn'st succeeding Times;
> Then shall thy Friend, nor thou refuse his Aid,
> Still Foe to Vice forsake his Cambrian Shade;
> In Virtue's Cause once more exert his Rage,
> Thy Satire point, and animate thy Page.[27]

During the following months Johnson rapidly modified this noble, Juvenalian projection of Savage as the exiled poetic conscience of his age. But its first impact was never forgotten. It leaves its imprint, and casts its shadow, everywhere in the *Life*.

It explains many of Johnson's extraordinary partialities, special pleadings and paradoxical defences of his friend. It suggests why Johnson, again and again, presents his reader with the dilemma of suspended moral judgement: 'The reigning Error of his Life was, that he mistook the Love for the Practice of Virtue, and was indeed not so much a good Man, as the Friend of Goodness.'[28]

It explains the heroic figure of the night-walks. And it explains, above all, perhaps, Johnson's overwhelming sense of loyalty, of emotional debt, which secretly animates his biography. Johnson was keeping faith with the man he knew Savage *might* have been; and more than this, with the man Savage wanted *him* to be in the future. *London* was in this sense a poetic pledge of friendship; and the *Life* its working-out and subtle fulfilment.

The publication of the poem on 13 May 1738 propelled Johnson for the first time to the edge of literary recognition, on his own account. The poem was printed by Cave, published and sold by the Pall Mall bookseller Robert Dodsley and quickly ran to a second edition. The work was unsigned, but Pope remarked that its author 'would soon be *deterré*'. Its authorship was immediately known to the large circle of Cave's contributors, such as Thomas Birch and Elizabeth Carter. There is some suggestion that it was Savage himself who brought the poem to Pope's attention, and perhaps circulated it to others.[29]

It is interesting, in view of Johnson's subsequent prevarications about the poem's links with Savage, that even at the time he submitted it with unusual sleight of hand. In a covering letter to Cave, written from Castle Street in April, he at first pretended it was the work of an unnamed friend – not his own, at all – and that this friend was in great poverty. Johnson never had recourse to such a subterfuge in his later career. He also made an unusual concession to Cave's editorial judgement, saying that he would 'take the trouble of altering any stroke of satire' in the poem which Cave might dislike. Both these manoeuvres, wholly uncharacteristic of the later, hugely self-confident Johnson, suggest how tentative and exposed the young author felt about the composition.

Johnson received only ten guineas from Dodsley for the copyright of *London*; but this was his first professional fee, and the success of the poem immediately brought in other work from Cave. From June 1738 he began as assistant editor on the Parliamentary Debates, published monthly in the *Gentleman's Magazine* as 'Debates in the Senate of Magna Lilliputia'; and in August he signed a contract for the translation of Paolo Sarpi.[30] He also followed up the Latin epigram to Savage, published in the April issue, with a number of occasional poems throughout the year. Johnson was thus quickly accepted into the inner circle of the magazine, which brought him into regular contact with its other contributors: Thomas Birch, Elizabeth Carter, and of course Savage.

His success also brought him for the first time in his life a regular freelance income. It was recorded, says Boswell, with 'minute and scrupulous accuracy' on a small-accounts sheet, and over the next eight months amounted to £49.7s.0d. By July 1739 it probably totalled between seventy and eighty guineas.[31] How much of this was absorbed by Elizabeth Johnson when she moved down to London, it is impossible to say; but from the summer of 1738

Johnson, with both lodgings and a basic freelance income, was slightly better off than Savage, and can never have been completely penniless again during the period of their friendship.

This too must have subtly altered their relationship, and Johnson's perceptions of Savage's shortcomings. Though Savage's poverty is represented as heroic in the night-walks, his total inability to manage money in a practical fashion now begins to come in for increasingly witty criticism. Savage was 'far better qualified' for the acquisition of knowledge than of riches: he was 'remarkably retentive of his Ideas, which, when once he was in Possession of them, rarely forsook him; a Quality which could never be communicated to his Money.'[32]

It also seems possible that Savage may sometimes have exaggerated his destitution to Johnson, as part of a general ploy of retaining his young protégé's sympathy. The night-walks which so impressed Johnson may partly have been staged for his benefit by Savage, deliberately acting out his role as the wandering 'Hermit' drifting through the underworld of the city.

By spring 1738 it is possible to track the two friends a little more closely. When Johnson brought Elizabeth to London, he established her in good West End lodgings: first at Woodstock Street, off Hanover Square; then at No. 6 Castle Street, off Cavendish Square. It is a surprise to realise that during the later period of their night-walks Johnson must always have had these lodgings close by. If he stayed out with Savage it must have been from choice, not from destitution; and one must conclude that part of his motivation was to avoid his wife. Whether Savage and Elizabeth Johnson ever met, it seems that Savage was rarely brought home as a house-guest. However, this may have been the result of Savage's complete lack of domestic virtues.

As we enter the section of Johnson's *Life* which draws on first-hand material dating from 1738 to 1739, it is this hopeless, cuckoo-like aspect of Savage's 'rambling Manner of Life' which Johnson turns to first. 'Whoever was acquainted with him, was certain to be solicited for small Sums'; and this would be followed by demands for hospitality. Johnson, himself undomesticated, with a profound aversion to regular hours, good furniture or smart clothes, nevertheless draws the picture of Savage as a house-guest in sharp strokes of comedy. Possibly here we are glimpsing a memory of Castle Street.

He was sometimes so far compassionated by those who knew both his Merit and his Distresses, that they received him into their Families, but they soon discovered him to be a very incommodious Inmate; for being always accustomed to an irregular Manner of Life, he could not confine himself to any stated Hours, or pay any Regard to the Rules of a Family, but would prolong his Conversation till Midnight, without considering that Business might require his Friend's Application in the Morning; nor when he had persuaded himself to retire to Bed, was he, without Difficulty, called up to Dinner . . .[33]

Savage's aim seemed to be 'the entire subversion of all Economy', and 'wherever Savage entered he immediately expected that Order and Business should fly before him . . . and that no dull Principle of domestic Management should be opposed to his Inclination, or intrude upon his Gaiety'.[34]

It is ironic that years later Mrs Thrale, or rather her servants at Streatham, would make similar complaints about Johnson's visits, when conversation was inevitably pressed into the early hours, and Johnson's re-emergence from the bedroom seldom impinged on breakfast.[35]

Johnson seems vaguely aware that Savage still had London friends who continued to shelter him in 1738; but he makes no specific reference to Thomson, Mendez, Birch or Pope. One family – unnamed by Johnson – supported Savage for several weeks while he began work on a new version of his *Tragedy of Sir Thomas Overbury* – but then they moved to another address and 'took Occasion to dismiss him'.[36]

One has the impression that Savage kept his friends in separate compartments – a characteristic of essentially solitary people – and rarely let one supporter know what another was doing for him. Johnson seemed to think that Savage was largely homeless throughout the time he knew him: 'He had seldom any Home, or even a Lodging in which he could be private, and therefore was driven into public Houses for the common Conveniences of Life, and Supports of Nature.' This meant that Savage would have to wash, shave, defecate and change his clothes – if he had any to change – in the back rooms of pubs and taverns; and failing this would simply wander off into the fields beyond Smithfield or Southwark.[37]

Johnson evidently soon began to accompany him on these wanderings, and saw the direct effects of Savage's poverty. When completely penniless 'he spent his Time in mean Expedients and tormenting Suspense, living for the greatest Part in Fear of Prosecution from his Creditors, and consequently skulking in the obscurest Parts of the Town, of which he was no Stranger to the remotest Corners'.[38]

To wander through London in tattered clothes, the remnants of his old aristocratic glory, provoked a thousand humiliations which Johnson grimly observed. He had first sketched these out in the character of Thales, jeered at by shopkeepers and courtiers alike:

> By Numbers here from Shame or Censure free,
> All Crimes are safe, but hated Poverty
> This, only this, the rigid Law persues,
> This, only this, provokes the snarling Muse;
> The sober Trader at a tatter'd Cloak,
> Wakes from his Dream, and labours for a Joke;
> With brisker Air the silken Courtiers gaze,
> And turn the varied Taunt a thousand Ways . . .
> This mournful Truth is ev'ry where confest,
> *Slow rises Worth, by Poverty deprest.*[39]

The question of Savage's clothes haunted Johnson, who had never forgotten the incident at Oxford, when a well-meaning friend had left a pair of old shoes outside his door. Convulsed with shame and anger, Johnson hurled them out of the window.[40] Savage told him of similar experiences.

'At this Time he gave another instance of the insurmountable Obstinacy of his Spirit; his Clothes were worn out, and he received Notice that at a Coffee-House some Clothes and Linen were left for him.' Instead of accepting this generous offer (which had been made anonymously, precisely to spare his feelings) Savage 'so much resented' the philanthropy that he refused to return to the coffee-house until the clothes were removed. When Johnson calls this 'insurmountable Obstinacy', one feels criticism and admiration trembling in the balance.[41]

On a later occasion, when a group of well-wishers decided to buy him a complete new outfit of clothes to get him through the winter of 1738, they unwisely sent round a city tailor to take his measurements and make an estimate of the cost. Savage's reaction, said Johnson, 'showed the Peculiarity of his character'. Johnson recalls it so accurately – even down to Savage's words, which he rarely quotes from memory elsewhere – that the 'friend' who witnessed it was probably Johnson himself, and the scene may have occurred in Castle Street: 'Upon hearing the Design that was formed, he came to the Lodging of a Friend with the most violent Agonies of Rage; and being asked what it could be that gave him such Disturbance, he replied with the utmost Vehemence of Indignation, "That they had sent for a Taylor to measure him."'

Johnson says that 'the Friend' never enquired how the affair of the winter clothes ended, 'for fear of renewing his Uneasiness'.[42]

Savage's explosive sense of *amour-propre* and independence fascinated Johnson by its very irrationality. He was always dependent on charity, pensions, or hospitality from others; but he could accept nothing – especially nothing as personal as clothes – which was not presented to him with due form, and as if it was his by right; or, as Johnson put it, 'by the Right of Conquest'.[43] He insisted that the world owed it to his genius, or to his birthright.

Johnson saw that this was absurd; but he was also attracted by it. It was ridiculous, but it was also nearly heroic. It showed too how utterly fickle were the favours of the world: 'The great Hardships of Poverty were to Savage not the Want of Lodging or of Food, but the Neglect and Contempt which it drew upon him . . . his Opinion in Questions of Criticism was no longer regarded, when his Coat was out of Fashion . . .'[44]

The fame of Savage's 'tattered cloak' even reached the stage when it was featured in a two-act farce by James Miller, produced in January 1738. Miller had already ridiculed Savage at the time of his affluence in 1734, by introducing a dandified bard into his comedy *The Mother-in-Law*, who loudly introduces himself into the drawing-rooms of the rich and famous, making great play with his poetical appearance and mannerisms and relentlessly importuning for patrons.

But the figure of Mr Bays the Poet who appears in Miller's *The Coffee-House* is a far crueller caricature. He is a penniless, irascible, grandiose eccentric who has been reduced to scribbling his verses in the corner of public rooms, 'a pleasant Parnassus, truly!' Short-tempered and self-important to the point of lunacy, Bays is mocked and insulted by the other habitués:

'Sir, I say that a poet is a shabby, rhyming, impertinent ass; a fellow that flatters the living, and tells lies of the dead; that talks of nothing but heroes and kings, and converses with nobody but fiddlers and pick-pockets; a mumping hungry pimp, that's always crowding at other people's tables . . .' This, with a vengeance, is an alternative and satiric version of the Outcast Poet: Grub Street turning on its own creation, and rejoicing in Savage's fall.

Bays's infuriated replies make sly reference to Savage's reputation as a coffee-house killer, and to his attacks on Lady Macclesfield in *The Bastard*. The stage-business indicated in one of his speeches suggests that he cannot distinguish between a quill pen and a duelling sword:

Bays: 'Pimp! pimp! that's not to be suffered. – A poet a pimp! that is not to be put up. Sir, I'll have instant satisfaction. – Paper and ink, here – more ink and paper, I say. – I'll draw my pen on you this moment, Sir, and will write a satire in the modern manner, that shall transmit you, your relations, friends, and acquaintances, to all future generations, as a pack of owls, bats, thieves, scoundrels, et cetera, et cetera, et cetera ... (*Walking about in a great rage.*)[45]

Johnson does not quote from this farce, but he seems to have seen it (or heard it painfully described by Savage), for he notes how the production deliberately guyed Savage's clothes and mannerisms. 'Mr Miller so far indulged his Resentment as to introduce him in a Farce, and direct him to be personated on the Stage in a Dress like that which he then wore; a mean Insult which only insinuated, that Savage had but one Coat ...'[46] He says Savage planned to reply with a lampoon on Miller, but finally decided it was beneath him to punish 'so impotent an Assault'. Johnson felt that such attacks on a writer's poverty were infinitely wounding. As Thales says:

> Fate never wounds more deep the gen'rous Heart
> Than when a Blockhead's Insult points the Dart.[47]

It seems odd that Johnson had no knowledge of Savage's social life at Richmond with Thomson, and at Hackney with Mendez during 1738. But Savage's policy of keeping Johnson apart from his other supporters can be glimpsed in the unpublished Latin appointments diary for 1738 kept by Thomas Birch, the antiquarian and *Biographical Dictionary* writer.

What is fascinating about this diary is that it shows Birch lunching, dining and going on elegant picnic expeditions up the Thames with all the inner circle of the *Gentleman's Magazine* throughout 1738. But it never once shows Johnson and Savage *together* in the same party. A typical series of entries for August, translated from Birch's dog-Latin, reads as follows:

8 August   First meeting with Eliza Carter, the learned young spinster.

15 August   Journey to Claremont House and dine at Richmond with James Thomson, Richard Savage, and Eliza Carter. Eliza gives me her poems.

22 August   Receive a Latin letter from Eliza Carter, and sup with her and with Samuel Johnson, Author of the poem entitled London.

25 August   Escort Eliza Carter to the Museum of the Society of Antiquaries, and supped with her and Samuel Johnson.[48]

In September there is an expedition to visit the grounds of Lord Burlington's House at Chiswick, actually organised by Savage, and including Birch, Mallet and Thomson (with whom they dine), but again excluding Johnson. Similarly, in November there is a big supper at the Mendez house in Hackney, which Johnson does not attend. There are other frequent meetings with Elizabeth Carter and Johnson, but again never with Savage present. Of course the evidence of the diary is fragmentary; yet it is curious that the two friends are never once recorded in each other's company by Birch. It could be coincidence, but it gives one pause for thought.

Was Savage deliberately keeping Johnson to himself? Or did he only include Johnson in the bohemian, back-street, perambulatory side of his life, when he could give free rein to the story of his misfortunes and persecutions, without the check of those who knew him of old? Was Savage even, perhaps, slightly ashamed of introducing the outlandish, intense young provincial to his smarter friends? It is difficult to gauge, on such slight evidence, the exact shifting nuances of their social relations in 1738. But the Savage who appears in the diary and letters of Birch, however fleetingly, does not seem to be quite the same desperate, drifting, solitary figure who is conjured up by Johnson.

Johnson's account gets steadily darker as the winter of 1738 approached. He describes Savage as obsessed with a number of schemes: the extension of his royal pension, the publication of his *Collected Works* (several times advertised in the *Gentleman's Maga-*

zine), the revision of his *Tragedy* and the escape to the rural seclusion of Wales.

Johnson gradually realised that each of these schemes was invested with powerful elements of fantasy and wish-fulfilment. They were really excuses for endless dreams, talk and self-dramatisation. The scheme for the *Collected Works* was typical. 'This Project of Printing his Works was frequently revived, and as his Proposals grew obsolete, new ones were printed with fresher Dates.' Each time a subscription came in, Savage merely went to a tavern and 'squandered whatever he obtained'. But he enjoyed himself immensely, and was never happier than when drawing someone like Johnson into the game: 'To form Schemes for the Publication was one of his favourite Amusements, nor was he ever more at Ease than with any Friend who readily fell in with his Schemes, he was adjusting the Print, forming the Advertisements, and regulating the Dispersion of his new Edition, which he really intended some time to publish . . .'[49]

Johnson now saw clearly the central delusion upon which all these fantasies were based. Savage could never face up to his real situation, and take positive control of his life. His night-walks were symptomatic of his dreamlike, labyrinthine journey through his own existence. He sleep-walked to his own disaster, never recognising the endless, somnambular, repetitious pattern. These circular, traumatised steps become one of the most powerful images in the later part of Johnson's biography. The man whom Johnson had first seen as his Virgilian guide through the dark city was also a man enclosed and entranced by its nightmare. Savage was a man 'intoxicated' and enthralled by his own interior images:[50]

By imputing none of his Miseries to himself, he continued to act upon the same Principles, and follow the same Path; was never made wiser by his Sufferings, nor preserved by one Misfortune from falling into another. He proceeded throughout his Life to tread the same Steps on the same Circle; always applauding his past Conduct, or at least forgetting it, to amuse himself with Phantoms of Happiness, which were dancing before him . . .[51]

Johnson brooded uneasily on the ritual pattern and symbolism in Savage's behaviour: the darkness, the intoxication, the amnesia, the self-circling treadmill steps, the dancing seductive fantasies. In a striking phrase, he spoke of Savage having 'lulled his Imagination' with 'ideal Opiates', as if poetry were a kind of self-administered drug. It was a notion, a terror, full of Romantic premonition. But he returned to a traditional, classical trope of darkness. Savage had 'willingly turned his Eyes from the Light of Reason, when it would have discovered the Illusion, and shewn him, what he never wished to see, his real State'.[52] The darkness of the night-walk might also be that of moral blindness.

If Johnson came to see Savage's failings so clearly, as their intimacy deepened in the autumn of 1738, why did he continue to defend him retrospectively in the *Life*? This is the question that evidently haunted Boswell – particularly since it was to Boswell that the sacred baton of friendship was eventually passed; as well as the sacred duty of the biographer to tell the truth as candidly as possible. For it is a mistake to believe that Johnson did not penetrate deeply into Savage's vanity, delusions and opportunism. The most dramatic and ironic revelation of the *Life* is that Johnson gradually realised in the daily and nightly round of their Grub Street existence together in 1738 that Savage was morally incapable of friendship in its true sense. Savage could be impetuously kind and generous (especially to those worse off than himself); but he was always fickle and untrustworthy. Such a perception, which seems to challenge the whole basis of their intimacy, is given by Johnson with unflinching, melancholy realism:

'He was compassionate both by Nature and Principle, and always ready to perform Offices of Humanity; but when he was provoked, and very small Offences were sufficient to provoke him, he would prosecute his Revenge with the utmost Acrimony till his Passion had subsided. His Friendship was therefore of little Value; for though he was zealous in the Support or Vindication of those whom he loved, yet it was always dangerous to trust him, because he considered himself discharged by the first Quarrel, from all Ties of Honour or Gratitude; and would betray those Secrets which in the Warmth of Confidence had been imparted to him. This Practice drew upon him an universal Accusation of Ingratitude . . .'[53]

This rueful and damaging admission deepens our whole sense of Johnson's powers as a biographer. He is not taken in by Savage, but still extends sympathy and insight. Young Johnson's extraordinary moral intelligence, and his own largeness of heart, become pre-eminent at this moment of crisis. He accepts this truth about Savage's character, but he sees it is not the whole truth. For in addition Johnson argues that Savage had an instinct of engagement with life, and with those around him, which amounted to genius. Observing him in the coffee-houses and taverns, Johnson saw a creative faculty at work that deeply impressed him and which he was to emulate himself for the rest of his career:

'His Judgment was accurate, his Apprehension quick, and his Memory so tenacious, that he was frequently observed to know what he had learned from others in a short Time better than those by whom he was informed . . . He had the peculiar Felicity, that his Attention never deserted him; he was present to every Object, and regardful of the most trifling Occurrences . . . He mingled in cursory Conversation with the same Steadiness of Attention as others apply to a Lecture, and, amidst the Appearance of thoughtless Gaiety, lost no new idea that was started nor any Hint that could be improved . . .'54

Johnson also felt that there remained an essential goodness in Savage's character, a generosity of spirit, which despite the weaknesses he displayed, and the humiliations he had suffered, allowed him to accept people for what they were. If Savage was often disenchanted, he was never embittered by life: 'His Judgment was eminently exact both with regard to Writings and to Men. The Knowledge of Life was indeed his chief Attainment, and it is not without some Satisfaction, that I can produce the Suffrage of Savage in favour of human Nature, of which he never appeared to entertain such odious Ideas, as some who perhaps had neither his Judgment nor Experience have published, either in Ostentation of their Sagacity, Vindication of their Crimes, or Gratification of their Malice.'55

It is clear that Johnson's own emotions are strongly engaged here, and perhaps we are dealing with conscious rationalisations about their friendship. One can feel deeper, less formulated attractions at work.56 Savage's seductive powers, as already suggested, had an ambivalent sexual quality about them for both women and men. There is no evidence of a conscious homosexual element in his personality (though the obsession with his mother might suggest an unconscious one to a psychoanalyst), and indeed he seems to have had many heterosexual liaisons. Yet something about his physical elegance, his supple wit and his moments of childlike vulnerability and vanity appealed to a protective instinct in his male companions and patrons.

I am certain this was the case for young Johnson, whose tenderness and compassion are so vividly reflected in the 'partiality' (Boswell's anxious word) of the *Life*. Savage drew from Johnson emotions and impulses that had been partly blocked in his marriage with Elizabeth, and which would emerge again, years later, in his relations both with Boswell and with Hester Thrale.

Part of Savage's mysterious charm, his magical 'fascination', lay in what Eliza Haywood identified – with a novelist's swift grasp of the animating principle – as his shape-shifting, changeling quality. When Johnson records Savage 'performing' Judge Page on the bench, he hit upon this theatrical, role-playing aspect of his personality. Savage could 'become' many people, almost at will, and one suspects that this is what made much of his conversation so entrancing. (It is interesting that Johnson rarely captures this conversational flow in action, though he alludes frequently to its effect; and Boswell would take up the rendering of conversation as a major element in his own biography.)

Savage's gift for self-invention, or for mimicry, must have been an essential attribute of his wit. In literary terms this enabled him to adopt many different personae with almost alarming speed: the romantic Hermit, the satiric Bastard, the poor poet 'Alexis', the cynical Iscariot Hackney, and finally the Arcadian Thales. In terms of his private life, it allowed him to be both the dejected orphan and the glorious 'son of the late Earl Rivers'. It may also have meant that in the end he did not really know *who* he was, or to whom he belonged, or where he fitted into the world.

Johnson came to realise some of this about Savage in the course of 1738, and probably a great deal more when he came to reflect upon it as he wrote the *Life* five years later. The difference between the two degrees of knowledge – the love of the friend and the judgement of the biographer – accounts for the underlying psychological drama of his book.

What Johnson finally saw as the moral meaning of Savage's existence – the discovery of which he enshrined as the central purpose of biography – lay in the capacity of even a flawed man to struggle nobly against the misfortunes of life. Savage was 'a Man equally distinguished by his Virtues and Vices'.[57] This idea was of immense personal importance to Johnson. If we look back at the seven symbolic words chosen for his great *Dictionary*, one interpretation of their significance lies in the curve or parabola of destiny which they seem to trace. From initial hopes and elevated ambitions, through the consolations of work and love, to the final catastrophe of loneliness and self-destruction, a vivid individual spirit is battling out its fate.

That fate was hard for Savage; but it is hard for anyone. Johnson could never accept the optimism of Shaftesbury any more than he could yield to the pessimism of Hobbes. Instead he clung to the redeeming virtues which may be discovered in human compassion and stoic resolution. These became the lasting spiritual tenets of the mature Johnson. There is also the final tantalising possibility, for a writer, that his work may afterwards secure some kind of immortality. Johnson regarded this last hope with a passionate irony. In July 1743, the month before Savage eventually died, Johnson would suddenly publish in the *Gentleman's Magazine* a short poem 'The Young Author' which he later guardedly told Boswell had been composed long ago at Oxford. Yet it also seems to be a reflection on what he had learned from his friendship with Savage in 1738:

> So the young author panting for a name,
> And fir'd with pleasing hope of endless fame,
> Intrusts his happiness to human kind,
> More false, more cruel than the seas and wind.
> 'Toil on, dull crowd,' in extacy, he cries,
> 'For wealth or title, perishable prize;
> 'While I these transitory blessings scorn,
> 'Secure of praise from nations yet unborn.'[58]

The sudden collapse of Savage's affairs in the winter of 1738–9 greatly increased Johnson's concerns and doubts. It began in September, with the King's announcement confirming the late Queen's extensive list of charities and pensions which he intended to continue in her memory. Though Stephen Duck and other writers were included in this list, Savage's name was missing. Cave's campaign in the *Gentleman's Magazine* had not borne fruit, and indeed the silent, unexplained omission of the 'Volunteer Laureate' from the official listings suggests that the £50 pension had never really been recognised as a formal grant by the royal household, but was seen more as one of Queen Caroline's private charities.

Savage wrote rapidly to all his shrinking band of supporters to break the news, and one of his letters, to Thomas Birch, has survived: 'I had done myself the Honour of calling you today, but am very much in a hurry. – I take this opportunity of letting you know that I am struck out (& am the only person struck out) of the late

Queen's List of Pensions.' Though Savage realised the full implications of the disaster – for the first time in a decade he was utterly without regular income or prospects – he makes no further reference to the matter in this insouciant note to Birch. Instead he blithely concentrates on arrangements for a visit to Burlington House and gardens with Thomson, Mendez and other friends.

The bustling, airy tone of the postscript wonderfully displays Savage's ability to flourish, unblinking, on the very brink of catastrophe: 'PS. Pray put your Letter to Mr Mendez in the penny post by Eight o'Clock on Monday Morning. – But above all do not disappoint me on any Account of your Company – We all being exceeding desirous of it. – I hope you have not forgot lending Miss Carter my Author to be Let.'[59]

Johnson says that despite this show of 'unclouded Gaiety',[60] Savage actually reacted with great 'Violence' to this final disappointment, and forced himself into a morning meeting of the Prime Minister's office. Again, this seems to be a replay of the original night-trespass on his mother's house, demanding recognition: 'Mr Savage who seldom regulated his Conduct by the Advice of others, gave way to his Passion, and demanded of Sir Robert Walpole, at his Levee, the reason of the Distinction that was made between him and the other Pensioners of the Queen, with a Degree of Roughness which perhaps determined [Walpole] to withdraw what had been only delayed.'[61]

After this disastrously ill-judged intervention, all hope of a royal or government pension was permanently extinguished. By the spring of 1739 Savage was reduced to 'the lowest Degree of Distress'. It is notable that Birch's Latin diary records many suppers with Johnson and Elizabeth Carter in January and February; and the opening of James Thomson's play, *Edward and Eleanor*, in March; but never once does Savage's name appear. Johnson, who probably saw more of him at this desperate period than anyone, summarised the professional situation bluntly: 'he had now no Prospect of Subsistence but from his Play, and he knew no Way of Living for the Time required to finish it.'[62]

At this new crisis in Savage's career, the Welsh retirement scheme arose – phoenix-like – to save him from the ashes of the London glass-houses, and what Johnson clearly saw as the imminent prospect of starvation. Once again his friends rallied round, and determined to save 'injur'd Thales' at the eleventh hour: 'His Distress was now publickly known, and his Friends, therefore, thought it proper to concert some Measures for his Relief . . .'[63]

These measures, which involved establishing a kind of Savage Relief Fund, also generated a good deal of revealing correspondence, as the friends began to wonder between themselves who or what exactly they were paying for. Of particular interest are a series of letters between Pope and Ralph Allen, reflecting on the whole anomalous problem of Savage; and two letters from Savage himself to Elizabeth Carter, attempting to explain the early history of his misfortunes.

How far Johnson knew the contents of these exchanges is doubtful. It is particularly striking that Savage admitted much more about the fabrications of his early biography to Elizabeth Carter (in order to get her sympathy) than he ever admitted to Johnson. Similarly, though Johnson knew that Pope was behind the Relief Scheme, he does not seem to have understood the rueful scepticism with which it was conceived. Johnson mentions neither Pope nor Elizabeth Carter by name at this point in his *Life*, but perhaps this was for reasons of discretion.

The basic idea of the fund was that a number of well-to-do friends should club together to supply Savage with an annual allowance of £50, to replace the royal pension. Pope proposed to launch this subscription with a payment of £10, which he hoped would be matched by his philanthropic friend Ralph Allen, by Solomon Mendez, James Thomson, David Mallet and by various well-wishers in the bookselling business, including possibly Cave and Dodsley.[64] Not everyone could afford the same amount, and in the event several pulled out after a few payments. But the whole point of the subscription was to establish Savage safely in Wales, with quarterly instalments paid through an agent, thereby ensuring that he would never return to the city.

According to Savage, Pope grandly assured him that 'in a short Time, he should find himself supplied with a Competence, *without any Dependence on those little Creatures which we are pleased to call the Great*'.[65] In fact Pope's surviving letter of 18 May 1739 to Ralph Allen suggests a more hard-headed, and last-ditch, charity. The plan is presented to Allen as 'sending a Man to be Saved, both in this World & in the next (I hope). He is to cost me ten pound a year, as long as he thinks fit to live regularly, & if you will let him cost you as much, we shall want few further Aids, & I believe you don't care how long our Benevolence may last, tho' I think it can't be many years.'[66] The last phrase seems to imply that Savage had never really recovered his health.

Johnson realised that what had been the Hermit's grand ideal of rural retirement, and Thales's dream of honourable retreat ('Some secret Cell, ye Powers, indulgent give'), had dwindled down to a humiliating piece of private charity, a whip-round to send a cantankerous poet out to grass. This 'happy and independent Subsistence' was intended to force Savage 'to live privately in a cheap Place, without aspiring any more to Affluence, or having any further Care of Reputation'.[67]

Still Savage retained his fantasies. He could gladly accept the offer, though his intentions for the subscription were very different from those who proposed it. They planned 'that he should continue an Exile from London for ever, and spend all the remaining Part of his Life at Swansea'. But Savage planned merely to taste the delights of country life 'for a short Time', to rewrite his play and prepare his *Collected Works*, and then come storming back to London, and live in glory 'upon the Profits'.

Meanwhile, to avoid arrest by his creditors, Savage was directed by his benefactors to take up lodgings in the Liberties of the Fleet, a small area of streets round Ludgate in which a debtor's writ could not normally be served. Johnson evidently visited him there, for he noted Savage's efforts of economy, when the first instalments of charity arrived. They sent him 'every Monday a Guinea, which he commonly spent before the next Morning', and survived the remainder of the week 'after his usual Manner', trusting to 'the Bounty of Fortune' until Monday came round again.[68]

Savage's departure was planned for June 1739, but was continuously delayed from one week to the next. There were disagreements over the details of the allowance; rows over clothes; and last-minute attempts to seek a reconciliation with Lord Tyrconnel. Johnson seems to have had increasing doubts about the whole scheme, as it threatened to destroy Savage's sense of pride and liberty, the last things that he possessed.

Pope, perhaps realising the awkward responsibilities he was taking on as manager of the subscription, tried a diplomatic move in Tyrconnel's direction. Lady Macclesfield's legitimate daughter by Colonel Brett had recently married Sir William Leman, and Pope – a master of social manoeuvres – saw in Sir William a possible new champion for Savage's affairs. Accordingly, Pope drafted a long, tactful letter for Savage to send to Sir William, begging him to intervene on his behalf with Lord Tyrconnel. He asked Savage to copy it and despatch it without delay. Nothing could have better demonstrated the psychological chasm between Savage and his well-meaning benefactors.

Savage evidently showed the intended instrument of peace to Johnson, in one of his characteristic fits of outrage. Johnson sided wholly with Savage, and scornfully quoted extracts of Pope's letter in his *Life*, though without explicitly identifying its author. Savage was to say that he humbly 'solicited Sir William's Assistance, *for a Man who really needed it as much as any Man could well do'*; that he was 'retiring *for ever to a Place where he should no more trouble his Relations, Friends, or Enemies'*; and that he 'confessed, that his *Passion* had *betrayed* him to some Conduct, with Regard to Lord Tyrconnel, *for which he could not but heartily ask his Pardon'*.[69]

Savage refused outright to copy this letter, saying that its style was too supplicatory and abject, and that he despised Lord Tyrconnel's pardon '*and would not hypocritically ask it'*.[70] Though Johnson must have realised that this manoeuvre of Pope's was almost the only alternative to the humiliation of the subscription, he warmly applauded Savage's refusal. He thought it 'very justly observed', and Savage's response to Pope as 'full of masculine Resentment and warm Expostulations'. Savage later claimed that Pope had yielded to his arguments and agreed that the letter 'ought to be suppressed'. But Pope, who would prove generous and patient towards Savage over the final four years, later gave a very different reaction in a letter that Johnson never saw.

Looking back at this episode in 1742, Pope wrote reproachfully to Savage:

. . . What was done more in relation to the Lord [Tyrconnel], but trying a method we thought more likely to serve you, than threats and injurious language? You seemed to agree with us at your parting, to send some letters, which after all were left in your own hands, to do as you pleased . . . Indeed I was shocked at your strong declarations of *vengeance* and *violent measures* against him, and am very glad you now protest you meant nothing like what those words imported.[71]

The figure that Savage presented to Johnson in those last few weeks in London is so noble and high-principled that one might almost suspect a curious overlapping, or collusion perhaps, between art and life. One wonders if Savage had actually begun to model himself consciously on Johnson's Thales, the honourable poet driven from the corrupt city. It is almost as if Savage was trying to fulfil the ideal, poetic projection that Johnson had initially created for him in all its Juvenalian grandeur.[72] The poet was trying to live up to his own biography:

> At length awaking, with contemptuous Frown,
> Indignant Thales eyes the neighb'ring Town.[73]

Savage was shaping and adjusting his life-story up to the very eve of departure. This is revealed by two letters he now sent Johnson's fellow-contributor to the *Gentleman's Magazine*, Elizabeth Carter. Johnson never saw these letters, but Savage may well have intended him to at some later date.

Miss Carter (1717–1806) was the youngest and most prodigiously talented of all Cave's contributors, a poet and translator, who had just published her first book of verse at the age of twenty-one. She lived with her father, the Rev. Nicolas Carter, in Kent, but frequently came up to London to see Cave and dine with friends from the magazine, such as Birch and Johnson. In spring 1739 she spent several months in town. Johnson indeed seems to have been half in love with her (with his characteristic *tendresse* for attractive young bluestockings), and he composed several poems in her honour.

In 1738 he wrote to Cave: 'I have composed a Greek Epigram to Eliza, and think she ought to be celebrated in as many languages as Lewis le Grand.' He tenderly recorded a visit she made to Twickenham, in a surprisingly puckish version of the Daphne myth, 'To Eliza plucking Laurel in Mr Pope's Gardens' which contains such a roguish line as 'Cease, lovely thief! my tender limbs to wound'. (Later Johnson accorded Miss Carter the signal honour of contributing two essays to his *Rambler*, and praised her for being able to 'make a pudding as well as translate Epictetus'.[74]) Savage cannot have overlooked these affectionate overtures of the susceptible young Johnson, and for this reason perhaps he decided to enlist Elizabeth Carter's sympathies in his cause, before leaving.

That at any rate was the intention of a long letter he sent her in May, enclosing a copy of the 1727 'Newgate' pamphlet, which was to become so central to Johnson's biography. He had previously sent her his *Author to be Let* (perhaps a less well-judged choice) through Birch, but he now concentrated on rewriting the story of his early years as contained in the 'Newgate' document. He affirmed that 'as to the matters of fact contained, there are not above two or three that are false or mistaken ones'; but went on to adjust the story at numerous points concerning his supposed nurse ('quite a fictitious character'), his relations with Sir Richard Steele, Wilks the actor and Mrs Oldfield.

The overall effect of his comments was to insist on the independence of his behaviour with regard to his many patrons, throughout his life. Stress was laid on his emotional deprivations at an early age: 'The person who took care of me, and as tenderly as *the apple of her eye* (this expression is in a letter of hers, a copy of which I found many years after her decease among her papers) was one Mrs Lloyd, a lady that kept her chariot, and lived accordingly. But alas! I lost her when I was but seven years of age . . .'[75].

Savage was becomingly modest about his poetical gifts, which he said the 'Newgate' writer had over-praised. But as to what the pamphleteer 'says on my moral character, though he may have embellished even that a little too much, I hope at least that in some measure he may be thought authentic'.

All this, with its appeals and disclaimers and innocent ambiguities ('partly true, and partly not so'), shows Savage at his most beguiling. Johnson would undoubtedly have used the material verbatim if it had ever been passed on to him. But it was not, because Savage now made a terrible error in his assessment of Miss Carter.

Savage assumed she could be won over by a final paragraph of wildly hyperbolic praise. In a curious reversal of his strategy with Lady Macclesfield, he cast himself as the abject and insignificant poet at the feet of an adorable, perfect, unearthly Muse. The naïve miscalculation of this reveals much more than duplicity. It reveals delusion. Savage thought he could make Elizabeth Carter believe anything at all, simply by enchanting her with words. This much is evident as the paragraph unfurls like one of Savage's elaborate obeisances:

> Now, dear Miss Carter, will you be so good to pardon me for troubling you with so inaccurate a letter, where so much is said to so little purpose on so insignificant a subject, as the person whose Life you are going to peruse? All the merit I can discern he may pretend to, is that of being fully sensible of your transcen-

dent perfections, of desiring eagerly to copy them where he can, and of being allowed to admire them where he cannot . . .

The letter continues to the end in this style, concluding 'with utmost value and veneration', and describing Miss Carter as 'one finished master-piece of nature'.[76]

Of course, this was the age of the fulsome compliment. But Savage went to extremes, just as he went to extremes in his attacks on Lord Tyrconnel. Praise and blame, for him, seemed interchangeable currency, to be lavished as recklessly as the money which was not really his either. Words and guineas were all part of his fantasy existence, to be expended as the fit took him.

Elizabeth Carter's reply has not survived, but the clear-headed young authoress evidently accused him of bad faith and firmly instructed him to mend his ways. This emerges from Savage's second letter, which now swings back to a mode of familiar mockery, strongly reminiscent of his original attacks on Lady Macclesfield.

He insists that everything he said in praise of Miss Carter was literally true; but he insists with such vehemence that he parodies himself in the role of poetical suitor. The underlying message seems to be this: how could Elizabeth Carter have been such a fool as to believe him in the first place? Challenged in one role, Savage swiftly slips into another, and the truth of his feelings becomes impossible to guess – even, perhaps, impossible for himself:

Dear Madam, Be pleased to accept my thanks for your pious intention of making me a saint. I am truly desirous of becoming so, because, as saints, they say, are allowed the happiness of conversing with Angels, I may by that means be so blest, as in some measure to become worthy of the Conversation of Miss Carter.

I entreat you would not be so unkind as to accuse me of hyperbolical compliments. I never used one expression to you, but I always thought it fell short of your accomplished beauty, genius, learning, and virtue; nay, I farther believe, that the strongest hyperbole, in any dead or living language whatsoever, would give but a faint resemblance of those ideas which I have formed of your perfections. Believe me to be, with sincerest veneration, dear Madam, your most affectionate and devoted servant, R. Savage.[77]

If Savage had hoped to create a last-minute ally out of Elizabeth Carter, or even to strengthen his hand with Johnson, he signally failed. Her own biographer, Montagu Pennington, later remarked: 'Notwithstanding the flattery, there never was much acquaintance between Savage and Miss Carter. She never spoke of him with any regard, nor indeed much pity. She thought very ill of his moral character, and was not greatly delighted with his poetry. Perhaps it was natural to Johnson, who had been both a witness and a partaker in his distresses, to think more highly of his genius than it really deserved, but Miss Carter had no such bias, and there was nothing to make Savage particularly interesting but his misfortunes.'

Yet perhaps this verdict is too severe. One takes from this episode an impression, not of Savage's deviousness or malice but of his vanity and innocence. If the 'pious' and brilliant Miss Carter had been a little more worldly-wise, a little more humorous, she might have unlocked Savage's heart and much more of his true history. In the end this was left to Johnson alone.

As Savage's departure for Wales became imminent, Johnson's doubts about the whole scheme came crowding in. It seemed more and more like a banishment on dishonourable terms: chained to a subscription, exiled in the provinces, cut off from the Grub Street life that had so long sustained him. Moreover Johnson would lose his first great ally in the literary world. That spirit of outrage, of protest, of incorrigible survival, would be taken from him. As he had grown to know him, he felt that Savage's whole concept of rural retirement was based on his poetic fantasies of the Hermit, innocently woven in the comforts of Richmond and Greenwich, but ludicrously innocent of the realities of boorish provincial existence which he himself knew so well. Johnson gently mocked this dream of Arcadia in one of the most skilful passages in the *Life*:

As he was ready to entertain himself with future Pleasures, he had planned out a Scheme of Life for the Country, of which he had no Knowledge but from Pastorals and Songs. He imagined that he should be transported to Scenes of flow'ry Felicity, like those which one Poet has reflected to another, and had projected a perpetual Round of innocent Pleasures, of which he suspected no Interruption from Pride, or Ignorance, or Brutality.[78]

This criticism has a double irony. For Johnson himself was partly responsible for this Arcadian dream of Savage's. The year before, in *London*, he had projected precisely such a bucolic paradise as part of Thales's vision of freedom and independence. By going to the country, by settling on some splendid abandoned estate, Thales would break free from all the corruptions and compromises of the city. Food, lodgings and the sustaining beauty of the natural world would become his by right; and the night-walks of the nightmare metropolis would be metamorphosed into the sweet ramblings of a summer evening amid the song of birds. It is a Juvenalian counterpoint; but it was also one of Johnson's most romantic endorsements of Savage's hopes:

> Could'st thou resign the Park and Play content,
> For the fair Banks of Severn or of Trent;
> There might'st thou find some elegant Retreat,
> Some hireling Senator's deserted Seat;
> And stretch thy Prospects o'er the smiling Land,
> For less than rent thy Dungeons of the Strand,
> There prune thy Walks, support thy drooping Flow'rs,
> Direct thy Rivulets, and twine thy Bow'rs;
> And, while thy grounds a cheap Repast afford,
> Despise the Dainties of a venal Lord:
> There ev'ry Bush with Nature's Music rings,
> There ev'ry Breeze bears Health upon its Wings;
> On all thy Hours security shall smile,
> And bless thine Evening Walk and Morning Toil.[79]

Now that Johnson saw how this shining Arcadian prospect had shaped itself in reality for Savage, he was full of foreboding. Much of the emotion he felt on the loss of his friend must have been generated by this sense of a final delusion invading Savage's destiny, after so many other bitter failures and acts of self-destruction. There is evidence, as near as Johnson ever comes to admitting it, of passionate arguments between the two men on the practical wisdom of the subscription scheme. Savage argued there was no alternative, and that he would yet return triumphantly from the hills, like Thales. Johnson insisted that one more resolute effort to support himself, after all the disasters, would yet save the day. But Savage would only reply with his fantasies of the Hermit wandering through Arcadia.

This scene, one of the most remarkable in the biography, is

placed with touching humour a few days before Savage finally left the city. Johnson's tone is so delicate – plaintive, melancholic, mocking – that it hovers almost like the nightingale's song which it evokes. This is an absurd comparison, of course, unless one can now see what Johnson saw in his friend's mournful and enraptured face:

> With these Expectations he was so enchanted, that when he was once gently reproach'd by a Friend for submitting to live upon a Subscription, and advised rather by a resolute Exertion of his Abilities to support himself, he could not bear to debar himself from the Happiness which was to be found in the Calm of a Cottage, or lose the Opportunity of listening without Intermission, to the Melody of the Nightingale, which he believ'd was to be heard from every Bramble, and which he did not fail to mention as a very important Part of the Happiness of a Country Life.[80]

CHAPTER 9

ARCADIA

With Savage's departure for Wales in July 1739, the old intimacy was broken for ever. Johnson too immediately began planning to leave London, and there is a strong sense that he felt a chapter in his own life was over. We do not know where the tearful parting took place, but Johnson presents Savage as a hostage to fortune like himself, though with the added chain of financial dependence. 'He was furnished with fifteen Guineas, and informed, that they would be sufficient, not only for the Expence of his Journey, but for his Support in Wales for some Time ... He promised a strict Adherence to his Maxims of Parsimony, and went away in the Stage Coach; nor did his Friends expect to hear from him, till he informed them of his Arrival at Swansea.'[1]

The parsimony was, of course, imaginary. Within a fortnight, a letter arrived at Dodsley's bookshop to say that Savage was 'yet upon the Road' and could not proceed even as far as Bristol without a further remittance. Pope duly despatched all the remaining money of the annual subscription that he could obtain, and hoped to hear from him in Swansea in the autumn.

In fact Savage lingered in Bristol until 1740, using the excuse that there was an embargo on civilian shipping because of the imminent war with Spain. He postponed the delights of rural retirement for a lively round of 'publick Feasts' and invitations to the houses of the rich Bristol merchants, many of whom had heard his story and were eager to entertain such a raconteur and celebrity from London. They 'gratified his vanity', observed Johnson sadly, 'and therefore easily engaged his Affection'.[2]

Meanwhile Johnson himself set out for the Midlands, leaving Elizabeth in Castle Street and hoping to secure yet another post as a schoolmaster. One such plan was for the mastership at Appleby, near Lichfield, which was worth a mere £60 a year: some indication of his desperate desire to free himself from the toils of free-lance work for Cave. But this opportunity fell through, because he did not have the requisite MA degree, and also perhaps because of his physical disabilities. Pope was trying to help him, as he was helping Savage, though Johnson would never have considered financial aid, even at this juncture. A brief note from Pope to his friend Jonathan Richardson, the printer, placed inside a copy of Johnson's *London*, vividly suggests Johnson's position at this time: one more gifted poet defeated by the capital and doomed to provincial obscurity.

> This [*London*] is imitated by one Johnson who put in for a Publick-school in Shropshire, but was disappointed. He has an infirmity of the convulsive kind, that attacks him sometimes, so as to make him a sad Spectacle. Mr P[ope] from the Merit of this Work which was all the knowledge he had of him endeavour'd to serve him without his own application; & wrote to my Lord Gore, but he did not succeed. Mr Johnson published afterwards another Poem in Latin with Notes the whole very Humorous call'd the Norfolk Prophecy. P[ope].[3]

Failing to find work, Johnson returned to his old school-friend John Taylor, at Ashbourne; and lingered for the rest of the winter around Lichfield, carousing with Gilbert Walmsley and flirting with Molly Ashton, and wondering no doubt what had become of Savage in Arcadia. It was only on his return to London, in spring 1740, to the ailing Elizabeth, that he began to get news.

Johnson was never to see Savage again, and this loss of direct contact greatly affects the final pages of his biography. This was the section which he subsequently rewrote with such care, using materials that Edward Cave obtained from Bristol. These included a dozen or so letters and an unpublished poem, 'London and

Bristol Delineated'. For the first time Johnson had something like a continuous sequence of correspondence with which to work, and he uses this with masterly effect to construct a detailed narrative of Savage's last days.

This strong narrative framing also distances Johnson from his subject, and prepares for a final magisterial summary of Savage's character and career. So the physical distance from his old friend also produces an emotional withdrawal in the biography, and this seems to allow Johnson to concentrate more objectively on the moral dilemma posed by the whole pattern of Savage's career. The passionate advocate is subsumed in the judicial intelligence, and the reader is asked, again and again, to stand back and make a judgement. Dramatically speaking, Johnson drives steadily towards this climax, which requires both a literary and a moral decision on all that has gone before. But the final verdict is held in suspense until the very last paragraphs.

Although Johnson eventually obtained remarkably full details of Savage's Bristol days, there remain two areas in which he lacked information. The first concerns Pope's handling of the subscription, throughout the last four years, and his reflections on Savage's behaviour. The second covers the period of more than eighteen months which Savage spent in Wales between early 1740 and summer 1741, which Johnson sketches in a couple of pages, deliberately omitting Savage's last entanglement with a final Muse-figure, Mrs Bridget Jones of Llanelli.

Pope's letters, alternating between tender anxiety and maddened irritation, are probably a model of the experience undergone by all Savage's previous patrons – from Richard Steele to Lord Tyrconnel – in attempting to support Savage and cope with his irrational resentments and outrageous extravagance. Not knowing the details of Pope's involvement, month after month, Johnson sided with Savage's claims that his subscribers 'had no sooner banished him to a remote Corner, than they reduced his Allowance to a Salary scarcely equal to the Necessities of Life'.[4] In fact Savage, from the moment he took the road to Bristol, spent his allowance as fast as he received it, then wrote endless letters complaining of his treatment, so that he quickly alienated all the subscribers, with the single exception of Pope.

This situation emerges as early as December 1739, when Pope journeyed to Bristol, being himself harassed and ill, and seeking a period of peace and convalescence with Ralph Allen. On his arrival he heard that Savage was still in the city, despite his promise to go to Swansea weeks before, and causing a great stir about his ill-treatment by London friends. Significantly Pope could not face a direct confrontation with Savage in this mood, but exchanged letters with him, before swiftly escaping out of harm's way, to Bath. A letter to David Mallet, written from Bath on 17th December, clearly depicts the developing situation and foresees little peace in Arcadia:

> There [at Bristol] was Mr Savage *to be* found, but indeed I could not persuade myself to *find* him, thinking it would have given him some Confusion (as it would have given me,) to meet the face unawares of a Friend, with whom he had broken his Word. But I wrote him a very sorrowful Letter, which he answered in a higher Key than I deserved, and a much harsher than his other Friends deserved. However it ended in a promise to go in a few days to Swansea ... I have renewed my orders since for prompt payment of my part of the 'Subscription for his Retirement' (for so he calls it) to *his own hands* this Xmas. For he declares against all Measures, by which any of us pretend to put him into a 'State of Infancy', & the Care of another.[5]

This was precisely the position that Johnson had warned Savage against, when he abandoned all attempts at supporting himself. But not knowing the patience and delicacy with which Pope tried to manage Savage's finances for him at a distance, Johnson quickly assumed that his friend was being victimised once more. Savage gradually 'broke off all Correspondence with most of his Contributors, and appeared to consider them as Persecutors and Oppressors, and in the latter Part of his Life, declared, that their Conduct toward him, since his Departure from London, *had been Perfidiousness improving on Perfidiousness, and Inhumanity on Inhumanity*.'[6]

Johnson allowed for Savage's 'satirical Exaggerations' of their behaviour, but still found it difficult to vindicate their treatment of a man who, 'upon the Faith of their Promise, had gone into a kind of Banishment'. According to Johnson, Savage's situation deteriorated still further when he eventually reached Swansea in 1740, 'where he lived about a Year very much dissatisfied with the Diminution of his Salary'.[7]

In fact Johnson discovered very little about this Swansea period, during which Savage succeeded in being taken in as an honoured house-guest by a wealthy local barrister, John Powell; and paying protracted court to a celebrated local beauty, Mrs Bridget Jones. It is curious to see that in these respects Savage's final adventures among the well-to-do provincial squirearchy were not entirely unlike Johnson's own period of retirement at Lichfield, in the company of Gilbert Walmsley and Molly Aston. Johnson could have discovered indirect evidence for this late halcyon period in a number of poems which Savage sent to Cave at the *Gentleman's Magazine* in 1741, and which he certainly saw in print. But he preferred to account for these months as being largely given over to work on the new version of Savage's *Tragedy* and a last attempt to publish his *Collected Works* – by another subscription scheme, of course.

Yet Savage's dream of 'Cambria's shore' as a place for idyllic retirement had been reinforced by Johnson's Thales, with his picture of rambling manorial estates and private incomes sprouting as easily as vegetable gardens and cornfields, through which a poet might wander at his ease, plucking poetry and money from Nature's bounty. Moreover, Savage's fellow-poet John Dyer was now settled in his native Carmarthenshire, and there is some evidence that Savage used this connection to establish himself in Swansea Society, in his usual search for patrons and supporters.

His poems to John Powell and Bridget Jones suggest that his old fascination had not faded, and that for some months he was remarkably successful in the role of London celebrity, and the Arcadian existence came close to being realised. Most surprising of all, it seems that he nearly succeeded in making a Society marriage into the prosperous, landowning Jones family of Llanelli, whose estates overlooked the Bristol Channel on a beautiful bay twelve miles up the coast from Swansea on the Gower peninsula. This indeed would have been an achievement worthy of Thales.

John Powell, the barrister, was a member of one of the most influential families in Swansea, with large estates in Brecon and Radnorshire and professional connections with the Duke of Beaufort who controlled the region politically. Powell had been educated at Cambridge and was appointed successively Burgess of Swansea in 1728, Alderman in 1731 and Portreeve of the city for periods of office between 1733 and 1747. Savage's elegant panegyric to his talents and comfortable way of life was published in the *Gentleman's Magazine* in 1742.

It describes him as a generous and 'dear associate' and is clearly the tribute of poet to patron. Among the Welsh rural gentry of 'unread squires illiterately gay' Powell is witty, learned and accomplished. Most of all, he 'renders all, around him, blest' – a clear indication of Savage's gratitude for financial support and hospitality. More than this, Powell's relaxed and easy life of the country squire, withdrawn (according to Savage) from political faction and urban business, is held up as a model of the Arcadian mode, surprisingly like a Welsh version of the Hermit-figure.

Savage pictures him pacing the Carmarthenshire shoreline, stately and philosophic, having survived all the 'sudden shocks' of life – 'Love, wealth and fame (tyrannic passions all!)' – and content with 'competence, on rural plains'. Unmoved by emotional storms, he draws wisdom from everything that art, science and Nature can freely provide:

> Calm, on the beach, while madd'ning billows rave,
> He gains philosophy from ev'ry wave;
> Science, from ev'ry object round, he draws;
> From various nature and from nature's laws.
> He lives o'er ev'ry past, historic age;
> He calls forth ethics from the fabled page.[8]

For a moment Savage seems tantalisingly close to his dream, the Wanderer poised to enter safe haven after all the tempests.

But how could he secure himself permanently on the peaceful shores of Carmarthenshire? Savage must have kept quiet about the humiliations of his subscription, and decided upon a new part for 'the son of the late Earl Rivers': that of a desirable and well-connected suitor from London. We do not know exactly how he obtained a footing with the Jones family of Llanelli, but Powell obviously knew them socially ('Llannelly's *fair*' is mentioned in his poem, as a romantic reference well-understood by Powell).

Bridget Jones was then a widow of twenty-seven, her husband Thomas having died in January 1740, at the very moment of Savage's arrival in Swansea. She had one small son and a comfortable income, and was much inclined to remarry, should a suitable match appear. Indeed, she subsequently remarried twice, ending her days as the distinguished wife of the High Sheriff of the County.[9]

John Dyer too visited the town and admired the lady, whose dark-eyed melancholy beauty was renowned through the whole area, making her an object of amorous speculation and a proper subject for poetry. One local tradition says that both Dyer and

Savage whiled away summer months on an idyllic farm, Soho House, at Llanelli, the guests of William Rees, a gentleman-farmer who had been educated like Dyer at Westminster School.[10]

The story of Savage's courtship appears in a sequence of four poems which he sent to the *Gentleman's Magazine* after he had returned to Bristol, in 1742. Johnson saw all these but preferred to remain silent over the whole episode, either believing it was improper to relate or perhaps finding some subtle betrayal of the Arcadian motif, that the Outcast Poet should have come so close to worldly – and specifically sexual – happiness, in his final years. One might even wonder if, for one moment, Johnson was slightly jealous of his incorrigible old friend's romantic daring.

The first poem is formal, short and decorous, and shows Savage finding a suitable poetic *entrée* into the family's affections. It is an epitaph for Bridget's much-loved grandmother, who had recently died, and who was known for her seigneurial kindness, keeping an open table for friends and visitors alike and acting as 'the parent of the poor'. Savage unblushingly describes her as 'the friend, who spared th' assistant loan'.[11] Whether he secretly included himself among the number of her debtors, he clearly puts himself forward as an accepted friend of the household:

> . . . at her board, with decent plenty blest,
> The journeying stranger sat a welcome guest.[12]

With the next poem, Savage has leapt forward into the role of the grief-struck Hermit, wandering the Cambrian shore in search of happiness and love. Having learned from his encounter with Elizabeth Carter, he sent Bridget a more carefully chosen present: not the 'Newgate' pamphlet of his real tribulations but the poetic version of *The Wanderer*. The title of the accompanying poem points out to the eligible widow exactly how she is to regard its author: 'Verses sent to Mrs Bridget Jones, with the *Wanderer*, a Poem; alluding to an Episode, where a young Man turns Hermit, for the Loss of his Wife Olympia.'

In case this was not sufficiently clear, Savage eloquently explained his intentions in a tremulous stanza (one cannot help wondering if he had actually provided himself with a lost wife, as well as a lost mother, for this occasion):

> Tell her, my muse, in soft, sad, sighing breath,
> If she his piercing grief can pitying see,

Worse, than to him was his OLYMPIA's death,
From her each moment's absence is to me.[13]

We know nothing of Bridget Jones's response to this overture, or for how long during 1740 and 1741 Savage pressed home his suit. But press home he did, for his next poem, 'The Employment of Beauty', is an 85-line enumeration of her physical charms, starting in businesslike fashion with her feet ('these curious pedestals') and continuing upwards via 'faultless' waist, 'snow-white' hands, 'blushing' nipples and 'crescent' ears, to a pair of 'lucid' shoulders spread with magnificent hair which 'softens light with shade'.[14]

The 'sublime' descriptive style of this love-poem is so gloriously mannered – Mrs Jones's nostrils are presented as 'two little porches' drawing in 'aromatic flowers' – that one suspects Savage of a secret parody, which the innocent widow was not entirely intended to perceive. Either that, or Savage, in one more transformation, was throwing himself into the traditional role of the Welsh bard, whose linguistic ingenuity was supposed to carry all before it by sheer virtuosity. One has a glimpse of 'the son of the late Earl Rivers', his cloak tossed back over his shoulder, reciting passionately in a candlelit Llanelli drawing-room.

Savage's last poem, which appears to date from February 1742, is a valediction to Bridget Jones couched in the form of a Valentine's Day verse-letter. We learn from this that his suit has been rejected, and that he is about to leave Wales:

> Cambria farewell! – my Chloe's charms no more
> Invite my steps along Llannelley's shore . . .
> I watch'd the seas, I pac'd the sands with care,
> Escap'd, but wildly rush'd on beauty's snare.
> Ah! – better far, than by that snare o'erpower'd,
> Had sands engulph'd me, or had seas devour'd.[15]

This poem returns to the passionate, autobiographical manner of *The Wanderer*, and one is particularly surprised that Johnson did not quote from it, since the theme of the lost Arcadia re-emerges strongly, as the magic place which 'wraps sweet ruin in resistless spells'. His silence is perhaps explained by another of Savage's strange dream-sequences in which he imagines himself making love to Bridget, in the transparent guise of Adonis making love to his 'Chloe'. The passage has a physical energy and explicitness which reflects genuine sexual passion, recalling some of Savage's early

'Songs', and probably intended both to shock Bridget Jones and to reproach her:

> All she resigns, as dear desires incite,
> And rapt he reach'd the brink of full delight.
> Her waist compress'd in his exulting arms,
> He storms, explores, and rifles all her charms;
> Clasps in extatic bliss th' expiring fair,
> And, thrilling, melting, nestling, riots there.[16]

The entire episode, though it is only a partial glimpse of Savage's struggles to find happiness in Wales, suggests how powerfully his fantasies still drove him on, just as Johnson had feared. But it also reveals something of Savage's restless sexual nature, which Johnson found less easy to write about, precisely because it echoed the profound dissatisfactions in his own heart.

As a friend, Johnson had submerged his own sexual feelings into Savage's fantasies about his mother. Her refusal of social recognition had been made to embody the entire pattern of emotional rejection in Savage's life. Johnson shared this burden as far as he could with Savage, and responded to it with all the loyalty that masculine complicity allowed. But as a biographer it sometimes forced upon him these strange, decorous silences, when he felt it improper and inappropriate to write what – after all – he must have known about his friend's dreams and sufferings. Savage had sought love in Arcadia, and once again the poet had been cast out.

So Johnson says nothing. His whole account of the Swansea period amounts to this: Savage 'contracted, as in other Places, Acquaintance with those who were most distinguished in that Country, among whom he has celebrated Mr Powell and Mrs Jones, by some Verses which he inserted in the *Gentleman's Magazine*'.[17]

No one really knows when, or under what circumstances, Savage finally returned from Swansea to Bristol. On the evidence of the 'Valentine's Day' poem, it could have been any time between spring 1741 and spring 1742. Perhaps Savage shuffled between the two ports, across the Bristol Channel, exploiting hospitality as he had done before between Richmond and London. Pope mentions sending extra money at Christmas 1741, though made 'peevish' by Savage's 'strange behaviour', which suggests a hint of the affair with Mrs Jones. 'I was in haste to relieve him, tho' I think nothing will relieve him.'[18] Several of the contributors to the subscription had by now ceased payment, including Solomon Mendez, offended by Savage's rudeness and continual demands for further financing.

In April 1742 Pope wrote to Ralph Allen, sending replacement funds but admitting a good deal of irritation. 'Pray forward the enclosed to the simple Man it is directed to. I could not bring myself to write to him sooner, & it was necessary to tell him how much I disapproved of his language and conduct. – What a pleasure it had been to me had he been a better Man whom my small Charity had been a true relief to: or were he less miserable, that I might bestow it better without abandoning him to Ruin.'[19] Pope's use of 'simple' – in its original sense of 'foolish' – is now intentionally cutting.

Johnson says that Savage finally came back to Bristol when he had completed the new version of *Sir Thomas Overbury*, and began making plans to have it staged in London. But when Edward Cave obtained the manuscript of the play, six years after Savage's death, it was found to be unfinished.[20] Johnson adds that when Savage proposed to bring the play to London himself, this scheme was 'warmly opposed' by Pope who wanted to prevent him returning to the capital. Instead, Pope advised him 'to put it into the hands of Mr Thomson and Mr Mallet, that it might be fitted for the Stage, and allow his Friends to receive the Profits, out of which an annual Pension should be paid him'.[21]

According to Johnson, Savage rejected this suggestion with 'the utmost Contempt'. He felt that his subscribers were trying to keep him '*in Leading-strings*', and were dishonourably proposing 'to *pension him out of the Profits of his own Labours*'[22] Certainly, had the play been finished, such a plan looked very much as if Pope and the others were manipulating Savage like a child, and by withholding money attempting to prolong his 'Banishment' as long as possible.

But again, Johnson was not aware of Pope's side of this correspondence. A rather different picture emerges from a letter which Pope sent to Savage in September 1742, by which time Savage had evidently been in Bristol for several months. Pope looks back at the whole sorry saga of Savage's retirement, reasons patiently with him and quietly defends his fellow-subscribers. Had Johnson seen this letter, he would have found Savage's case less easy to argue.

I am sorry to say there are in your letter so many misunderstandings, that I am weary of repeating what you seem determined not to take rightly. I once more tell you, that neither I, nor any one who contributed at first to assist you in your retirements, ever desired you should stay out of London, for any other reason than that your debts prevented you staying in it.

No man desired to confine you to the country, but that the little they contributed might support you better there than in a town. It was yourself who chose Swansea for your place; you no sooner objected to it afterwards (when Mr Mendez stopt his allowance, upon complaint that you had used him ill) but I endeavoured to add to it, and agreed to send remittances to any other country place you pleased. I indeed apprehended Bristol was too great a city to suit a frugal expence; however I sent thither all I could, and now with as good a will, I add this little more at your desire, which I hope will answer the end you propose of making easy your journey to London. I heartily wish you may find every advantage, both in profit and reputation, which you expect from your return and success; not only on the stage, but in everything you shall commit to the press.[23]

It is difficult to mistake the kindness of this. Pope enclosed a bill for five guineas, which would easily have covered the stagecoach fare to London, had Savage cared to use it for such purpose.

It is only over the matter of the play that Pope reveals real exasperation. 'What mortal would take your play ... out of your hands, if you could come, and attend to it yourself? It was only in defect of that, these offices of the two gentlemen you are so angry at, were offered. What interest but trouble could they have had in it?'[24]

However, this note is softened when Pope adds that though the other subscribers cannot be prevailed upon to continue his pension in London, he himself 'could contribute to assist' Savage there, if he could be satisfied that it would be 'effectually so'. None of this seems very much like banishment. One can well understand the weary sigh with which Pope remarked in a covering note to Allen that 'Savage plagues me with his Misunderstandings & Miseries together'.[25]

In fact, one may wonder if Savage had any real plans to leave Bristol in 1742. Johnson remarks that on his return from Swansea 'he was not only caressed and treated' with all the splendour of his previous visit, 'but had a Collection made for him of about thirty

Pounds' – more than his whole annual subscription from London put together.[26]

Yet by the end of the year, the old pattern of his city life reasserted itself. 'All the Charms of his Conversation could not compensate' for his hopeless irregularity as a house-guest. He harassed friends with his 'nocturnal Intrusions'; he exhausted them with his talk and his drinking; and he finally repelled them with his endless schemes and demands. His clothes, like his novelty value, started to wear thin. He began to be pursued by small debtors, and slowly reverted to the tramp-like existence of his former days, lodging at taverns and wandering the streets at night.

Here Johnson resumes his narrative with a sombre power that gathers force steadily to the very end of his biography. We feel him living with Savage's humiliation, following his footsteps through the city, and carrying us with him on the endless, fatal round. 'While he was thus spending the Day in contriving a Scheme for the Morrow, Distress stole upon him by imperceptible Degrees . . . He now began to find every Man from home at whose House he called; and was, therefore, no longer able to procure the Necessaries of Life, but wandered about the Town slighted and neglected, in quest of a Dinner, which he did not always obtain.'[27]

Harassed by debtors, repulsed by friends, Savage reverted to a nocturnal existence, his health declining from lack of food and sunlight. 'His Custom was to lye in Bed the greatest Part of the Day, and to go out in the Dark with the utmost Privacy, and after having paid his Visit, return again before Morning to his Lodging, which was in the Garret of an obscure Inn. Being thus excluded on one hand, and confined on the other, he suffered the utmost Extremities of Poverty, and often fasted so long, that he was seized with Faintness, and had lost his Appetite, not being able to bear the smell of Meat, 'till the Action of his Stomach was restored by a Cordial.'[28]

This grim, lethargic life was partly forced on Savage by municipal laws, which prevented bailiffs arresting anyone for debt between the hours of sunset and sunrise. Night thus became the only time Savage could venture out from his hiding-place, which was a back-street tavern called the White Lion. He was also drinking heavily, and one may suspect in the grip of terrible moments of suicidal depression. He was forty-four, and his whole glorious career of adventure had dwindled down to nothing.

Johnson probably feared the depression more than any other part of Savage's sufferings. Solitude, poverty, the cold of winter, the pains of hunger and the sick hangovers from drinking, were as nothing compared to those visitations of suicidal horror that Savage had so unforgettably described in *The Wanderer*. Johnson's reaction was resolutely to deny that Savage ever gave way to them.

In reality, he cannot have known exactly how Savage coped with these dark hours; but Johnson now writes as if he were standing by Savage's shoulder. 'It is observable,' he says with the force of an eyewitness, 'that in these various Scenes of Misery, he was always disengaged and cheerful; he at some Times pursued his Studies, and at others continued or enlarged his epistolary Correspondence.' Johnson even attempts a sorrowful witticism to show Savage's indomitable spirits. Savage was never 'so far dejected' that he ever tried to procure an increase in his subscription 'by any other Methods than Accusations and Reproaches'.[29] In Johnson's eyes, Savage remained staunchly in his role as the Outcast and Accuser, always refusing to beg or demand pity.

At least in his outward bearing, Savage may have justified his friend's belief. An explosive note from him arrived at Ralph Allen's in December, which prompted an answering outburst from Pope when he heard of it. 'I am vexed at this wrongheaded Fool, for troubling You, & I hope You'll discourage such correspondence.' Nevertheless Pope, who had heard rumours of the threatening bailiffs, hastily despatched yet another five pounds to Savage, and urged him to extricate himself.[30] Johnson did get to hear of this remittance, and stoically observed the result: 'In this Distress he received a Remittance of five Pounds from London, with which he provided himself a decent Coat, and determined to go to London, but unhappily spent his Money at a favourite Tavern. Thus he was again confined to Bristol, where he was every Day hunted by Bailiffs.'[31] As it turned out, this was Savage's last chance to escape from Bristol.

Johnson accepted the fact that *any* available funds would inevitably be spent in a tavern by this stage in Savage's decline. This sense of an unavoidable destiny is oddly emphasised by a printer's error that crept into the second edition of the *Life*. The figure of five pounds was mistakenly changed to 'fifty', and although Johnson both corrected and annotated this edition carefully he overlooked the tenfold increase in the size of Pope's supposed emergency payment. He thus allowed it to appear that Savage had spent an entire annual subscription within a few days on clothes and drink. In reading over his own narrative of Savage's 'unhappy' extravagance,

Johnson simply missed the discrepancy because it was exactly what Savage might have done anyway.

On the night of 10th January 1743, Savage slipped out from the White Lion to dine with one of his few remaining friends in the city, William Saunders, a minor canon of the cathedral. Saunders, who had been educated at Balliol, seems to have had his own drink-related problems, for he subsequently lost his post in April.[32] The party went on so long that when Savage staggered back to his inn after dawn he was surprised by a group of bailiffs waiting for him on the stairs. He was arrested for a debt of eight pounds, brought against him by a certain Mrs Read who owned a coffee-house in Princes Street. Savage said at the time that his whole finances amounted to 'three Pence halfpenny'.

He was taken to the bailiff's office, a kind of private prison, where he was held for five days, to see if he could raise bail before being committed to the public jail. Even at this juncture Savage's charm did not fail him: the bailiffs treated him 'with the utmost Civility', did not inform the management of the White Lion of his predicament and allowed him complete freedom to write letters and send messages.

Savage accepted his arrest with extraordinary equanimity. It seems almost to have been a relief to him. Comfortably housed and fed by the bailiff's office, he could now revert to his most familiar role, that of the persecuted poet who defies his destiny with mag-nificent nonchalance. Johnson was so struck by this reaction that he illustrated it by one of the longest single quotations from Sav-age's letters which the *Life* contains. It is taken from the missive which Savage sent to William Saunders on the morning after his arrest, which Johnson felt – surely correctly – was 'too remarkable to be omitted'.

In the first Place I must insist, that you will industriously conceal this [arrest] from Mrs S——; because I would not have her good Nature suffer that Pain, which, I know, she would be apt to feel on this Occasion. Next I conjure you, dear Sir, by all the Ties of Friendship, by no Means to have one uneasy Thought on my Account; but to have the same Pleasantry of Countenance and unruffled Serenity of Mind, which (God be praised!) I have in this, and have had in a much severer Calamity. Furthermore, I charge you, if you value my Friendship as truly as I do yours, *not* to utter, or even harbour the least Resentment against Mrs

Read. I believe she has ruin'd me, but I freely forgive her; and (tho' I will never more have any Intimacy with her) would, at a due distance, rather do her an Act of Good, than ill Will. Lastly, (pardon the Expression) I *absolutely command* you not to offer me any pecuniary Assistance, nor to attempt getting me any from any one of your Friends.[33]

What is remarkable is not merely the effortless pose that Savage strikes, but the transparent implication that Saunders will do *exactly the opposite* of what Savage requests, in every detail. The letter amounts to a businesslike list of everything that Saunders should immediately do and feel on Savage's behalf; but the commands are issued in splendid negatives. One feels that the arrest has actually lifted Savage out of his sense of depression and dreadful obscurity, and induced a state of mania. Once again he has become a cause, a notoriety, an issue.

As on the previous occasion of his arrest for murder (that 'much severer Calamity'), he is all-commanding and all-forgiving. He will be as magnanimous to Mrs Read as he was once to Jane Leader, even though both have 'ruined' him. One wonders incidentally about that 'Intimacy': the virulence with which Mrs Read subsequently pursued her lawsuit – Savage was soon calling her 'Madam Wolf-Bitch' – suggests the possibility of a last sexual entanglement.

The arrest had finally restored to Savage, by a peculiar paradox, his ideal of aristocratic status and poetic destiny. God had willed that 'the son of the late Earl Rivers' should suffer at exactly this date and in this fashion. It is on this exalted note that Savage concludes his letter to Saunders.

The civil Treatment I have thus far met from those, whose Prisoner I am, makes me thankful to the Almighty, that, tho' He has thought fit to visit me (on my Birth-night) with Affliction; yet (such is his great Goodness!) my Affliction is not without alleviating Circumstances. I murmur not, but am all Resignation to the *divine Will*. As to the World, I hope that I shall be endued by Heaven with that Presence of Mind, that serene Dignity in Misfortune, that constitutes the Character of a true Nobleman; a Dignity far beyond that of Coronets; a Nobility arising from the just Principles of Philosophy, refined and exalted, by those of Christianity.[34]

It is no surprise to find that within a few weeks of this Olympian epistle, Savage had quarrelled bitterly with that 'poor creature' Saunders and dismissed him as a thoroughly 'worthless fellow'.[35] He had probably made the mistake of taking Savage at his word.

At all events, Savage obtained no bail, and was committed to the debtors' section of the Bristol Newgate Prison. He was to remain there for the last six months of his life, while Mrs Read's lawsuit came up regularly before the courts, in May, June and July, but was never concluded.

By a peculiarity of the eighteenth-century debtors' legislation, it emerges that Savage's subsistence was paid for by Mrs Read herself, and must eventually have cost her quite as much as the original debt at issue. On Savage's side it appears that he frequently had sufficient funds to discharge at least part of the debt: one gift of five guineas somehow arrived from Beau Nash in Bath, an indication that the author of *The Bastard* still had his fashionable connections. But Savage chose deliberately to refuse payment, on the grounds that it was beneath his dignity to obtain his freedom through charity.

Johnson again uses Savage's letters to show how characteristically the humiliation of imprisonment was transformed into martyrdom. When a circle of Bristol acquaintances offered a collection of money to release him, he refused the proposal with 'Disdain'. Urged to apply to other friends in London, he announced that this would amount to writing 'mendicant Letters'. He would only accept release by the reinstatement of what he regarded as proper acknowledgement of his social claims. '. . . He had too high a Spirit, and determined only to write to some Ministers of State, to try to regain his Pension.'[36]

As to his original subscribers, they had '*lost the Profits of his Play which had been finished three Years*', and he would publish a pamphlet to unveil their infamy and '*how he had been used*'.[37] His imprisonment steadily became a fantasy of self-justification.

In fact, part of Savage's strategy was to hide his real state and to keep secret both his incarceration in Newgate and his rapidly declining health from those he regarded as most influential in London. While he wrote angry, high-handed letters to Pope which completely omitted all reference to his imprisonment, he also sent desperate requests to other friends to keep his Newgate address silent and provide him with immediate money.

One of the most mysterious of these requests refers to a sister, at an unknown London lodgings, who will surely help him once apprised of his terrible position. 'For God's sake call on my dear sister and let her know the state of my affairs.'[38] If this was a natural sister, referred to years later by Benjamin Victor as living in Dublin and married to the sculptor John Vannost, then this is the nearest we come to a glimpse of Savage's true birth. It is possible that in a moment of desperation he had let slip a vital fragment of his hidden past. But equally Savage could be referring, in his imperious fashion, to Bessy Rocheford or even Lady Macclesfield's legitimate daughter Marguerite. We cannot tell, and Johnson certainly knew nothing of this puzzling last clue.[39]

In April, Savage received what appears to be a final dismissal from Pope. The date is uncertain, but it strongly suggests that Pope still had no idea of the imprisonment at this time. Savage had simply become intolerable in his demands and his accusations.

Sir, I must be sincere with you, as our correspondence is now likely to be closed. Your language is really too high, and what I am not used to from my superiors; much too extraordinary for me, at least sufficiently so, to make me obey your commands, and never more presume to advise or meddle in your affairs, but leave your own conduct entirely to your own judgement.[40]

It is likely, none the less, that Savage continued to write, though there is no record of any further gifts from Twickenham. Johnson believed that one last letter arrived from Pope just a few days before Savage's death, containing 'a Charge of very atrocious Ingratitude'. It is impossible to believe Pope would have written this had he known of Savage's real circumstances. Johnson says that Savage returned 'a very solemn Protestation of his Innocence, but however appeared much disturbed at the Accusation'.[41]

Johnson clearly blamed Pope for his behaviour, but the evidence of the letters which he did not see suggests that all along Pope had acted with exceptional generosity and forbearance. He was in reality one of Savage's last true friends. But for Johnson, the idea that Savage was abandoned in his last extremity seemed intolerable.[42]

Nothing impressed Johnson more than Savage's ability to adapt to the daily life of the Newgate jail. He accepted his confinement with apparent good humour, 'recover'd his usual Tranquillity, and cheerfully applied himself to more inoffensive Studies'.[43] He wrote letters and poetry, received visitors, 'and diverted himself in the Kitchen with the Conversation of the Criminals'. He was 'always ready to perform any Offices of Humanity to his fellow Prisoners'.[44]

Savage made one last conquest for his cause, in some ways the most remarkable of all. He completely captivated the hard-bitten, long-serving Keeper of Bristol Newgate, Abel Dagge. Much of Johnson's information about Savage's last weeks came from Mr Dagge, who evidently fell under the spell of his distinguished poet-prisoner, allowed him a very free regime, and even secretly attempted to obtain his release by offering Mrs Read a three guinea down-payment on Savage's debt from his own purse. It was refused, with the comment that she was determined to keep Savage in confinement for 'a twelvemonth'.[45]

The result, as Johnson tenderly records, was an extraordinary last period of security, 'a Freedom from Suspense, and Rest from the disturbing Vicissitudes of Hope and Disappointment', which amounted almost to happiness. It was as if Savage had finally found a home, and a father-figure to look after him. 'He was treated by Mr Dagge, the Keeper of the Prison, with great Humanity; was supported by him at his own Table without any certainty of Recompense, had a Room to himself, to which he could at any Time retire from all Disturbance, was allowed to stand at the Door of the Prison, and sometimes taken out into the Fields; so that he suffered fewer Hardships in the Prison, than he had been accustomed to undergo in the greatest part of his Life.'[46]

The irony here, which Johnson could appreciate more than any other, was that Savage actually found his long-dreamed Arcadia in the conditions of his final incarceration. Not only did Abel Dagge befriend him and take care of him, he also took the sick man for long walks in the countryside, talking and drinking along the way, as Savage always loved to do. Several of these expeditions are mentioned in Savage's letters, and the note of pastoral pleasure emerges with the old, childlike simplicity of the Wanderer's happiest moments:

One day last week Mr Dagge, finding me at the Door, asked me to take a walk with him, which I did a mile beyond Baptist Mill in Gloucestershire; where, at a public-house, he treated me with ale and toddy. Baptist Mill is the pleasantest walk near this city. I found the smell of the new-mown hay very sweet, and every breeze was reviving to my spirits . . .[47]

If this was not exactly the state of rural contentment that Thales had imagined, Savage celebrated it none the less and saw himself as strangely blessed. He wrote one other letter, to an unidentified 'Friend' in London, which Johnson quotes at length as an example of his 'Fortitude' and unbroken poetic belief in himself.

Johnson does not say who the 'Friend' was. But the play which Savage makes in this letter, with the theme of the Nine Muses and the singing birds – and particularly the nightingale – seems to recall unmistakably their last conversation before his departure from London four years previously. One would like to believe that this was Savage addressing his old friend one last time, and teasing him with the paradox of his Arcadian destiny, about which they had so often argued in the toils of Grub Street:

> I now write to you from my Confinement in Newgate . . . where I enjoy myself with much more Tranquillity than I have known for upwards of a twelvemonth past; having a Room entirely to myself, and persuing the Amusement of my poetical Studies, uninterrupted and agreeable to my Mind. I thank the Almighty, I am now all collected in myself, and tho' my Person is in Confinement, my Mind can expatiate on ample and useful Subjects, with all the Freedom imaginable. I am now more conversant with the Nine than ever; and if, instead of a Newgate Bird, I may be allowed to be a Bird of the Muses, I assure you, Sir, I sing very freely in my Cage; sometimes indeed in the plaintive Notes of the Nightingale; but, at others, in the chearful strains of the Lark.[48]

The last poem Savage wrote in Newgate, still unpublished at the time of his death in August 1743, was however a bitter satire. This was 'London and Bristol Delineated', a poem largely intended as an attack on all those who had failed to come to his aid in Bristol:

> In a dark Bottom sunk, O Bristol now,
> With native Malice, lift thy low'ring Brow! . . .
> What Friendship can'st thou boast? what Honours claim?
> To Thee each Stranger owes an injur'd Name . . .
> Thy Sons, though crafty, deaf to Wisdom's Call;
> Despising all Men and despis'd by all.
> Sons, while thy Cliffs a ditch-like River laves,
> Rude as thy Rocks, and muddy as thy Waves . . .[49]

Savage circulated this poem in manuscript, and it was said to have so offended the City Fathers that a group of Bristol merchants 'by way of revenge' were clubbing together to oppose Savage's release at the July court hearing by maintaining his legally-required prison subsistence in perpetuity.[50] When he sent a copy to the *Gentleman's Magazine* even Edward Cave refused to publish it, on the grounds that it imperilled his release and even perhaps his life. Johnson too exclaimed at its astonishing imprudence. 'A Prisoner! supported by Charity! . . . he could forget on a sudden his Danger, and his Obligations, to gratify the Petulance of his Wit, or the Eagerness of his Resentment, and publish a Satire by which he might reasonably expect, that he should alienate those who then supported him, and provoke those whom he could neither resist nor escape.'[51]

Yet Johnson also saw that this final act of defiance was perfectly in accord with everything that had gone before. Even in death, Savage 'returned Reproach for Reproach, and Insult for Insult', and maintained his fighting stance, the sword of his wit untipped against the society that had rejected him. Johnson acknowledged this by printing the poem in full in the last pages of his *Life*.

If this was an act of loyalty to Savage, it may also have been a recognition of something far deeper than satire which the poem contained. Johnson drew particular attention to the 'Spirit and Elegance' of the first part of the verse, which does not concern Bristol at all, but rather looks back at his happy memories of London. It draws, in particular, a magical picture of the River Thames, an image of power and wealth, effortlessly bringing the riches of the world to the quaysides of the capital.

In this image, Savage seems to revert to his earliest dreams of fame and glory. To Johnson it must have instantly recalled his conversations with Thales at Greenwich, and their first meetings along the great river-bank when friendship was pledged and Arcadia glimpsed:

> Now silver Isis bright'ning flows along,
> Echoing from Oxford's Shore each classic Song;
> Then weds with *Tame*; and these, O London, see
> Swelling with naval Pride, the Pride of Thee!
> Wide deep unsullied *Thames* meand'ring glides
> And bears thy Wealth on mild majestic Tides . . .
> Social, not selfish, here, O Learning trace
> Thy Friends, the Lovers of all human Race![52]

This was the last poem that Savage wrote. It contains no other revelations of his past, no claims, no promises, no greetings. Death came suddenly, taking him, as so often in his life, unaware of his predicament. As Johnson says, 'all his Schemes' were suddenly destroyed.[53]

Savage was seized with a pain in his 'Back and Side' which was 'not suspected to be dangerous', but he retired to his room 'growing daily more languid and dejected'. He rapidly became feverish, and despite all Abel Dagge's ministrations slipped into a coma. The little we know of his symptoms suggests liver failure, probably brought on by drinking. Johnson narrates his end with studied care and simplicity, but suggests some mystery that still haunted his final moments.

The last Time that the Keeper saw him was on July the 31st, 1743; when Savage seeing him at his Bed-side said, with an uncommon Earnestness, *I have something to say to you, Sir*, but after a Pause, moved his Hand in a melancholy Manner, and finding himself unable to recollect what he was going to communicate, said *'Tis gone*. The Keeper soon after left him, and the next Morning he died. He was buried in the Church-yard of St Peter, at the Expence of the Keeper.[54]

The overwhelming impression of this quiet death-scene is that Johnson bitterly regretted not being at Savage's bedside himself, to take that hand and hear that last secret.

Johnson concludes his *Life* with a careful summary of all Savage's contradictions and with a noble assertion of his genius. If he was frequently a vain and self-deluded man, and an untrustworthy friend, yet the hardships he suffered should make us forgive him. 'For his Life, or for his Writings, none who candidly consider his Fortune, will think an Apology either necessary or difficult.'[55]

It is the testimony of an enduring intimacy, which no amount of moral censure had finally shaken. One might say that against his better judgement – against his judgement as a biographer – young Johnson stood with his friend in defiance of the whole eighteenth-century world.

Yet in his closing lines there lies a curious irony. Johnson does appear to revert to the traditional eighteenth-century idea of biography as a moral exemplum. From this perspective, Savage's whole career must be condemned, for it shows that 'nothing will supply the Want of Prudence, and that Negligence and Irregularity, long continued, will make Knowledge useless, Wit ridiculous, and Genius Contemptible'.[56]

Those are the words on which the biography, as we now have it, actually ends. Is it, at the very last, a damnation?

It would be easy to think so, and to find the great Boswellian moralist finally in the ascendant. As so often in this story, there is just one fragment – a single word scrawled on a manuscript – which challenges the conventional conclusion, and tips the drama back towards its essential human mystery.

When Johnson was correcting his *Life* for the second edition, he wrote against that final, sad, dismissive passage the one word: 'Added'. This was not how he had originally intended to conclude his biography. It was a solemn, placatory afterthought; a conciliatory gesture to the forces of social opinion, which became so powerful in his own life.

His original ending, which stands now as the penultimate paragraph, had been altogether different. It defiantly evokes the world of Grub Street, his own world, and romantically challenges the reader to accept the conditions of Savage's existence. It urges empathy before judgement. 'Those are no proper Judges of his Conduct who have slumber'd away their Time on the Down of Plenty, nor will a wise Man easily presume to say, "Had I been in Savage's Condition, I should have lived, or written, better than Savage."'[57]

Through the force of Johnson's art, it is these words that are always remembered and quoted as his real conclusion about Richard Savage.

CHAPTER 10

CHARON

According to Pope's letters, there was a ferryman called Holmes who ran the boats up the Thames from Hungerford Stairs, near Charing Cross, to Richmond.[1] I identify with this shadowy, background figure who carried goods and messages along the river which runs so powerfully through the heart of Savage's story. The biographer is a kind of ferryman, perhaps even a kind of Charon, crossing back and forth between the Past and Present, over the dark river of Oblivion. Now, briefly, I want this ferryman to speak *in propria persona* of what he experienced in Johnson and Savage's company, and how he tried to give an account of it.

This book is not a complete biography of either writer, but the fragment of two lives brought together for a period of some two years. I have tried to approach this central period of intimacy – that so puzzled Hawkins and Boswell – from a number of different angles, to throw as much light as possible on what is really an astonishing lack of solid evidence or definite fact. It must never be forgotten that this is the story of a friendship which lacks all the normal biographical sources. There are no authenticated letters between the two men, no mention of each other in private journals, not even a single surviving account from an eyewitness of seeing the two in each other's company. It was, as I have said, an invisible friendship from the start.

Savage's story, as first presented in his imaginary obituary, has a strong and even melodramatic plot. But the simple chronology of his life has not entirely shaped my own narrative. I have instead looked at the overall outline of his life through various retellings, and in terms of carefully varied perspectives: Johnson's early romantic longings and frustrations; the legend of the night-walks; the theme of the cruel mother; the creation of the Outcast Hermit-bard; the representative episode of the trial for murder and Johnson's defence; the problems of eighteenth-century patronage; and the dream of Arcadia which acted so powerfully and so differently on both men.

At the same time I have tried to give the sparest, most sharply focused account of their friendship and Johnson's complex and subtle shifts of empathy and antagonism towards Savage. To do this, I have found myself constantly cutting away the period setting, removing the elements of historical furniture and dress, to avoid anything like a pageant novel of eighteenth-century life and manners. Though there are glimpses of eighteenth-century London, of the rumbustious world of the theatre, the magazines, and Opposition politics, these have been deliberately reduced to the thinnest of backdrops. Instead I have tried to see Johnson and Savage almost as our contemporaries, living before our eyes, creating their own intensely atmospheric world of hope, ambition, suffering and endurance. It is the quality of that friendship I have tried to carry back, over the dark river, and the impact it has had on the art of biography ever since.

It is fair to say that the picture that emerges does not agree with much current Johnsonian scholarship, still shaped as it is by the overwhelming figure that Boswell so magnificently created. My view of young Johnson's frustrated but impassioned sexual nature, his romanticism and credulity, his emotional and moral instability, is not the conventional one. Certain specific points, like the role of the Thales-figure in defining Savage, may be challenged. All I can say is that I have given the evidence as I have found it, and allowed the story to create its own emotional and artistic logic.

No doubt Johnson changed and matured a great deal in the years before he met Boswell at Davies bookshop in Covent Garden in 1763. But the friendships formed in our early years are sometimes the most profound and the most revealing; and this friendship is the one that I believe influenced Johnson for the rest of his life as a writer. If it does not quite fit the great Johnsonian image, then this small fragment of biography may slightly alter it hereafter. The ferryman delivers his cargo as best he can, and sets it down on the shore to await valuation.

Previous biographers, including Boswell, have made the central mystery of Savage turn on the question of his birthright. Were his claims true or false? This fixation with a question that can never finally be answered – though I have summarised some of the considerations in an Appendix – has obscured what I believe has always been the real enigma. It is why young Johnson, along with many others, was so fascinated by Savage that he was instinctively prepared to believe him. Something about Savage, and his ability to exploit or live out the image of the unrecognised and persecuted man of genius, held Johnson – and Johnson's age – in a grip of guilty enchantment. I have tried to show this enchantment at work, and to suggest that against all expectation it heralds the coming of the Romantic generation.

I believe in fact that biography itself, with its central tenet of empathy, is essentially a Romantic form; and that Johnson's friendship with Savage first crystallised its perils and its possibilities.

In the process of transforming that friendship into a *Life* Johnson brought a new and recognisably modern English genre into being. It was no longer based on classical models – Plutarch, Tacitus, Sallust – even though Johnson would still claim their authority for his use of intimate detail to display character (as in his famous apologia for biography in *Rambler* 60). It now drew essentially on popular and indigenous English forms, of varying degrees of respectability. The scandal romance, the sensational Newgate confession, the sentimental ballad of folk archetypes (the Cruel Lover, the Poor Poet), the journalistic investigation and profile, the theatrical comedy of manners and the revelations of courtroom drama: all these shaped the narrative forms of the new biography, and continue to affect it to this day.

By first absorbing and largely mastering them in his *Life*, Johnson created a new hybrid, non-fiction form of enormous energy and potential. He also gave it his own distinctive stamp, by critically relating Savage's work to his life (and accepting how often these seemed at odds with each other); and by subjecting the whole pattern of Savage's career to a profound moral scrutiny. In Johnson's hands, biography became a rival to the novel. It began to pose the largest, imaginative questions: how well can we know our fellow human beings; how far can we learn from someone else's struggles about the conditions of our own; what do the intimate circumstances of one particular life tell us about human nature in general? This seems to me the historic significance of Johnson's *Life of Richard Savage*.

Whenever modern biographers set out on the long journey of research and writing, somewhere behind them walk the companionable figures of these two eighteenth-century presences, talking and arguing through a labyrinth of dark night streets, trying to find a recognisable human truth together.

Finally I should say that if my book's title strikes some curious chord in the reader's mind, it came to me on such a night in the small, deserted public garden that now stands behind St John's Gate in the City, when a light winter rain was falling like a mist around the lamps. The echo you hear, of course, is of *Dr Jekyll and Mr Hyde*.

APPENDIX

Note on Savage's birth and identity

Savage's version

Savage stated that he was the illegitimate son of Lady Macclesfield and Earl Rivers, born in Holborn on 10th January 1698.[1] He said he was christened Richard Savage at St Andrew's, Holborn, with Earl Rivers as his godfather. He believed he had an illegitimate sister Ann, born three years previously from the same parents, who also survived into adulthood.[2] He believed he was brought up, under another name, by his godmother Mrs Lloyd who was in correspondence with Lady Macclesfield's mother, Lady Mason. He said that after Mrs Lloyd's death, Lady Macclesfield secretly tried to ship him off to the Plantations and then apprenticed him as a shoemaker in Holborn. He discovered his true identity, he said, about this time (1714) through reading 'convincing Original Letters' of Mrs Lloyd, left his apprenticeship, researched his family background and started using his real name, 'Richard Savage'.[3] When arrested for a treasonous publication in 1715 he gave his name to the court as 'Richard Savage, son of the late Earl Rivers', which was not challenged. He gave further public details of his claim in Jacob's *Poetical Register*, 1719.[4] In 1726 Savage convinced two members of the Rivers family to subscribe to his *Poems*: Countess Bessy Rocheford and John Savage (the Earl's cousin and heir). In 1729 he began receiving a pension of £200 per annum from Lady Macclesfield's nephew, Lord Tyrconnel, which he accepted as a recognition of kinship.

Lady Macclesfield's version

Lady Macclesfield had two illegitimate children by Earl Rivers, a girl in 1695 and a boy on 16th January 1697.[5] (Note that this was not the date claimed by Savage.) The boy was christened Richard Smith at St Andrew's, Holborn on 18th January 1697, and his godmother signed her name in the register as Dorothy Ousley.[6] (Note her name was not Lloyd.) He was put out to nurse to Mary Peglear, who was told his name was Richard Lee; and then transferred to a second nurse, Ann Portlock, who called him Richard Portlock.[7] Lady Macclesfield said both illegitimate children subsequently died. The girl, Ann Savage, was given a formal funeral at Chelsea Church in 1698, attended by the Ousleys, which is fully documented.[8] The boy, Richard Portlock, is registered as buried in St Paul's, Covent Garden, in November 1698, which is also documented.[9] Lady Macclesfield subsequently confirmed the children's death when Earl Rivers enquired about bequests for his Will.[10] She also told her second husband, Colonel Brett whom she married in 1700, that both children were dead.[11] She never publicly recognised Richard Savage's claim to be her son; and when she paid him money in 1726 to suppress the *Miscellaneous Poems*, this was either to soothe or to silence him. She believed Savage was either a blackmailing impostor, or else a deluded troublemaker who was actually a son of one of his nurses. (Ann Portlock did have her own baby son in 1697.[12]) When Savage was convicted of murder in 1727, Lady Macclesfield made no attempt to plead for his life, and completely disowned him.

Her version appears more consistent and better documented than Savage's. But it is not water-tight. First, because the Richard Portlock who was buried at St Paul's, Covent Garden, *could* have been Mrs Portlock's own baby or even her husband (who was, confusingly, also named Richard), since no details of age or parentage are given in the register.[13] Second, because Lord Tyrconnel did recognise Richard Savage to some degree by supporting him with a pension. And third, because Lady Macclesfield never sued either Aaron Hill in 1724, or Samuel Johnson in 1744, for publishing libels against her on Savage's behalf.

Biographer's version

Historical certainty is impossible in such a case, and after such a lapse of time. The key documents, what Savage called the 'convincing Original letters' from Mrs Lloyd and Lady Mason, have not survived if they ever existed. What documents do survive tend to support Lady Macclesfield. Savage made a number of claims which can be shown to be false: viz. his exact date of birth in Holborn; the name of his godmother; the survival of his supposed sister Ann Savage. Nevertheless, he knew a surprising number of details which suggests he had access to 'Original' documentation of some kind.

Moreover, the whole pattern of his public writing, and relentlessly pursued claims against Lady Macclesfield, suggests that he passionately – and even pathologically – believed in his own claims. He also convinced a large number of his contemporaries of their truth: Sir Richard Steele, Eliza Haywood, Aaron Hill, Lord Tyrconnel, and of course Samuel Johnson. He had no fear of libel and was prepared to shame or even blackmail Lady Macclesfield. Under sentence of death in 1727 he never changed his story; and to the end of his life he insisted on it, as in his private letters to Elizabeth Carter.

He did not resemble his father physically: being small, dark and melancholy in manner, whereas Earl Rivers was notably tall, blond and raffishly extrovert. But he always deported himself with aristocratic style, spoke with great wit and elegance, and had an irascible, impulsive streak which could have been inherited from the adventurous Rivers family. His originality of mind, his gift for poetry and his psychological instability were entirely his own. His love of gossip, anecdotes and scandal (which Pope cultivated for *The Dunciad*) were clearly the product of his Grub Street life. His ability to charm and fascinate people as varied as Martha Sansom, Lord Tyrconnel, Johnson, and Abel Dagge suggests a kind of romantic genius.

Later biographers and scholars – notably Boswell, the Victorian antiquary Moy Thomas and the modern academic Tracy – have remained sceptical of his claims, though Tracy is much inclined to give him the benefit of the doubt. For myself, I cannot believe that Savage was a conscious impostor. The whole pattern of his life and friendships suggests something different; and I do not think Johnson, however loyal and infatuated, would have failed to see through a simple fraud. Much of the evidence, documentary and otherwise, is reconciled if we assume that through the disrupted, unhappy circumstances of his childhood, Savage was genuinely deluded about his identity.

There is one further tragic consideration, if we accept anything that Savage said about the personal sufferings of being an orphan or bastard. In childhood and adolescence he lost three people in succession whom he may have looked upon as mother-figures: a nurse, Mrs Portlock; an affectionate 'godmother', Mrs Lloyd; and a wealthy aristocrat, Lady Macclesfield. We could say that it was Richard Savage's peculiar fate to lose his mother three times over, and to be left with nobody to love him but the Muse of Poetry.

ACKNOWLEDGEMENTS

For kind permission to draw upon copyright texts, editions, and manuscripts, my grateful acknowledgements are due to the Oxford University Press, the Cambridge University Press, the Bodleian Library, and the British Library.

This book would not have been possible without the pioneering work of Clarence Tracy, of Acadia University, Nova Scotia, who first edited Richard Savage's poems, produced a variorum edition of Johnson's *Life of Savage*, and wrote a brilliant monograph on Savage's life, *The Artificial Bastard*. The extent of my debt will appear in the References. Among Johnson scholars, I have drawn particularly on the learned studies by James L. Clifford, Walter Jackson Bate, Thomas Kaminski and John Wain. Full details of these and other works appear in my Select Bibliography. Several librarians have helped me greatly, especially those at the British Library, the Bodleian Library, the London Library, Lincoln's Inn Library, the Inner Temple Library and the Library of St John's Gate, Clerkenwell.

My knowledge of the eighteenth century has been transformed by two works of outstanding scholarship: *Grub Street* (1972) by Pat Rogers; and *Alexander Pope: A Life* (1985) by Maynard Mack, which is virtually an encyclopaedia of the whole period from the South Sea Bubble via Button's Coffee-house to Arcadia. I have also learned a great deal – though probably not enough – from the shrewd and kindly comments of Dr Roger Lonsdale of Balliol College, Oxford, on a draft of this book in its most unbuttoned state. Dr Isabel Rivers, of St Hugh's College, Oxford, gave me valuable advice about the eighteenth-century philosophical debate concerning human evil, cruelty, and the natural affections, which started with Shaftesbury and has never really ended. Nor have I forgotten the first time I read *The Vanity of Human Wishes*, in a tutorial given by Professor George Steiner at Churchill College, Cambridge, some thirty years ago.

As to the whole problem of re-imagining what eighteenth-century London was really like, I have returned again and again to the London street maps of Jean Rocque (1746); the paintings of William Hogarth, Sir Joshua Reynolds, and Canaletto; the music of William Boyce and Handel; the architecture of Hawksmoor and Wren; the vivid street vernacular recorded in three decades of cross-examination at the Old Bailey; and endless solitary walking in the back streets between Gough Square, Smithfield, St Paul's and the Thames.

My particular thanks go to Peter Janson-Smith, who kept up my spirits from the time of our first twilight encounters with Savage in 1984; Ion Trewin for his encouragement and advice during the early drafts; Philip Howard of *The Times* who sent me inky postcards wondering if I was lost in Grub Street; the musicologists Olive Baldwin and Thelma Wilson who put me on the trail of new Savage poems at the Bodleian; Ismena Holland for her generous support; Douglas Matthews for harvesting the Index; Simone Mauger for her tender editing; and Richard Cohen who handles a manuscript as skilfully as he does a sword-fight, and indeed in a rather similar fashion, for which I am truly grateful.

To those in what Johnson (or was it Savage?) called 'the Wilds of Kent' and 'the Groves of Norfolk', my love.

R.H.

SELECT BIBLIOGRAPHY

1. Primary Sources

Johnson's works have been beautifully edited and I give here the most easily available editions. Savage's works by contrast are still scattered, his letters remain uncollected and many editions are rare. So I have supplied British Library Catalogue numbers where helpful, together with an indication where his letters – in print and manuscript – may be found. Other biographical materials about both authors can be found under Secondary Sources.

Samuel Johnson, *Life of Savage*, edited by Clarence Tracy from the first edition (1744), Oxford, 1971

Samuel Johnson, *The Complete English Poems*, edited by J. D. Fleeman, Penguin, 1971

Samuel Johnson, *The Letters of Samuel Johnson*, Vol. I: 1731–72, edited by Bruce Redford, Oxford, 1992

Samuel Johnson, *The Oxford Authors: Samuel Johnson* (Works), edited by Donald Greene, Oxford, 1989

Samuel Johnson, 'The Life of Edward Cave' (anon.), in the *Gentleman's Magazine*, February 1754

*

Richard Savage, *The Poetical Works of Richard Savage*, edited by Clarence Tracy, Cambridge University Press, 1962

Richard Savage, *The Tragedy of Sir Thomas Overbury*, 1724 (BL 11775.f.34)

Richard Savage, *Miscellaneous Poems*, 1726 (BL 1509/623)

Richard Savage, *The Bastard*, 1728 (BL C.57.h.4)

Richard Savage, *The Wanderer*, 1729 (BL 11633.bbb.32[2])

Richard Savage, *An Author to be Let*, 1729 (BL WP 2367. a. 84)

Richard Savage, *A Collection of Pieces in Verse and Prose . . . on Occasion of the DUNCIAD*, 1732 (BL 992.h.9[6])

Richard Savage, *Letters* to be found in:

(a) Johnson, *Life of Savage*, op. cit.

(b) Aaron Hill (ed.), *The Plain Dealer*, no. 73, 30 November 1724

(c) James Thomson, *Letters and Documents*, edited by A. D. McKillop, University of Kansas Press, 1958

(d) Leonard Howard (ed.), *Letters and State Papers*, 1756

(e) Montagu Pennington, *Memoirs of the Life of Mrs Elizabeth Carter*, 1808

(f) Thomas Birch, unpublished papers, British Museum Sloane MS 4318

(g) *The Gentleman's Magazine*, 1787

Richard Savage, 'Eleven Songs' in Bodleian Library (Music) Harding Mus. E. 143 (1720)

2. *Secondary Sources*

Paul Alkon, 'The Reception of Johnson's *Life of Savage*', in *Modern Philology*, no. 72, 1974

Walter Jackson Bate, *Samuel Johnson*, Hogarth Press, 1984

Edmund Bergler MD, 'Richard Savage', in *American Imago: A Psychoanalytic Journal of the Arts and Sciences*, IV, 1947

Thomas Birch, unpublished Diary, British Museum Add. MS 4478c (1737–9)

Thomas Birch, unpublished papers, British Museum Sloane MS 4318

James Boswell, *Life of Johnson* (1791), edited by R. W. Chapman, Oxford, 1980

James Boswell, *London Journal, 1762–1763*, edited by Frederick A. Pottle, Heinemann, 1950

Benjamin Boyce, 'Johnson's *Life of Savage* and Its Literary Background', in *Studies in Philology*, 53, 1956

Dorothy Brewster, *Aaron Hill*, 1913

Robert Carruthers, *The Life of Alexander Pope*, 1857. (This contains Pope's Notes on 'The Case of Richard Savage and Gregory', from the Mapledurham Mss.)

Theophilus Cibber, *The Lives of the Poets* (with Robert Sheil), 5 vols., 1753

James L. Clifford, *Young Samuel Johnson*, Heinemann, 1955

Thomas Cooke, *The Life of Mr Richard Savage Who was Condemned for the Murder of Mr James Sinclair . . .* (anon., with Aaron Hill and 'Mr Beckingham'), 1727

Daniel Defoe, *Roxana* (1724), edited by David Blewitt, Penguin, 1982

Robert DeMaria, *The Life of Samuel Johnson*, Blackwell, 1993

European Magazine, no. VI, 1874. (This contains twelve letters to Savage from Aaron Hill and David Mallet.) (BL PP.5459.Z)

Henry Fielding, *The Covent Garden Journal*, no. 51, 1752

Henry Fielding, *Jonathan Wild* (1743), edited by David Noakes, Penguin, 1983

Henry Fielding, *Tom Jones* (1749), edited by R. P. C. Mutter, Penguin, 1966

Robert Folkenflik, *Samuel Johnson, Biographer*, Cornell University Press, 1978

Paul Fussell, *Samuel Johnson and the Life of Writing*, Chatto, 1972

Donald J. Greene, *The Politics of Samuel Johnson*, Yale, 1960

Sir John Hawkins, *The Life of Samuel Johnson Ll.D*, 1787

Eliza Haywood, *Memoirs of a Certain Island Adjacent to the Kingdom of Utopia*, 1724

Aaron Hill, see *European Magazine*, for twelve letters to Savage

Aaron Hill (editor), *The Plain Dealer*, 1724

Aaron Hill, *Works* (contains his letters), 4 vols., second editor, 1754

Aaron Hill, *Dramatic Works*, 2 vols., 1760

William Hogarth, *Graphic Works*, compiled by Ronald Paulson, The Print Room, 1989

Leonard Howard (editor), *Letters and State Papers*, II, 1756

Mary Hyde, *The Impossible Friendship: Boswell and Mrs Thrale*, Harvard, 1972

Giles Jacob (editor), *The Poetical Register*, 1719

Thomas Kaminski, *The Early Career of Samuel Johnson*, Oxford, 1987

Thomas Kaminski, 'Was Savage "Thales"?', in *Bulletin of Research in the Humanities*, no. 85, 1982

Hugh Kingsmill, *Johnson without Boswell*, Methuen, 1940

Joanna Lafler, *The Celebrated Mrs Oldfield*, Southern Illinois University Press, 1989

Bryant Lillywhite, *London Coffeehouses*, Allen and Unwin, 1963

Jack Lindsay, 'Richard Savage: First Poet of Colour', in *Life and Letters Today*, no. XXII, 1939

Roger Lonsdale (editor), *The New Oxford Book of Eighteenth-Century Verse*, Oxford, 1984.

Maynard Mack, *Alexander Pope: A Life*, Yale University Press, 1985

Dorothy Marshall, *Dr Johnson's London*, Wiley, 1968

Frank McLynn, *Crime and Punishment in Eighteenth-Century England*, Routledge, 1992

James Miller, *The Mother-in-Law* (play), 1734

James Miller, *The Coffee-House* (play), 1738

Samuel Monk, *The Sublime*, 1935

Sylvia Myers, *The Blue Stocking Circle*, Oxford, 1990

Newgate Life, 1727 – see Thomas Cooke

John Gough Nicols, 'The Autobiography of Sylvanus Urban (Edward Cave)', (anon.) in the *Gentleman's Magazine*, 1856

Montagu Pennington, *Memoirs of the Life of Mrs Elizabeth Carter*, 1808

William Pinks, *A History of Clerkenwell*, 1865

Alexander Pope, *Correspondence*, edited by George Sherburn, 5 vols., Oxford, 1956

Public Records Office, SP 35/7/78. (This contains the Secret Service Report on Savage, 1717.)

Jean Rocque, *A Guide to the Streets of London*, 1746

Pat Rogers, *Grub Street: Studies in a Subculture*, Methuen, 1972

Pat Rogers, *Samuel Johnson*, Oxford Pastmasters, 1993

Niall Rudd, *Johnson's Juvenal*, Bristol Classical Press, 1981

Edward Ruhe, 'Birch, Johnson and Carter: an Episode of 1738–9', in *Publication of the Modern Language Association*, no. 73, 1958

James Sambrook, *James Thomson (1700–1748): A Life*, Oxford, 1991

Martha Sansom, *The Memoirs of Clio*, 1752

Select Trials for Murder, Robberies, Rapes, Sodomy ... in the Old Bailey, 1742. (An earlier edition, 2 vols, 1734, can be found at BL 6495. aaa. 14.)

Anna Seward, *The Swan of Lichfield: Correspondence of Anna Seward*, edited by Hesketh Pearson, Hamish Hamilton, 1936

James Sutherland, 'Richard Savage', in *The Times Literary Supplement*, 1st January 1938

W. Moy Thomas, 'Richard Savage', in *Notes and Queries*, 2nd Series, VI (1858) in 4 sections: pp. 361–5; 385–9; 425–8; 445–9

James Thomson, *Letters and Documents*, edited by A. D. McKillop, University of Kansas Press, 1958

Hester Thrale, 'Anecdotes of the Late Samuel Johnson Ll.d', in *Johnsoniana*, edited by Robina Napier, 1884

Clarence Tracy, 'Johnson and the Art of Anecdote', in *University of Toronto Quarterly*, no. 15, 1945

Clarence Tracy, *The Artificial Bastard: A Biography of Richard Savage*, Toronto University Press, 1953

Anon., *A Trip thro London*, 1728

Benjamin Victor, *Original Letters*, I, 1776

John Wain, *Samuel Johnson*, Macmillan, 1974

G. F. Whicher, *The Life and Romances of Mrs Eliza Haywood*, 1915

Kai Kin Yung (editor), *Samuel Johnson 1709–84: A Bicentenary Exhibition*, Arts Council of Great Britain, 1984.

REFERENCES

Full details of the abbreviated titles used in these notes may be found in the Select Bibliography, listed under the author's or editor's name.

Chapter One: Death

1 Our main sources are Thomas Cooke (1727), Samuel Johnson (1744), James Boswell (1791), W. Moy Thomas (1858), and Clarence Tracy (1953). See Select Bibliography under these authors.
2 Hawkins, *Johnson*, pp. 51–2
3 Boswell, *Johnson*, p. 118
4 *Gentleman's Magazine*, September 1743, p. 490
5 Johnson, *Letters*, I, pp. 32–3
6 Ibid., p. 33
7 Clifford, *Young Johnson*, p. 266
8 Johnson, *Poems*, p. 87

Chapter Two: Love

1 Johnson, *Life*, p. 114
2 Johnson, *Poems*, p. 61
3 Boswell, *Johnson*, pp. 73–4
4 Ibid., p. 74
5 Kaminski, *Early Johnson*, p. 4
6 Clifford, *Young Johnson*, p. 124
7 Ibid., p. 161
8 Boswell, *Johnson*, p. 106. It has been suggested that Johnson suffered from a neurological disease, Tourette's syndrome, 'associated with psychological causes, like suppressed rage'. DeMaria, *Johnson*, p. 6.
9 Clifford, *Young Johnson*, p. 153
10 Boswell, *Johnson*, p. 1385n
11 Johnson, *Letters*, I, p. 6

12 Ibid.
13 Ibid., p. 9
14 Ibid.
15 Boswell, *Johnson*, p. 66
16 Seward, *Correspondence*, pp. 115–16
17 Boswell, *Johnson*, p. 69
18 Clifford, *Young Johnson*, p. 152
19 Ibid., p. 341, n. 18; Seward, *Correspondence*, p. 128
20 Bate, *Samuel Johnson*, p. 62
21 Johnson, *Poems*, p. 25
22 Boswell, *Johnson*, pp. 704–5
23 Bate, *Samuel Johnson*, p. 59
24 Boswell, *Johnson*, p. 66
25 Johnson, *Poems*, p. 37
26 Ibid., p. 52
27 Clifford, *Young Johnson*, p. 157; Boswell, *Johnson*, p. 708
28 Ibid.
29 Clifford, *Young Johnson*, p. 145
30 Seward, *Correspondence*, p. 77
31 Boswell, *Johnson*, p. 68n
32 Seward, *Correspondence*, p. 77
33 Boswell, *Johnson*, p. 68
34 Ibid., pp. 67–8n
35 Johnson, *Poems*, p. 52
36 Boswell, *Johnson*, p. 67n
37 Ibid., p. 69
38 Clifford, *Young Johnson*, p. 147
39 Bate, *Samuel Johnson*, p. 146
40 Ibid., p. 151
41 Johnson, *Letters*, I, pp. 43–4
42 Clifford, *Young Johnson*, pp. 156, 298–9
43 Ibid., p. 298
44 Hawkins, *Johnson*, p. 89
45 Bate, *Samuel Johnson*, p. 178
46 Boswell, *Johnson*, p. 98
47 *The Rambler*, nos. 145, 156, 161, 170, 171

48 Hawkins, *Johnson*, p. 88
49 Bate, *Samuel Johnson*, p. 184
50 Seward, *Correspondence*, p. 116
51 Clifford, *Young Johnson*, p. 220
52 Ibid.
53 Johnson, *Poems*, p. 202n
54 Clifford, *Young Johnson*, p. 293
55 Johnson, *Poems*, p. 73
56 Hawkins, *Johnson*, pp. 315–16
57 Boswell, *Johnson*, p. 129
58 Ibid., p. 130
59 Thrale, *Anecdotes*, p. 12
60 Ibid., p. 66
61 Bate, *Samuel Johnson*, pp. 263–4
62 Johnson, *Letters*, I, pp. 22–4
63 Boswell, *Johnson*, p. 709
64 Clifford, *Young Johnson*, p. 146
65 Bate, *Samuel Johnson*, p. 264

Chapter Three: Night

1 Kaminski, *Early Johnson*, p. 83
2 Boswell, *Johnson*, p. 119
3 Ibid.
4 Johnson, *Works*, p. 256
5 Boswell, *Johnson*, p. 174
6 Ibid., p. 121
7 Ibid., p. 119
8 See Pat Rogers, *Grub Street*. The original site was Milton Street, but by the 1740s the term was largely used as an adjective for journalism and hack-writing. Compare the modern use of 'Fleet Street'. And see Pope's magnificent invocation to 'the Grub

Street race' in *The Dunciad*, I, lines 29–44

9 Savage, *Poetical Works*, pp. 123–4
10 Ibid., p. 124
11 Ibid., p. 126
12 Johnson, *Life*, p. 74
13 Johnson, *Poems*, p. 67
14 Clifford, *Young Johnson*, pp. 202–3
15 Johnson, *Works*, p. 403
16 Ibid., p. 353
17 Hawkins, *Johnson*, p. 53
18 Ibid., p. 54
19 Johnson, *Poems*, p. 62
20 Kaminski, *Early Johnson*, p. 91
21 Johnson, *Poems*, p. 75
22 Hawkins, *Johnson*, pp. 53–4
23 Tracy, *Bastard*, pp. 30–1
24 Johnson, *Life*, p. 137
25 Ibid., p. 91
26 Ibid., p. 92
27 Ibid., p. 93
28 Ibid., p. 96
29 Ibid., p. 93
30 Ibid.
31 Ibid.
32 Ibid.
33 Savage, *Poetical Works*, p. 229
34 Ibid., p. 230
35 Johnson, *Life*, p. 93
36 Ibid., p. 94
37 Ibid., p. 97
38 Hill, *Works*, I, p. 252
39 Johnson, *Life*, p. 97
40 Ibid., p. 96
41 Ibid., p. 12

Chapter Four: Mother

1 Johnson, *Letters*, I, p. 36
2 Boswell, *Johnson*, p. 123
3 Johnson, *Letters*, I, p. 35n
4 J. D. Fleeman in *The Library*, no. 22, 1967
5 Boswell, *Johnson*, p. 474
6 Johnson, *Works*, p. 206
7 Ibid., p. 207
8 Johnson, *Life*, p. 138
9 Bate, *Samuel Johnson*, p. 222
10 Johnson, *Works*, p. 207
11 Johnson, *Life*, p. 6
12 Ibid.
13 Ibid., p. 39
14 Ibid., p. 38
15 *Dictionary of National Biography*; Tracy, *Bastard*, pp. 9–11; W. Moy Thomas in *Notes and Queries*, 1858
16 *Dictionary of National Biography*. Colley Cibber draws an affectionate sketch of Lady Macclesfield in his play *The Careless Husband*, 1704.
17 Boswell, *Johnson*, p. 127
18 Montagu Pennington, *Memoirs*, I, pp. 58–64
19 Johnson, *Life*, pp. 6–10
20 Ibid., p. 11
21 Ibid., p. 12
22 Ibid., p. 136
23 Ibid., pp. 14–15
24 Ibid., p. 13
25 Ibid., p. 16
26 Montagu Pennington, *Memoirs*, I, pp. 58–64
27 Johnson, *Life*, pp. 18–19
28 Ibid., p. 19
29 Montagu Pennington, *Memoirs*, I, pp. 58–64
30 T. Cibber, *Lives of the Poets* (1753), V, pp. 32–3
31 Johnson, *Life*, p. 21
32 Ibid., p. 20
33 Tracy, *Bastard*, p. 30
34 Savage, *Poetical Works*, p. 26

35 Johnson, *Life*, p. 12
36 Public Records Office, SP 35/7/78. The file was first discovered by Professor James Sutherland in 1937.
37 Tracy, *Bastard*, p. 38
38 Giles Jacob, *Poetical Register* (1719), vol. I
39 Ibid., vol. 2, pp. 125–7
40 Johnson, *Life*, p. 17; Boswell, *Johnson*, p. 143
41 Johnson, *Life*, p. 24
42 Bodleian MS: Harding. Mus.E.143 (1720). This discovery was originally made by Olive Baldwin and Thelma Wilson, musicologists, of Pilgrim's Hatch, Essex, in 1991; and generously communicated to me at Rewley House, Oxford.
43 Ibid.
44 Ibid.
45 Tracy, *Bastard*, p. 41
46 Savage, *Poetical Works*, p. 46
47 Ibid.
48 Ibid., pp. 46–7
49 *The Dunciad*, II, lines 149–54
50 Savage, *Poetical Works*, pp. 44, 50
51 Haywood, *Utopia* (1724), I, pp. 176–87
52 Ibid., pp. 183–6
53 Ibid., p. 183
54 Johnson, *Life*, p. 37
55 Thomson, *Letters*, p. 47
56 Hill, *Works*, vol. 3
57 Johnson, *Life*, p. 22
58 Ibid.
59 Savage, *Poetical Works*, p. 59
60 Johnson, *Life*, p. 23
61 *European Magazine*, 1784; and *Notes and Queries*, 1954, p. 388ff

62 Hill to Savage, 1st May 1723, in *European Magazine*, 1784
63 Hill to Savage, 13th August 1724, ibid.
64 Savage, *Poetical Works*, p. 53
65 Johnson, *Life*, p. 11n
66 Ibid., p. 26
67 Ibid., p. 25
68 Ibid.
69 Johnson, *Works*, pp. 534–5
70 Ibid., p. 527
71 Johnson, *Life*, p. 25
72 Ibid.
73 Savage, *Poetical Works*, p. 47
74 Ibid., p. 48

Chapter Five: Bard

1   Sambrook, *Thomson*, p. 25
2   Ibid., p. 28
3   Ibid., p. 27
4   Ibid., pp. 29–31
5   Ibid., p. 32
6   Thomson, *Letters*, p. 27
7   *Newgate Life*, 1727, p. 20
8   Savage, *Poetical Works*, p. 107
9   Thomson, *Letters*, p. 48
10 Ibid., p. 47
11 Ibid.
12 Ibid.
13 Ibid., p. 52, n. 10
14 Ibid., p. 34. (Developing theories of the 'Sublime' can be traced from the classical Greek of Longinus through to Edmund Burke's famous treatise *On the Sublime* (1757). See Samuel Monk, *The Sublime*, 1935.)
15 Ibid., p. 49
16 Savage, *Poetical Works*, p. 102
17 Ibid., pp. 114–15
18 Thomson, *Letters*, p. 50
19 Tracy, *Bastard*, p. 75, n. 55
20 Ibid., p. 68

21 Savage, *Poetical Works*, pp. 56–7
22 *Newgate Life*, 1727, p. 18
23 Johnson, *Life*, pp. 28–9
24 Ibid., p. 27
25 *Newgate Life*, 1727, p. 19
26 Tracy, *Bastard*, pp. 89–90
27 Virgil, *Eclogues*, VIII, line 49. The translation of the whole passage from Virgil is of great interest. It reads: 'So savage Love taught the Mother to stain her hands / with the blood of her children; you too are a cruel Mother. / A cruel Mother: but crueller than the Boy was wicked? / That Boy was wicked; but you too are a cruel Mother.' *Eclogues*, VIII, lines 47–50
28 Savage, *Poetical Works*, p. 265
29 Ibid., p. 266
30 Ibid.
31 Ibid., p. 267
32 Ibid., p. 268
33 Ibid.
34 Ibid.
35 Ibid., p. 269

Chapter Six: Murder

1 *Select Trials*, pp. 77–8
2 Johnson, *Life*, p. 30
3 *Select Trials*, p. 79
4 Johnson, *Life*, p. 31
5 Johnson, *Works*, p. 7
6 *Newgate Life*, 1727, p. 21
7 *Select Trials*, p. 82
8 Johnson, *Life*, p. 32
9 Carruthers, *Pope*, p. 424
10 Johnson, *Life*, p. 31
11 *Select Trials*, p. 80
12 Ibid.
13 Johnson, *Life*, p. 32
14 Ibid., p. 33
15 Ibid., p. 34
16 Ibid.
17 *Select Trials*, p. 78
18 Ibid.
19 Ibid., p. 79
20 Carruthers, *Pope*, p. 424
21 *Select Trials*, p. 79
22 Ibid.
23 Carruthers, *Pope*, p. 424
24 *Select Trials*, p. 80
25 Ibid., p. 81
26 Ibid.
27 Ibid.
28 Ibid., p. 79
29 Johnson, *Life*, pp. 31–3
30 Ibid., p. 33
31 Ibid., pp. 33–4
32 *Newgate Life*, 1727, p. 22
33 Johnson, *Life*, p. 34
34 Ibid., p. 35
35 Ibid.
36 Carruthers, *Pope*, p. 424
37 Howard, *State Papers*, II, pp. 675–7
38 *Newgate Life*, 1727, pp. 26–7
39 Howard, *State Papers*, II, pp. 657–80
40 *Select Trials*, p. 79
41 Ibid., p. 78
42 Ibid., p. 81
43 Ibid., p. 78
44 Johnson, *Life*, p. 36
45 Ibid.
46 Howard, *State Papers*, II, pp. 675–7
47 Johnson, *Life*, pp. 37–8
48 Ibid., p. 38
49 Ibid., p. 39
50 Ibid., p. 37
51 Howard, *State Papers*, II, pp. 675–80
52 Johnson, *Life*, p. 38
53 Ibid., p. 40
54 Ibid., p. 42

55   Savage, *Poetical Works*, p. 91
56   Johnson, *Life*, p. 42
57   Savage, *Poetical Works*, p. 129
58   Johnson, *Life*, p. 40

Chapter Seven: Fame

1   Johnson, *Life*, p. 39
2   Savage, *Poetical Works*, p. 89
3   Ibid.
4   Fielding, *Covent Garden Journal*, no. 51, 27 June 1752. Savage's 'Works' were of course an invention, and Fielding was thinking of the *Newgate Life*.
5   See also Dorothy Marshall, *London*, pp. 11–12.
6   Mack, *Pope*, p. 457
7   Johnson, *Life*, p. 44
8   Ibid., p. 43
9   Ibid., p. 44
10   Ibid., p. 70
11   *Gentleman's Magazine*, 1737, pp. 113–14
12   Johnson, *Life*, p. 71
13   Ibid., p. 72
14   Tracy, *Bastard*, p. 93
15   Johnson, *Life*, p. 75
16   Savage, *Poetical Works*, p. 96
17   Ibid., p. 93
18   Johnson, *Life*, p. 44
19   Ibid., p. 62
20   Savage, *Poetical Works*, p. 97
21   But Roger Lonsdale has recently championed Aaron Hill's poetry; see *The New Oxford Book of Eighteenth-Century Verse* (1984)
22   Savage, *Poetical Works*, p. 95
23   *Memoirs of Viscountess Sundon* (1847), II, pp. 241–2
24   Johnson, *Life*, p. 79
25   Tracy, *Bastard*, p. 117
26   Savage, *Poetical Works*, pp. 171–2

27   Ibid., p. 170
28   Johnson, *Life*, p. 79
29   Ibid., p. 60
30   Ibid., p. 51
31   Ibid.
32   Hill, *Works*, I, p. 50
33   Johnson, *Life*, p. 61
34   Ibid., p. 53
35   *European Magazine*, 1784
36   Johnson, *Life*, p. 58
37   Ibid., p. 53
38   Ibid., p. 54
39   Savage, *Poetical Works*, p. 130
40   Ibid., p. 137
41   Ibid., pp. 141–6
42   Ibid., p. 146
43   Ibid., pp. 154–5
44   Ibid., p. 158
45   Ibid., p. 159
46   Johnson, *Life*, p. 139
47   Savage, *Poetical Works*, p. 124
48   Ibid., p. 128
49   Ibid., pp. 133–4
50   Ibid., p. 155
51   Ibid., p. 143
52   Johnson, *Life*, p. 52
53   Ibid.; Savage, *Poetical Works*, p. 52
54   Ibid., p. 158
55   Ibid., p. 106
56   Ibid., p. 127
57   Ibid., p. 124
58   Ibid., p. 114
59   Johnson, *Life*, p. 45
60   Cibber, *Lives of the Poets* (1753), V, p. 266n
61   Johnson, *Life*, p. 45
62   Ibid.
63   *An Author to be Let* (1729), p. 7. A further glimpse into the Grub Street that Savage had escaped, appears in his revealing reference to William Pattison (1706–27), the 'Unfortunate Poet' who

died of smallpox aged twenty-one. Pattison came from Peasmarsh, near Rye in Sussex; he attended Sidney Sussex College, Cambridge, and convinced of his genius left early to find a patron and literary fortune in London. His despairing letters are dated from Button's Coffee-house throughout 1727 and in a poem entitled 'Effigies of Authors', addressed to Pope's friend Lord Burlington, he describes himself as passing the nights on a bench in St James's Park. Overwhelmed by poverty, he sought an immediate subscription for publishing his *Poetical Works*, and while transcribing them for the press the bookseller Edmund Curll gave him shelter in his garret; but he died before they were completed, penniless, miserable, and unrecognised. Savage accused Curll of starving young Pattison to death. See DNB; and *An Author to be Let*, p. 3.

64 Johnson, *Life*, pp. 63–4
65 Ibid., p. 65
66 Ibid.
67 Ibid., p. 64
68 Ibid.
69 Ibid., pp. 59–60
70 Ibid., p. 69
71 Boswell, *Johnson*, p. 118n
72 Johnson, *Life*, pp. 65–6
73 Tracy, *Bastard*, p. 121
74 Ibid., p. 120

75 Johnson, *Life*, p. 70
76 Tracy, *Bastard*, p. 123
77 Mack, *Pope*, p. 439
78 Tracy, *Bastard*, p. 124
79 Savage, *Poetical Works*, pp. 194–5
80 Johnson, *Life*, pp. 85–6
81 Ibid., p. 83
82 Ibid.
83 Tracy, *Bastard*, p. 128
84 Ibid., p. 106
85 Johnson, *Life*, p. 85n
86 Ibid., pp. 84–5n
87 Ibid., p. 85n
88 Birch, BM Sloane MS 4318
89 Savage, *Poetical Works*, p. 205
90 Ibid., pp. 207–8
91 Johnson, *Life*, p. 87
92 Ibid., p. 90
93 Savage, *Poetical Works*, p. 209
94 Thomson, *Letters*, pp. 106–7
95 Hill, *Works*, I, pp. 317–8
96 Ibid., p. 318
97 Savage, *Poetical Works*, p. 216
98 Hill, *Works*, I, pp. 323–4
99 Ibid., p. 328
100 Johnson, *Life*, p. 68
101 Ibid.
102 Ibid., p. 91

Chapter Eight: Friendship

1 Hawkins, *Johnson*, p. 52
2 Johnson, *Life*, pp. 135–6
3 Clifford, *Young Johnson*, p. 173
4 Thomson, *Letters*, p. 110
5 Ibid., p. 112
6 Johnson, *Letters*, I, p. 12
7 Ibid., p. 6
8 Kaminski, *Early Johnson*, p. 21
9 Johnson, *Poems*, p. 61
10 Ibid. DeMaria (p. 49) suggests the name is based on

'Thales of Miletus' (600 BC), one of the Seven Sages of Greece; but he was known primarily as an astronomer. Niall Rudd also suggests 'Thaletes of Crete' (700 BC), an obscure poet who rid Sparta of the plague. My own suggestion is simpler. Johnson used a masculine version of 'Thalia', the classical Muse of bucolic poetry and mocking comedy, as peculiarly appropriate to the author of *The Wanderer* and *The Bastard*.

11 Savage, *Poetical Works*, p. 206
12 Johnson, *Poems*, p. 63
13 Ibid., p. 66
14 Savage, *Poetical Works*, p. 146, as quoted in Chapter 7, p. 150

15 Johnson, *Life*, p. 4
16 Kaminski, *Early Johnson*, p. 100; and article, 'Was Savage "Thales"?' in *Bulletin of Research in the Humanities*, no. 85 (1982), pp. 322–35. But Pat Rogers recognises in Thales 'a figure with some resemblance to Savage'. Rogers, *Johnson*, p. 47
17 Boswell, *Johnson*, p. 93
18 Hawkins, *Johnson*, pp. 55–6, 86
19 Boswell, *Johnson*, p. 91n
20 Tracy's suggestion in Savage, *Poetical Works*, p. 210
21 Savage, *Poetical Works*, p. 210
22 Boswell, *Johnson*, p. 91n
23 Kaminski, *Early Johnson*, p. 225, n. 20
24 Johnson, *Letters*, I, p. 16

25 Nicols, *Gentleman's Magazine*, 1856, p. 275
26 Mrs Thrale's annotated copy of the 1816 edition is held at Harvard. See *The Life of Samuel Johnson* (1938), ed. Edward G. Fletcher, vol. I, p. 77. I am grateful to Lili Pohlmann and Peter Janson-Smith for this shrewd *aperçu*.
27 Johnson, *Poems*, p. 68
28 Johnson, *Life*, p. 74
29 Pope, *Letters*, IV, p. 194, n. 1
30 Johnson, *Letters*, I, p. 18
31 Boswell, *Johnson*, p. 98; Kaminski, *Early Johnson*, p. 84
32 Johnson, *Life*, p. 102
33 Ibid., p. 98
34 Ibid., p. 99
35 Thrale, *Anecdotes*, pp. 109, 115
36 Johnson, *Life*, p. 108
37 Ibid., p. 104
38 Ibid.
39 Johnson, *Poems*, pp. 65–6
40 Hawkins, *Johnson*, p. 11
41 Johnson, *Life*, p. 109
42 Ibid., p. 112
43 Ibid., p. 100
44 Ibid., p. 101
45 Miller, *The Coffee-House* (1738), Act 1, scene 11
46 Johnson, *Life*, p. 100
47 Johnson, *Poems*, p. 65
48 Birch, Diary, BM Add. MS 4478c.
49 Johnson, *Life*, p. 103
50 Ibid., p. 74
51 Ibid.
52 Ibid.
53 Ibid., p. 138
54 Ibid., p. 136
55 Ibid., pp. 136–7
56 See John Wain, *Samuel*

Johnson, Chapter 7, 'The Friend of Goodness', for a brilliant assessment of these 'hidden springs of Johnson's deep feelings' which Savage touched.

57 Johnson, *Life*, p. 135
58 Johnson, *Poems*, pp. 50–1
59 Birch, BM Sloane MS 4318
60 Johnson, *Life*, p. 109
61 Ibid., p. 108
62 Ibid., p. 109
63 Ibid., p. 110
64 Ibid.; Tracy, *Bastard*, p. 138. Johnson only mentions Pope's name in later editions of the *Life*.
65 Johnson, *Life*, p. 110
66 Pope, *Letters*, IV, p. 180
67 Johnson, *Life*, p. 110
68 Ibid., p. 111
69 Ibid., p. 113
70 Ibid.
71 Pope, *Letters*, IV, p. 418
72 Even Kaminski, Boswell's most meticulous defender, accepts that this curious reversal of identification may have taken place: '... Savage may have chosen to live out Thales's heroic rejection of London for Wales. He was not above such theatricality.' Kaminski, 'Was Savage "Thales"?', p. 326
73 Johnson, *Poems*, p. 62
74 Johnson, *Letters*, I, p. 17; Johnson, *Poems*, p. 68. See Sylvia Myers, *Blue Stocking*
75 Montagu Pennington, *Memoirs*, I, pp. 58–64
76 Ibid.
77 Ibid.
78 Johnson, *Life*, p. 111
79 Johnson, *Poems*, p. 67
80 Johnson, *Life*, p. 111

Chapter Nine: Arcadia

1 Johnson, *Life*, pp. 114–5
2 Ibid., p. 115
3 Boswell, *Johnson*, pp. 104–5
4 Johnson, *Life*, p. 117
5 Pope, *Letters*, IV, p. 210
6 Johnson, *Life*, p. 117
7 Ibid., p. 116
8 Savage, *Poetical Works*, pp. 255–6
9 Tracy, *Bastard*, p. 140
10 Private correspondence, Mr Conway Davies, Cardiff
11 Savage, *Poetical Works*, p. 246
12 Ibid.
13 Ibid., p. 249
14 Ibid., p. 248
15 Ibid., p. 250
16 Ibid., p. 252
17 Johnson, *Life*, p. 116
18 Pope, *Letters*, IV, p. 432
19 Ibid., pp. 391–2
20 Tracy, *Bastard*, p. 143
21 Johnson, *Life*, p. 116
22 Ibid.
23 Pope, *Letters*, IV, pp. 417–18
24 Ibid., p. 418
25 Ibid., p. 417
26 Johnson, *Life*, p. 118
27 Ibid., p. 119
28 Ibid., p. 120
29 Ibid.
30 Pope, *Letters*, IV, p. 431
31 Johnson, *Life*, p. 120
32 Ibid., p. 122n
33 Ibid., pp. 122–3
34 Ibid., p. 123
35 Ibid., p. 122n
36 Ibid., p. 124

37 Ibid., p. 125
38 Tracy, *Bastard*, p. 149
39 Writing from Dublin, in an undated letter of the 1750s to his friend John Ellis in London, Benjamin Victor suddenly remarks: 'your favours ... to Mrs Vannost, whom at my request you greatly obliged, by giving her the picture of that odd being, her brother, *Richard Savage*, son of the late Earl Rivers.' Benjamin Victor, *Original Letters*, I, p. 264. Not the least tantalising revelation here, is that somewhere there may still be a painting of Savage.
40 Pope, *Letters*, IV, p. 392
41 Johnson, *Life*, p. 135
42 Ibid., p. 133
43 Ibid., p. 125
44 Ibid., p. 133
45 Ibid., p. 134n
46 Ibid., p. 126
47 *Gentleman's Magazine*, 1787, pp. 1040–1
48 Johnson, *Life*, p. 125
49 Savage, *Poetical Works*, pp. 258–9
50 Johnson, *Life*, p. 134n
51 Ibid., p. 132
52 Savage, *Poetical Works*, pp. 257–8
53 Johnson, *Life*, p. 134
54 Ibid., p. 135
55 Ibid., p. 139
56 Ibid., p. 140
57 Ibid.

Chapter Ten: Charon

1 Pope, *Letters*, IV, p. 475

Appendix

1 Jacob, *Poetical Register*; Savage's letter to Mrs Carter, in Montague Pennington, *Memoirs*
2 Haywood, *Utopia*, 1724; Savage's letters from Bristol, *Gentleman's Magazine*, 1787; Benjamin Victor, *Original Letters*
3 *Newgate Life*, 1727; letters to Mrs Carter, ibid.; Preface to *Miscellaneous Poems*, 1726; Haywood, *Utopia*, 1724
4 Jacob, *Poetical Register*, 1719; Secret Service report, Public Records Office, 1717
5 Tracy, *Bastard*, p. 11
6 Ibid.
7 W. Moy Thomas, 'Savage', 1858, pp. 361–5
8 Tracy, *Bastard*, p. 9
9 W. Moy Thomas, 'Savage', 1858, p. 365
10 Jacob, *Poetical Register*, 1719; Preface to *Miscellaneous Poems*, 1726
11 Mrs Thrale, in Tracy, *Bastard*, p. 4
12 Tracy, *Bastard*, p. 11
13 W. Moy Thomas, 'Richard Savage', 1858, pp. 361–5

INDEX